The Writer's Control of Tone

The Writer's Control of Tone READINGS, WITH ANALYSIS, FOR THINKING AND WRITING ABOUT PERSONAL EXPERIENCE

EDITED BY *Edward M. White*

CALIFORNIA STATE COLLEGE, SAN BERNARDINO

 W · W · NORTON & COMPANY · INC · NEW YORK

ISBN   0   393   09894   X

Copyright © 1970 by W. W. Norton & Company, Inc. Library of Congress Catalog
Card No. 78-95545. Printed in the United States of America.
    5 6 7 8 9 0

Contents

Introduction

WRITING FOR SOMEBODY · *One day, half an hour before I was due to teach yet another composition class, a salesman came to my office with some odd machinery. He had overlays, underlays, a five- (or was it six-? seven-?) color teaching program—a mass of technicolor technology ready to help my freshmen turn out five hundred interesting words. Hurrah for the twentieth century, I said to myself, and asked him to do his thing for my class, to treat me as one of the students.*

That class led me to change my concept of what the teaching of writing is all about. It also brought home to me unforgettably just how corrupt the usual composition game really is. The machine taught in unintended ways.

The crucial moment for me came about half way through the lesson, one obviously planned to inculcate the virtues of simple concrete language. Projected prettily on the blackboard was a sentence in yellow, I think it was, designed as an example of over elaborateness. Embedded in a description of a wintry city street, the delinquent sentence was overloaded with adverbs and adjectives: every third word or so was "glittering," "shiny," or the like. The turquoise overlay to follow would show the offending words struck out or subdued. But before the turquoise came the teaching.

"Would you," teacher-salesman pointed benignly at me, "come to the board and correct the sentence, please."

What a sensation. The doctorate, the professorial and administrative dignities, the years of more or less professional writing dropped away like rotted paper clothing, leaving me a thin, shivering third grader again. I straggled to the board and, good student that I always was, sized up the situation easily enough. Cross out

---

Part of this introduction appeared in another form in *College English* (Nov., 1969). Reprinted with the permission of the National Council of Teachers of English.

the words put up there to be crossed out, please teacher, and get rewarded by teacher's praise and class approval.

But the chalk froze in my hand. I was absolutely unable to lift my arm.

Time passed. I heard a few of my students—they were my students, I was really the teacher—begin to titter at the dummy up there who couldn't do what everybody could see was supposed to be done. The pressure from the class behind me was immense: just please the teacher, play the game.

"I can't do it," I said to teacher-salesman. Now the class really did titter. He looked puzzled, patronizing. "Well, now," he started to explain. But he stopped. That's the professor, he was thinking. There was a hint of panic in his eyes.

"I've done too much writing," I finally choked out, struggling hard back into my role. "This has nothing to do with writing." He protested, talking of weak adjectives, weak students. "But why?" I asked, gaining strength as I started to understand what had happened, "why am I writing or rewriting this? What am I saying? Who am I talking to? How can anyone write unless he has something to say to somebody?"

I left his sentence on the board, asked him to sit down, please, and spent the rest of the class hour discussing tone with the class. Why on earth, my first question went, would anybody want to describe a wintry city scene? The response was quick. A letter to a grandmother, a friend, a lover. A story. An essay on pollution. In each case, of course, the sentence took on a different tone. We were talking about writing.

But what was going on when I went to the board was not writing instruction; it was a socialization experience. The uncanny aura of third grade was everywhere, like a faded perfume, in the colored ink of the overlays. Here was a large and (the salesman, shaken, assured me) highly successful college program that pretended to teach writing, but was really an elaborate lesson in how to play the academic game. The whole point was to figure out the response the program called for, to satisfy the needs of the machine. Writing for nobody is not writing at all.

I have come to think that far too much college composition is a corrupt enterprise, writing for nobody. The student has nothing to say, imagines no audience who could care about what he has to say, but turns out his words on paper nonetheless. I am convinced that the most important job before teachers of writing is to resist *and protest against the dehumanizing effect of materials and essay assignments that turn writing into academic gamesmanship. Writing has to be hard because writing and thinking go together, and thinking is hard. But, even though writing is hard, it is still human and personal. It is my hope that those using this text will understand that writing for somebody, and as somebody, makes writing worth reading.*

TONE AND EXPERIENCE · *By focusing on ways of writing about personal experience, this text seeks to solve the most common writing problem that students face: to be forced to write an essay when they have nothing to say. Since a writer has something to say only when he has some personal knowledge of his subject, and some real feelings about it, personal experience is uniquely appropriate as subject material. Everyone has things in his past worth writing about, and almost everyone is interested in remembering, assessing, and retelling this past experience.*

The challenge for a writer dealing with personal experience is to treat his subject so that it has more than private meaning. I have prepared this text in order to help those of you learning how to write to deal with personal experience so that such experience becomes meaningful to others as well as to yourself. Since you have plenty to write about, you can attend specifically to the writer's obligation to say something which someone else will want to hear. It is this sense of a writer's responsibility to his reader that all writing courses seek to teach in one way or another—writing as a human transaction between the author and the audience.

The term for the relationship of reader to writer (and to subject) is tone, and that is the central rhetorical concept this text seeks to clarify: how is a writer to gain understanding of and some control over his relationship to his subject and his reader? Since tone is a matter of relationship, it is a narrower and clearer term than "style," which includes all aspects of how something is said: diction, syntax, rhythm, metaphor, point of view, and so forth. Tone is itself a metaphor, from "tone of voice," the inflection that can make the same words either a friendly greeting or a sneer. It is hard to define a particular tone, just as it is hard to describe precisely any human relationship; nonetheless, all writing has some tone, since all writing is a matter of communication and hence relationship. For a writer, understanding his own tone is one way of understanding what he has to say about his subject and why he is asking a reader to hear him out.

In conversation, tone is conveyed in many ways: a twist of the lips, a warm smile, a shrug, a side glance, a slang or professional term, a stamp of the foot. But a writer is limited to what he can put on paper: particular words arranged in particular ways, with a very few punctuation marks. In a sense, then, tone is clear and technical. The vocabulary of anger differs from that of joy. A period is not a semi-colon.

Tone is a useful concept for writers partly because it is technical and hence unambiguous. But in another sense, tone is an exceedingly complex matter: the choice of tone so expresses the purpose of a piece of writing that this choice governs and directs everything else. When we speak of tone, then, we eventually consider almost every aspect of writing. A badly organized paper is not faulty because it is badly organized; it is faulty because a reader cannot follow what the writer is trying to say. To use "ain't" in a college essay is usually a mistake, not because it is bad grammar but because it tends to set up, or insert, a relationship between reader and writer that is not appropriate to the situation. Writing which communicates only to the author is fine in a diary but out of place in a classroom. A paper which simply accumulates other peoples' ideas is at fault because the writer has not considered how he should relate himself to the material and thus make the writing his own.

Tone, then, is a matter of technique which can be discussed clearly, while, at the same time, it is a matter of scarcely understood emotional responses and implicit ideas which technical devices manage to convey. A writer who can achieve consistency of tone, and an appropriate tone, in personal experience essays has taken a large step toward the expressive and ordered thinking and writing that define good expository prose.

ORGANIZATION · The three sections of this text ask you to focus upon increasingly complicated problems of tone in reading and writing. Since each of the sections deals with a specific kind of problem, the readings are examples of the ways various writers have handled one kind of "assignment." Thus, this book differs from the conventional reader by seeking to relate directly the reading and writing which go on together in the writing course.

The first section contains essays and a story which center upon descriptions of an adult as seen by the writer when he was a child. But, of course, descriptions convey attitudes as well as information;

*it is the writer's relationship to the person being described which
makes these descriptions worth reading. Each of these writers is
primarily concerned with portraying a close relative so precisely
that the reader can immediately understand the meaning of the
relationship between child and adult. Although an awareness of the
reader is always present, and sometimes (as with E. E. Cummings)
influences the tone in important ways, the writer's major concern in
this section is to establish the exactly appropriate tone for his subject. We observe the writer in the act of coming to see and understand a significant influence over his childhood; we often notice as
well that the writer is coming to see himself with penetrating clarity
at the same time.*

*The second section also presents descriptions, but these descrip-
tions are of institutions, and the writers seek to convey analysis as
well as attitude. That is, the writers in this section are very much
concerned with the reader, who must be made aware not only of
how it was in the school (or wherever) but how the writer sees the
institution now, from a different perspective. This design calls for
control over two points of view at the same time: the view of the
institution from the inside, as seen by those who run it or are committed to it, and the perspective of the outsider who can see far
more clearly exactly what was going on by the use of outsiders'
terms and concepts. Jules Henry asks what is really being learned
while the grade school teacher thinks she is teaching music; Johnie
Scott finds Harvard part of "the Education Game" from the perspective of the black ghetto. The problem for the writer is to control
the double view of the institution so that the description makes the
reader share the writer's attitude.*

*The third section offers a group of selections in which the
writer-reader relationship becomes central. The writers here are
dealing with small, everyday experiences which hardly seem worth
writing about. The writer's job is to make the reader see the importance of the apparently unimportant. A reader is always about
to ask why he should spend his time hearing about someone else's
life or opinions or research. By choosing apparently insignificant
matters as subject material, then controlling tone so as to convey
large meanings, these writers forcibly demonstrate that the real substance of a piece of writing is the author's treatment of his topic,
not the topic itself. Mary McCarthy implies that we should attend
to a petty incident of child abuse because that incident will tell us
something about concentration camps and tyranny; James Joyce*

asks us to value a child's tears over a closed carnival because these tears help us see the meaning of growing up in an environment hostile to the imagination.

STUDENT WRITING · *While the selections are worth reading for all kinds of reasons, the primary reason for their choice and arrangement is to help you to write well. Of course good writing— like any skill—does not come easily. While personal experience seems perhaps an easier subject than great ideas or great literature, the difficulties and possibilities of such writing are in fact immense; the challenges are worthy of the best students and the best teachers.*

Each of the three sections suggests its own topic for exercises or essays. The first section calls for description of an adult you knew when you were a child; the description should convey an attitude as well as information. You may wish to follow Baldwin and Anderson and seek to investigate in depth the way a child is shaped by his reaction to the parent. Or you may even find ways to shape these essays into fictional forms with still larger emotional and symbolic content.

The second section calls for a description and evaluation of an institution you have known well. A school is the most obvious choice for a student; the selections (with two exceptions) deal with schools and the values they teach. But a Sunday school, a summer camp, a dancing school, a club or fraternity serve equally well, as long as you are able to see the values of the group from an outside perspective as well as that of a participant.

The third section is designed to help you write about a personal experience, the large meaning of which is not readily apparent to the reader. The basic problem, of course, is to decide what matters about the experience to the reader as well as to yourself; to convey meaning as well as emotion or personality calls for careful attention to tone. It is your responsibility as a writer to demonstrate to your reader what you are saying and why you are asking to be read.

REWRITING · *Tone is more often discovered than planned. In the course of writing about personal experience (or anything else, for that matter) you choose words which express your attitudes; these choices, emerging from subconscious as much as conscious intention, generally define emotions, responses, and assumptions previously left unstated and dimly discerned. The writing and careful reading of first drafts is as much a matter of coming to know what you mean as it is a matter of communicating known facts and ideas. But the first draft is rarely consistent and almost never appropriately structured. It is in the cutting, expanding, rearranging, and focusing that occur during rewriting that an essay takes shape.*

Thus, control of tone comes normally in rewriting. Usually (not always) spelling, punctuation, sentence structure, and the like are made to conform with standard English usage. Contradictions in tone are eliminated or reconciled as you become increasingly precise about your relationship to your subject and your reader. Organization becomes more and more clear as you understand more completely what you have to say and why it is important. The first draft is often an uncontrolled outpouring of ideas and reactions; perhaps it should be. But rewriting can be practiced and learned. The sample of student writing in the appendix includes both first and second drafts; the two drafts are intended to serve as an example of the dramatic improvement rewriting can bring about, as well as an encouragement to those who use this text to attend to rewritten papers as fully as to original drafts.

Acknowledgments

Harold C. Martin, *now president of Union College, first made me aware of the value of "tone" as a concept for teaching composition. The staff meetings he ran for Harvard's General Education A, and the texts he edited with Richard Ohmann helped shape my attitudes toward freshman composition; this book is indebted to those meetings and texts in many ways. A creative leave for Spring term 1969, granted me by California State College, San Bernardino, gave me time to complete and rewrite the book.*

Part One CONTROLLING

ATTITUDES: CHILD AND ADULT

It is particularly valuable for a writer to examine closely the way other writers control tone. While it is easy to feel the differences among the selections here, it is not quite so easy to discover how these writers have achieved their distinct tones. Notice, for example, these three descriptions of parents:

My sole consolation when I went upstairs for the night was that Mamma would come in and kiss me after I was in bed. But this good night lasted for so short a time: she went down again so soon that the moment in which I heard her climb the stairs, and then caught the sound of her garden dress of blue muslin, from which hung little tassels of plaited straw, rustling along the double-doored corridor, was for me a moment of the keenest sorrow. —PROUST

He was, I think, very handsome. I gather this from photographs and from my own memories of him, dressed in his Sunday best and on his way to preach a sermon somewhere, when I was little. Handsome, proud, and ingrown, "like a toe-nail," somebody said. But he looked to me, as I grew older, like pictures I had seen of African tribal chieftains: he really should have been naked, with war-paint on and barbaric mementos, standing among spears. He could be chilling in the pulpit and indescribably cruel in his personal life and he was certainly the most bitter man I have ever met; yet it must be said that there was something else in him, buried in him, which lent him his tremendous power and, even, a rather crushing charm. —BALDWIN

It will be admitted, that a man of the opinions, and the character, above described, was likely to leave a strong moral impression on any mind principally formed by him, and that his moral teaching was not likely to err on the side of laxity *or indulgence. The element which was chiefly deficient in his moral relation to his children was that of tenderness. I do not believe that this deficiency lay in his own nature. I believe him to have had much more feeling than he habitually showed, and much greater capacities of feeling than were ever developed.* —MILL

The first phrase of the Proust passage emphasizes the child's feelings: "My sole consolation. . . ." We are asked to sense the child's intense emotional relationship with his mother, whose goodnight kiss is "consolation" for deep unhappiness. The personal pronoun "my" opens the passage, and personal pronouns are repeated throughout, often next to active verbs: "I went upstairs," "kiss me," "I heard her climb." The nouns are predominantly concrete ones, such as "bed," "dress," "straw," and these nouns with their fullness of detail serve as well to bring us close to the scene, make us feel its intimacy. And, of course, to call the parent "Mamma" is to insist upon the closeness of the relationship between parent and child, and to insist that the reader see the relationship from the child's perspective.

The first phrase of the Baldwin passage asks the reader to see the father from a middle distance: "He was, I think, very handsome." The father is "he," not "daddy" or (as with Mill) " a man", we are asked to see him through the hesitating reflection of a thoughtful writer: "I think," "I gather." Abstract words ("handsome," "ingrown") are balanced by concrete ones ("Sunday best," "like a toe-nail"), and colorless verbs ("he was,""somebody said") are balanced by vivid ones ("to preach a sermon," "buried in him") as the style seeks to evaluate without losing physical touch. Of course the gain in abstraction involves a loss in intimacy; the more powerful words tend to be at one remove from the man, as in the simile of the naked savage. Thus the tone of the passage supports its meaning; we stand with the adult thinker, removed from his subject somewhat ("it must be said"), considering the effect of intimacy with a complicated father on a child's later life.

The Mill passage uses almost wholly abstract and passive language to convey the writer's emotional detachment from his father: "It will be admitted that a man of the opinions and character above described, was likely. . . ." The father becomes almost an abstract force with "opinions," "character," "teachings," even "elements" and a "deficiency" as if he were a chemical compound. The verbs are the abstract and neutral ones of cool scientific inquiry, and concrete nouns are scarce. The analysis is in some ways comparable to Baldwin's, with the same sort of distant evaluation ("I believe him to have had"), but Mill allows himself none of the words which Baldwin and Proust use to bring us close to the man described. Here the tone is a chill detachment; the writer invites us to consider a person toward whom he feels neither love nor hate nor anything but a kind of rational curiosity.

The search for exactly the right words and structures to embody exactly the right ideas and relationships is a major part of writing and (particularly) rewriting. But even a summary examination of these typical passages shows that such simple matters as the kind of noun or the voice of a verb have a large effect upon the tone of an essay. The incongruity of Mill calling his father "Pop" or Proust calling his mother "a woman" demonstrates the firmness with which each has defined his attitudes. It is such control of language, expressing control of attitude, that this section seeks to help you observe and attempt.

The writing you will be doing in connection with this section poses a number of specific practical problems. The first is to decide what adult had enough, and interesting enough, impact upon you as a child to be worth writing about; in order for a description of a person to mean much to anyone, the importance of the person must be clear to the writer. The second practical problem has to do with conveying that importance to a group of readers.

Even though the reader of a college paper is normally the instructor who assigns it, it is probably more useful for you to imagine an audience made up of fellow students. An essay is a kind of public act, and to write for a general audience with a known background helps avoid the special problems that come with special relationships. But an awareness of audience remains only one step toward control of tone. It is the writer's relationship to his subject that will determine in large part how he wants his audience to react; the decisions about tone can only emerge after the writer has a full sense of what he is saying. Thus the practical problem of tone tends to begin with the basic question of topic: what do you have to say about your subject that is interesting enough to call for the time and attention of busy readers?

Since this question of topic is so much a matter of understanding one's attitudes and assumptions, the problem of tone often emerges clearly only after a good first draft has been written. A writer can't choose a tone the way he picks a pencil from a box; the choice is *the gradual result of a series of decisions which the writer comes to recognize in the course of writing and rewriting. For example, anyone writing about his childhood is immediately forced into some important decisions: are his parents to be "Mom and Dad," "Mother and Father," "Ma'am and Sir," or perhaps a distant "the adults" or "the others"? How does he see himself as a child: "I" or "the child" or perhaps a name different from his own? Is the past still active and immediate in the imagination—and therefore expressed in active verbs, concrete nouns, detailed incidents—, or has it become more intellectualized, passive, abstract? What are the alternative tones available which might be effective? To ask questions of this sort about tone is one practical way to discover what is most worth saying to one's audience; what matters about the topic is what needs to be made clear, and this discovery of what matters is the most important work of the early draft.*

No one tone is "right" or "wrong," "better" or "worse" than another in the abstract; a letter to a grandfather will surely have a different tone from that to a lover, and neither is "wrong" because it is different. But the two relationships will each demand an appropriate tone, and something is wrong if we write to a lover as if to a grandfather! As the paper begins to take shape, the questions about topic recur: what attitude should the writer take to the subject? What kind of relation should be set up—or has somehow developed—between writer and reader? The problem must be dealt with afresh each time a paper is written or (particularly) rewritten. The tone that is right for the paper at hand is the one most appropriate to the subject and the occasion.

E. E. Cummings

ABOUT MY FATHER

I wot not how to answer your query about my father. He was a New Hampshire man, 6 foot 2, a crack shot & a famous fly-fisherman & a firstrate sailor (his sloop was named The Actress) & a woodsman who could find his way through forests primeval without a compass & a canoeist who'd stillpaddle you up to a deer without ruffling the surface of a pond & an ornithologist & taxidermist & (when he gave up hunting) an expert photographer (the best I've ever seen) & an actor who portrayed Julius Caesar in Sanders Theatre & a painter (both in oils & watercolors) & a better carpenter than any professional & an architect who designed his own houses before building them & (when he liked) a plumber who just for the fun of it installed all his own waterworks & (while at Harvard) a teacher with small use for professors—by whom (Royce, Lanman, Taussig, etc.) we were literally surrounded (but not defeated)—& later (at Doctor Hale's socalled South Congregational really Unitarian church) a preacher who announced, during the last war, that the Gott Mit Uns boys were in error since the only thing which mattered was for man to be on God's side (& one beautiful Sunday in Spring remarked from the pulpit that he couldn't understand why anyone had come to hear him on such a day) & horribly shocked his pewholders by crying "the Kingdom of Heaven is no spiritual roofgarden: it's inside you" & my father had the first telephone in Cambridge & (long before any Model T Ford) he piloted an Orient Buckboard with Friction Drive produced by the Waltham watch company & my father sent me to a certain public school because its principal was a gentle immense coalblack negress & when he became a diplomat (for World Peace) he gave me & my friends a tremendous party up in a tree at Sceaux Robinson & my father was a servant of the people who fought Boston's biggest & crookedest politician fiercely all day & a few evenings later sat down with him cheerfully at the Rotary Club & my father's voice was so magnificent that he was called on to

Reprinted by permission of the publishers from E. E. Cummings, *i: Six Nonlectures* (Cambridge, Mass., Harvard University Press, 1953). Copyright, 1953, by E. E. Cummings.

5

impersonate God speaking from Beacon Hill (he was heard all over
the common) & my father gave me Plato's metaphor of the cave
with my mother's milk.

———

E. E. CUMMINGS (1894–1962) *is best known as a poet, though he
has also written fiction, most notably* The Enormous Room *(1922).
His father was a well-known pastor in Cambridge, Massachusetts,
as well as an English teacher at Harvard; the passage here is taken
from* i: Six Nonlectures *delivered at Harvard in 1953.*

1. *What is Cummings' relationship with his audience? What is
   the effect of the endlessly rolling second sentence upon the tone?
   How will people who knew and disapproved of his father respond to the terms of the description? Is there any evidence of
   an attempt to irritate the audience?*
2. *What is Cummings' relationship with his father? Demonstrate
   the way specific words, symbols (the "&", the parentheses), and
   structures help to define Cummings' feelings about his father.*
3. *How do the two relationships (Cummings to his audience, Cummings to his father) work together to make us feel about the
   elder Cummings as the writer wishes us to?*
4. *What other means does Cummings use to reinforce his purpose?
   What is the effect, for instance, of his use of metaphor—"surrounded (but not defeated)"—, or the construction of the paragraph?*

John Stuart Mill

MY FATHER'S CHARACTER AND OPINIONS

I was brought up from the first without any religious belief, in the ordinary acceptation of the term. My father, educated in the creed of Scotch Presbyterianism, had by his own studies and reflections been early led to reject not only the belief in Revelation, but the foundations of what is commonly called Natural Religion. I have heard him say, that the turning point of his mind on the subject was reading Butler's Analogy. That work, of which he always continued to speak with respect, kept him, as he said, for some considerable time, a believer in the divine authority of Christianity; by proving to him, that whatever are the difficulties in believing that the Old and New Testaments proceed from, or record the acts of, a perfectly wise and good being, the same and still greater difficulties stand in the way of the belief, that a being of such a character can have been the Maker of the universe. He considered Butler's argument as conclusive against the only opponents for whom it was intended. Those who admit an omnipotent as well as perfectly just and benevolent maker and ruler of such a world as this, can say little against Christianity but what can, with at least equal force, be retorted against themselves. Finding, therefore, no halting place in Deism, he remained in a state of perplexity, until, doubtless after many struggles, he yielded to the conviction, that, concerning the origin of things nothing whatever can be known. This is the only correct statement of his opinion; for dogmatic atheism he looked upon as absurd; as most of those, whom the world has considered Atheists, have always done. These particulars are important, because they show that my father's rejection of all that is called religious belief, was not, as many might suppose, primarily a matter of logic and evidence: the grounds of it were moral, still more than intellectual. He found it impossible to believe that a world so full of evil was the work of an Author combining infinite power with perfect goodness and righteousness. His intellect spurned the subtleties by which men attempt to blind themselves to this open contradiction. The Sabaean, or Manichaean theory of a Good and Evil Principle, struggling against each

From the *Autobiography* (1873).

other for the government of the universe, he would not have
equally condemned; and I have heard him express surprise, that no
one revived it in our time. He would have regarded it as a mere
hypothesis; but he would have ascribed to it no depraving influence.
As it was, his aversion to religion, in the sense usually attached to
the term, was of the same kind with that of Lucretius: he regarded
it with the feelings due not to a mere mental delusion, but to a
great moral evil. He looked upon it as the greatest enemy of morality: first, by setting up factitious excellencies—belief in creeds, de-
votional feelings, and ceremonies, not connected with the good of
human kind,—and causing these to be accepted as substitutes for
genuine virtues: but above all, by radically vitiating the standard of
morals; making it consist in doing the will of a being, on whom it
lavishes indeed all the phrases of adulation, but whom in sober
truth it depicts as eminently hateful. I have a hundred times heard
him say, that all ages and nations have represented their gods as
wicked, in a constantly increasing progression, that mankind have
gone on adding trait after trait till they reached the most perfect
conception of wickedness which the human mind can devise, and
have called this God, and prostrated themselves before it. This *ne
plus ultra* of wickedness he considered to be embodied in what is
commonly presented to mankind as the creed of Christianity. Think
(he used to say) of a being who would make a Hell—who would
create the human race with the infallible foreknowledge, and
therefore with the intention, that the great majority of them were
to be consigned to horrible and everlasting torment. The time, I
believe, is drawing near when this dreadful conception of an object
of worship will be no longer identified with Christianity; and when
all persons, with any sense of moral good and evil, will look upon it
with the same indignation with which my father regarded it. My
father was as well aware as any one that Christians do not, in general, undergo the demoralizing consequences which seem inherent
in such a creed, in the manner or to the extent which might have
been expected from it. The same slovenliness of thought, and sub-
jection of the reason to fears, wishes, and affections, which enable
them to accept a theory involving a contradiction in terms, prevents
them from perceiving the logical consequences of the theory. Such is
the facility with which mankind believe at one and the same time
things inconsistent with one another, and so few are those who
draw from what they receive as truths, any consequences, but those
recommended to them by their feelings, that multitudes have held
the undoubting belief in an Omnipotent Author of Hell, and have
nevertheless identified that being with the best conception they
were able to form of perfect goodness. Their worship was not paid
to the demon which such a being as they imagined would really

be, but to their own ideal of excellence. The evil is, that such a belief keeps the ideal wretchedly low; and opposes the most obstinate
resistance to all thought which has a tendency to raise it higher.
Believers shrink from every train of ideas which would lead the
mind to a clear conception and an elevated standard of excellence,
because they feel (even when they do not distinctly see) that such a
standard would conflict with many of the dispensations of nature,
and with much of what they are accustomed to consider as the
Christian creed. And thus morality continues a matter of blind tradition, with no consistent principle, nor even any consistent feeling, to guide it.

It would have been wholly inconsistent with my father's idea
of duty, to allow me to acquire impressions contrary to his convictions and feelings respecting religion: and he impressed upon me
from the first, that the manner in which the world came into existence was a subject on which nothing was known: that the question, "Who made me?" cannot be answered, because we have no
experience or authentic information from which to answer it; and
that any answer only throws the difficulty a step further back, since
the question immediately presents itself, Who made God? He, at
the same time, took care that I should be acquainted with what had
been thought by mankind on these impenetrable problems. I
have mentioned at how early an age he made me a reader of ecclesiastical history; and he taught me to take the strongest interest
in the Reformation, as the great and decisive contest against
priestly tyranny for liberty of thought.

I am thus one of the very few examples, in this country, of one
who has, not thrown off religious belief, but never had it: I grew up
in a negative state with regard to it. I looked upon the modern exactly as I did upon the ancient religion, as something which in no
way concerned me. . . .

My father's moral convictions, wholly dissevered from religion,
were very much of the character of those of the Greek philosophers;
and were delivered with the force and decision which characterized
all that came from him. Even at the very early age at which I
read with him the Memorabilia of Xenophon, I imbibed from that
work and from his comments a deep respect for the character of
Socrates; who stood in my mind as a model of ideal excellence:
and I well remember how my father at that time impressed upon
me the lesson of the "Choice of Hercules." At a somewhat later
period the lofty moral standard exhibited in the writings of Plato
operated upon me with great force. My father's moral inculcations
were at all times mainly those of the "Socratici viri;" justice, temperance (to which he gave a very extended application), veracity,
perseverance, readiness to encounter pain and especially labor; re-

gard for the public good; estimation of persons according to their merits, and of things according to their intrinsic usefulness; a life of exertion in contradiction to one of self-indulgent sloth. These and other moralities he conveyed in brief sentences, uttered as occasion arose, of grave exhortation, or stern reprobation and contempt.

But though direct moral teaching does much, indirect does more; and the effect my father produced on my character, did not depend solely on what he said or did with that direct object, but also, and still more, on what manner of man he was.

In his views of life he partook of the character of the Stoic, the Epicurean, and the Cynic, not in the modern but the ancient sense of the word. In his personal qualities the Stoic predominated. His standard of morals was Epicurean, inasmuch as it was utilitarian, taking as the exclusive test of right and wrong, the tendency of actions to produce pleasure or pain. But he had (and this was the Cynic element) scarcely any belief in pleasure; at least in his later years, of which alone, on this point, I can speak confidently. He was not insensible to pleasures; but he deemed very few of them worth the price which, at least in the present state of society, must be paid for them. The greater number of miscarriages in life, he considered to be attributable to the overvaluing of pleasures. Accordingly, temperance, in the large sense intended by the Greek philosophers—stopping short at the point of moderation in all indulgences—was with him, as with them, almost the central point of educational precept. His inculcations of this virtue fill a large place in my childish remembrances. He thought human life a poor thing at best, after the freshness of youth and of unsatisfied curiosity had gone by. This was a topic on which he did not often speak, especially, it may be supposed, in the presence of young persons: but when he did, it was with an air of settled and profound conviction. He would sometimes say, that if life were made what it might be, by good government and good education, it would be worth having: but he never spoke with anything like enthusiasm even of that possibility. He never varied in rating intellectual enjoyments above all others, even in value as pleasures, independently of their ulterior benefits. The pleasures of the benevolent affections he placed high in the scale; and used to say, that he had never known a happy old man, except those who were able to live over again in the pleasures of the young. For passionate emotions of all sorts, and for everything which has been said or written in exaltation of them, he professed the greatest contempt. He regarded them as a form of madness. "The intense" was with him a bye-word of scornful disapprobation. He regarded as an aberration of the moral standard of modern times, compared with that of the ancients, the great stress laid upon feeling. Feelings, as such, he considered to be no proper subjects of praise or blame. Right and wrong, good and bad, he regarded as qualities solely of conduct—of acts and omissions; there being no feeling which may not lead, and does not frequently lead, either to good or to bad actions: conscience itself, the very desire to act right, often leading people to act wrong. Consistently carrying out the doctrine, that the object of praise and blame should be the discouragement of wrong conduct and the encouragement of right, he refused to let his praise or blame be influenced by the motive of the agent. He blamed as severely what he thought a bad action, when the motive was a feeling of duty, as if the agents had been consciously evil doers. He would not have accepted as a plea in mitigation for inquisitors, that they sincerely believed burning heretics to be an obligation of conscience. But though he did not allow honesty of purpose to soften his disapprobation of actions, it had its full effect on his estimation of characters. No one prized conscientiousness and rectitude of intention more highly, or was more incapable of valuing any person in whom he did not feel assurance of it. But he disliked people quite as much for any other deficiency, provided he thought it equally likely to make them act ill. He disliked, for instance, a fanatic in any bad cause, as much or more than one who adopted the same cause from self-interest, because he thought him even more likely to be practically mischievous. And thus, his aversion to many intellectual errors, or what he regarded as such, partook, in a certain sense, of the character of a moral feeling. All this is merely saying that he, in a degree once common, but now very unusual, threw his feelings into his opinions; which truly it is difficult to understand how any one who possesses much of both, can fail to do. None but those who do not care about opinions, will confound it with intolerance. Those, who having opinions which they hold to be immensely important, and their contraries to be prodigiously hurtful, have any deep regard for the general good, will necessarily dislike, as a class and in the abstract, those who think wrong what they think right, and right what they think wrong: though they need not therefore be, nor was my father, insensible to good qualities in an opponent, nor governed in their estimation of individuals by one general presumption, instead of by the whole of their character. I grant that an earnest person, being no more infallible than other men, is liable to dislike people on account of opinions which do not merit dislike; but if he neither himself does them any ill office, nor connives at its being done by others, he is not intolerant: and the forbearance which flows from a conscientious sense of the importance to mankind of the equal freedom of all opinions, is the only tolerance which is commendable, or, to the highest moral order of minds, possible.

It will be admitted, that a man of the opinions, and the character, above described, was likely to leave a strong moral impression on any mind principally formed by him, and that his moral teaching was not likely to err on the side of laxity or indulgence. The element which was chiefly deficient in his moral relation to his children was that of tenderness. I do not believe that this deficiency lay in his own nature. I believe him to have had much more feeling than he habitually showed, and much greater capacities of feeling than were ever developed. He resembled most Englishmen in being ashamed of the signs of feeling, and by the absence of demonstration, starving the feelings themselves. If we consider further that he was in the trying position of sole teacher, and add to this that his temper was constitutionally irritable, it is impossible not to feel true pity for a father who did, and strove to do, so much for his children, who would have so valued their affection, yet who must have been constantly feeling that fear of him was drying it up at its source. This was no longer the case later in life, and with his younger children. They loved him tenderly: and if I cannot say so much of myself, I was always loyally devoted to him. As regards my own education, I hesitate to pronounce whether I was more a loser or gainer by his severity. It was not such as to prevent me from having a happy childhood. And I do not believe that boys can be induced to apply themselves with vigor, and what is so much more difficult, perseverance, to dry and irksome studies, by the sole force of persuasion and soft words. Much must be done, and much must be learnt, by children, for which rigid discipline, and known liability to punishment, are indispensable as means. It is, no doubt, a very laudable effort, in modern teaching, to render as much as possible of what the young are required to learn, easy and interesting to them. But when this principle is pushed to the length of not requiring them to learn anything *but* what has been made easy and interesting, one of the chief objects of education is sacrificed. I rejoice in the decline of the old brutal and tyrannical system of teaching, which, however, did succeed in enforcing habits of application; but the new, as it seems to me, is training up a race of men who will be incapable of doing anything which is disagreeable to them. I do not, then, believe that fear, as an element in education, can be dispensed with; but I am sure that it ought not to be the main element; and when it predominates so much as to preclude love and confidence on the part of the child to those who should be the unreservedly trusted advisers of after years, and perhaps to seal up the fountains of frank and spontaneous communicativeness in the child's nature, it is an evil for which a large abatement must be made from the benefits, moral and intellectual, which may flow from any other part of the education.

———

JOHN STUART MILL (1806–1873) *wrote the classic* On Liberty *(1859) and other political statements emphasizing his belief in the value of individual freedom and the power of logic over human behavior. The section here is from his* Autobiography *(1873), a document described by his contemporary Carlyle as "the life of a logic-chopping engine, little more of human in it than if it had been done by a thing of mechanised iron."*

1. The first long paragraph presents a logically developed argument against belief in a particular version of Christianity and against what Mill calls "the evil" of such a belief. What are the various stages of this argument? What is the attitude of the writer towards the argument (which is, of course, his father's), and what means does Mill use to convey this attitude? The second and third paragraphs discuss the effect his father's beliefs had upon the young Mill. Does he ask the reader to find this aspect of his education deserving of praise or blame, or does he use a language that discourages that sort of reaction?

2. The next three paragraphs of the selection describe the opinions of Mill's father on a number of other matters. What are these matters, and what attitude is Mill asking the reader to take toward them? Does Mill seem to defend his father from the harsh judgment of the reader at any point in these paragraphs? If so, how?

3. The last paragraph renders judgments on the father and the system of education the father used upon Mill. Find the sentences which state these judgments, and analyze the care and precision with which they are made.

4. The preface to this section gives a brief analysis of the tone of the first few sentences of the last paragraph. Does that analysis apply to the entire selection? Are there some slight, but important variations in tone in the selection? If so, where do they occur and what is their purpose?

5. Consider the two relationships defined by tone (Mill to his father as parent and teacher, Mill to the reader) and the judgments referred to in question 3. What is the connection between the judgments and the tone; how does the tone itself deliver the same sort of judgments that the assertions in the last paragraph do?

Marcel Proust

MAMMA'S GOOD-NIGHT KISS

My sole consolation when I went upstairs
for the night was that Mamma would come in and kiss me after I
was in bed. But this good night lasted for so short a time: she
went down again so soon that the moment in which I heard her
climb the stairs, and then caught the sound of her garden dress of
blue muslin, from which hung little tassels of plaited straw, rustling along the double-doored corridor, was for me a moment of the
keenest sorrow. So much did I love that good night that I reached
the stage of hoping that it would come as late as possible, so as to
prolong the time of respite during which Mamma would not yet
have appeared. Sometimes when, after kissing me, she opened the
door to go, I longed to call her back, to say to her "Kiss me just
once again," but I knew that then she would at once look displeased, for the concession which she made to my wretchedness and
agitation in coming up to me with this kiss of peace always
annoyed my father, who thought such ceremonies absurd, and she
would have liked to try to induce me to outgrow the need, the
custom of having her there at all, which was a very different thing
from letting the custom grow up of my asking her for an additional
kiss when she was already crossing the threshold. And to see her
look displeased destroyed all the sense of tranquillity she had
brought me a moment before, when she bent her loving face
down over my bed, and held it out to me like a Host, for an act of
Communion in which my lips might drink deeply the sense of her
real presence, and with it the power to sleep. But those evenings on
which Mamma stayed so short a time in my room were sweet indeed compared to those on which we had guests to dinner, and
therefore she did not come at all. Our 'guests' were practically
limited to M. Swann, who, apart from a few passing strangers, was
almost the only person who ever came to the house at Combray,
sometimes to a neighbourly dinner (but less frequently since his

Composite of excerpts from *Swann's Way* reprinted by permission of Random
House from *Remembrance of Things Past*, Modern Library Edition, by Marcel Proust,
trans. by C. K. Moncrieff. Copyright 1928 and renewed 1956 by The Modern Library,
Inc.

unfortunate marriage, as my family did not care to receive his wife) and sometimes after dinner, uninvited. . . .

I never took my eyes off my mother. I knew that when they were at table I should not be permitted to stay there for the whole of dinner-time, and that Mamma, for fear of annoying my father, would not allow me to give her in public the series of kisses that she would have had in my room. And so I promised myself that in the dining-room as they began to eat and drink and as I felt the hour approach, I would put beforehand into this kiss, which was bound to be so brief and stealthy in execution, everything that my own efforts could put into it: would look out very carefully first the exact spot on her cheek where I would imprint it, and would so prepare my thoughts that I might be able, thanks to these mental preliminaries, to consecrate the whole of the minute Mamma would allow me to the sensation of her cheek against my lips, as a painter who can have his subject for short sittings only prepares his palette, and from what he remembers and from rough notes does in advance everything which he possibly can do in the sitter's absence. But tonight, before the dinner-bell had sounded, my grandfather said with unconscious cruelty: "The little man looks tired; he'ld better go up to bed. Besides, we are dining late tonight."

And my father, who was less scrupulous than my grandmother or mother in observing the letter of a treaty, went on: "Yes; run along; to bed with you."

I would have kissed Mamma then and there, but at that moment the dinner-bell rang.

"No, no, leave your mother alone. You've said good night quite enough. These exhibitions are absurd. Go on upstairs."

And so I must set forth without viaticum; must climb each step of the staircase 'against my heart,' as the saying is, climbing in opposition to my heart's desire, which was to return to my mother, since she had not, by her kiss, given my heart leave to accompany me forth. That hateful staircase, up which I always passed with such dismay, gave out a smell of varnish which had to some extent absorbed, made definite and fixed the special quality of sorrow that I felt each evening, and made it perhaps even more cruel to my sensibility because, when it assumed this olfactory guise, my intellect was powerless to resist it. When we have gone to sleep with a maddening toothache and are conscious of it only as a little girl whom we attempt, time after time, to pull out of the water, or as a line of Molière which we repeat incessantly to ourselves, it is a great relief to wake up, so that our intelligence can disentangle the idea of toothache from any artificial semblance of heroism or rhyth-

mic cadence. It was the precise converse of this relief which I felt
when my anguish at having to go up to my room invaded my consciousness in a manner infinitely more rapid, instantaneous almost,
a manner at once insidious and brutal as I breathed in—a far more
poisonous thing than any moral penetration—the peculiar smell of
the varnish upon that staircase.

Once in my room I had to stop every loophole, to close the
shutters, to dig my own grave as I turned down the bedclothes, to
wrap myself in the shroud of my nightshirt. But before burying
myself in the iron bed which had been placed there because, on
summer nights, I was too hot among the rep curtains of the four-
poster, I was stirred to revolt, and attempted the desperate strata-
gem of a condemned prisoner. I wrote to my mother begging her
to come upstairs for an important reason which I could not put in
writing. . . .

My mother did not appear, but with no attempt to safeguard
my self-respect (which depended upon her keeping up the fiction
that she had asked me to let her know the result of my search for
something or other) made Françoise tell me, in so many words
"There is no answer"—words I have so often, since then, heard the
hall-porters in 'mansions' and the flunkeys in gambling-clubs and
the like, repeat to some poor girl, who replies in bewilderment:
"What! he's said nothing? It's not possible. You did give him my
letter, didn't you? Very well, I shall wait a little longer." And just
as she invariably protests that she does not need the extra gas
which the porter offers to light for her, and sits on there, hearing
nothing further, except an occasional remark on the weather which
the porter exchanges with a messenger whom he will send off suddenly, when he notices the time, to put some customer's wine on
the ice; so, having declined Françoise's offer to make me some tea
or to stay beside me, I let her go off again to the servants' hall, and
lay down and shut my eyes, and tried not to hear the voices of my
family who were drinking their coffee in the garden.

But after a few seconds I realised that, by writing that line to
Mamma, by approaching—at the risk of making her angry—so
near to her that I felt I could reach out and grasp the moment in
which I should see her again, I had cut myself off from the possibility of going to sleep until I actually had seen her, and my heart
began to beat more and more painfully as I increased my agitation
by ordering myself to keep calm and to acquiesce in my ill fortune.
Then, suddenly, my anxiety subsided, a feeling of intense happiness coursed through me, as when a strong medicine begins to take
effect and one's pain vanishes: I had found a resolution to abandon
all attempts to go to sleep without seeing Mamma, and had de-

cided to kiss her at all costs, even with the certainty of being in disgrace with her for long afterwards, when she herself came up to bed. The tranquillity which followed my anguish made me extremely alert, no less than my sense of expectation, my thirst for and my fear of danger.

Noiselessly I opened the window and sat down on the foot of my bed; hardly daring to move in case they should hear me from below. Things outside seemed also fixed in mute expectation, so as not to disturb the moonlight which, duplicating each of them and throwing it back by the extension, forwards, of a shadow denser and more concrete than its substance, had made the whole landscape seem at once thinner and longer, like a map which, after being folded up, is spread out upon the ground. What had to move—a leaf of the chestnut-tree, for instance—moved. But its minute shuddering, complete, finished to the least detail and with utmost delicacy of gesture, made no discord with the rest of the scene, and yet was not merged in it, remaining clearly outlined. Exposed upon this surface of silence, which absorbed nothing from them, the most distant sounds, those which must have come from gardens at the far end of the town, could be distinguished with such exact 'finish' that the impression they gave of coming from a distance seemed due only to their 'pianissimo' execution, like those movements on muted strings so well performed by the orchestra of the Conservatoire that, although one does not lose a single note, one thinks all the same that they are being played somewhere outside, a long way from the concert hall, so that all the old subscribers, and my grandmother's sisters too, when Swann had given them his seats, used to strain their ears as if they had caught the distant approach of an army on the march, which had not yet rounded the corner of the Rue de Trévise.

I was well aware that I had placed myself in a position than which none could be counted upon to involve me in graver consequences at my parents' hands; consequences far graver, indeed, than a stranger would have imagined, and such as (he would have thought) could follow only some really shameful fault. But in the system of education which they had given me faults were not classified in the same order as in that of other children, and I had been taught to place at the head of the list (doubtless because there was no other class of faults from which I needed to be more carefully protected) those in which I can now distinguish the common feature that one succumbs to them by yielding to a nervous impulse. But such words as these last had never been uttered in my hearing; no one had yet accounted for my temptations in a way which might have led me to believe that there was some excuse for my giving in to them, or that I was actually incapable of holding out against them. Yet I could easily recognise this class of transgressions by the anguish of mind which preceded, as well as by the rigour of the punishment which followed them; and I knew that what I had just done was in the same category as certain other sins for which I had been severely chastised, though infinitely more serious than they. When I went out to meet my mother as she herself came up to bed, and when she saw that I had remained up so as to say good night to her again in the passage, I should not be allowed to stay in the house a day longer, I should be packed off to school next morning; so much was certain. Very good: had I been obliged, the next moment, to hurl myself out of the window, I should still have preferred such a fate. For what I wanted now was Mamma, and to say good night to her. I had gone too far along the road which led to the realisation of this desire to be able to retrace my steps. . . .

My mother opened the latticed door which led from the hall to the staircase. Presently I heard her coming upstairs to close her window. I went quietly into the passage; my heart was beating so violently that I could hardly move, but at least it was throbbing no longer with anxiety, but with terror and with joy. I saw in the well of the stair a light coming upwards, from Mamma's candle. Then I saw Mamma herself: I threw myself upon her. For an instant she looked at me in astonishment, not realising what could have happened. Then her face assumed an expression of anger. She said not a single word to me; and, for that matter, I used to go for days on end without being spoken to, for far less offences than this. A single word from Mamma would have been an admission that further intercourse with me was within the bounds of possibility, and that might perhaps have appeared to me more terrible still, as indicating that, with such a punishment as was in store for me, mere silence, and even anger, were relatively puerile.

A word from her then would have implied the false calm in which one converses with a servant to whom one has just decided to give notice; the kiss one bestows on a son who is being packed off to enlist, which would have been denied him if it had merely been a matter of being angry with him for a few days. But she heard my father coming from the dressing-room, where he had gone to take off his clothes, and, to avoid the 'scene' which he would make if he saw me, she said, in a voice half-stifled by her anger: "Run away at once. Don't let your father see you standing there like a crazy jane!"

But I begged her again to "Come and say good night to me!" terrified as I saw the light from my father's candle already creeping up the wall, but also making use of his approach as a means of blackmail, in the hope that my mother, not wishing him to find me there, as find me he must if she continued to hold out, would give in to me, and say: "Go back to your room. I will come."

Too late: my father was upon us. Instinctively I murmured, though no one heard me, "I am done for!"

I was not, however. My father used constantly to refuse to let me do things which were quite clearly allowed by the more liberal charters granted me by my mother and grandmother, because he paid no heed to 'Principles,' and because in his sight there were no such things as 'Rights of Man.' For some quite irrelevant reason, or for no reason at all, he would at the last moment prevent me from taking some particular walk, one so regular and so consecrated to my use that to deprive me of it was a clear breach of faith; or again, as he had done this evening, long before the appointed hour he would snap out: "Run along up to bed now; no excuses!" But then again, simply because he was devoid of principles (in my grandmother's sense), so he could not, properly speaking, be called inexorable. He looked at me for a moment with an air of annoyance and surprise, and then when Mamma had told him, not without some embarrassment, what had happened, said to her: "Go along with him, then; you said just now that you didn't feel like sleep, so stay in his room for a little. I don't need anything."

"But, dear," my mother answered timidly, "whether or not I feel like sleep is not the point; we must not make the child accustomed . . ."

"There's no question of making him accustomed," said my father, with a shrug of the shoulders; "you can see quite well that the child is unhappy. After all, we aren't gaolers. You'll end by making him ill, and a lot of good that will do. There are two beds in his room; tell Françoise to make up the big one for you, and stay beside him for the rest of the night. I'm off to bed, anyhow; I'm not nervous like you. Good night."

It was impossible for me to thank my father; what he called my sentimentality would have exasperated him. I stood there, not daring to move; he was still confronting us, an immense figure in his white nightshirt, crowned with the pink and violet scarf of Indian cashmere in which, since he had begun to suffer from neuralgia, he used to tie up his head, standing like Abraham in the engraving after Benozzo Gozzoli which M. Swann had given me, telling Sarah that she must tear herself away from Isaac. Many years have passed since that night. The wall of the staircase, up which I had watched the light of his candle gradually climb, was long ago demolished. And in myself, too, many things have perished which, I imagined, would last for ever, and new structures have arisen, giving birth to new sorrows and new joys which in those days I could not have foreseen, just as now the old are difficult of comprehension. It is a long time, too, since my father has been able to tell Mamma to "Go with the child." Never again will such hours be

possible for me. But of late I have been increasingly able to catch,
if I listen attentively, the sound of the sobs which I had the
strength to control in my father's presence, and which broke out
only when I found myself alone with Mamma. Actually, their echo
has never ceased: it is only because life is now growing more and
more quiet round about me that I hear them afresh, like those convent bells which are so effectively drowned during the day by the
noises of the streets that one would suppose them to have been
stopped for ever, until they sound out again through the silent
evening air.

Mamma spent that night in my room: when I had just committed a sin so deadly that I was waiting to be banished from the
household, my parents gave me a far greater concession than I
should ever have won as the reward of a good action. Even at the
moment when it manifested itself in this crowning mercy, my
father's conduct towards me was still somewhat arbitrary, and
regardless of my deserts, as was characteristic of him and due to the
fact that his actions were generally dictated by chance expediencies
rather than based on any formal plan. And perhaps even what I
called his strictness, when he sent me off to bed, deserved that title
less, really, than my mother's or grandmother's attitude, for his
nature, which in some respects differed more than theirs from my
own, had probably prevented him from guessing, until then, how
wretched I was every evening, a thing which my mother and grandmother knew well; but they loved me enough to be unwilling to
spare me that suffering, which they hoped to teach me to overcome,
so as to reduce my nervous sensibility and to strengthen my will.
As for my father, whose affection for me was of another kind, I
doubt if he would have shewn so much courage, for as soon as he
had grasped the fact that I was unhappy he had said to my mother:
"Go and comfort him."

Mamma stayed all night in my room, and it seemed that she
did not wish to mar by recrimination those hours, so different from
anything that I had had a right to expect; for when Françoise (who
guessed that something extraordinary must have happened when
she saw Mamma sitting by my side, holding my hand and letting
me cry unchecked) said to her: "But, Madame, what is little Master
crying for?" she replied: "Why, Françoise, he doesn't know himself: it is his nerves. Make up the big bed for me quickly and then
go off to your own." And thus for the first time my unhappiness
was regarded no longer as a fault for which I must be punished, but
as an involuntary evil which had been officially recognised, a nervous condition for which I was in no way responsible: I had the
consolation that I need no longer mingle apprehensive scruples
with the bitterness of my tears; I could weep henceforward without

sin. I felt no small degree of pride, either, in Françoise's presence at this return to humane conditions which, not an hour after Mamma had refused to come up to my room and had sent the snubbing message that I was to go to sleep, raised me to the dignity of a grown-up person, brought me of a sudden to a sort of puberty of sorrow, to emancipation from tears. I ought then to have been happy; I was not. It struck me that my mother had just made a first concession which must have been painful to her, that it was a first step down from the ideal she had formed for me, and that for the first time she, with all her courage, had to confess herself beaten. It struck me that if I had just scored a victory it was over her; that I had succeeded, as sickness or sorrow or age might have succeeded, in relaxing her will, in altering her judgment; that this evening opened a new era, must remain a black date in the calendar. And if I had dared now, I should have said to Mamma: "No, I don't want you; you mustn't sleep here." But I was conscious of the practical wisdom, of what would be called nowadays the realism, with which she tempered the ardent idealism of my grandmother's nature, and I knew that now the mischief was done she would prefer to let me enjoy the soothing pleasure of her company, and not to disturb my father again. Certainly my mother's beautiful features seemed to shine again with youth that evening, as she sat gently holding my hands and trying to check my tears; but, just for that reason, it seemed to me that this should not have happened; her anger would have been less difficult to endure than this new kindness which my childhood had not known; I felt that I had with an impious and secret finger traced a first wrinkle upon her soul and made the first white hair shew upon her head.

MARCEL PROUST (1871–1922) *includes these autobiographical recollections in the first volume,* Swann's Way, *of his* Remembrance of Things Past *(1913–1927), an example of modern fiction technique seeking to recreate the workings of the mind.*

1. *The preface to this section refers to Proust's use of concrete nouns and active, sensual verbs to involve the reader intimately in the situation. Find additional examples of these stylistic devices, and discover other specific means the writer uses for the same ends. What is the connection between the tone of the passage and the personal and moral problems the passage considers?*

2. *In the paragraph beginning "I was well aware . . .", the writer*

speaks of the grave consequences of his appeal for the goodnight kiss, "consequences far graver indeed than a stranger would
have imagined." Part of the writer's problem here is to make
the reader feel that what seems rather slight is in fact "grave,"
important, worthy of his attention. What does Proust do in this
paragraph to help the reader share the narrator's sense of the
meaning of the event? Find similar examples elsewhere in the
selection.

3. The last two paragraphs of this selection give the writer's analysis of his "victory." How does this victory help define his relationship to his father? How does it help define the very
complicated relationship to his mother? Why do so many tears
and so much sorrow accompany what he calls "a sort of puberty
of sorrow" and "emancipation from tears"?

Sherwood Anderson

I DISCOVER MY FATHER

You hear it said that fathers want their sons to be what they feel they cannot themselves be, but I tell you it also works the other way. A boy wants something very special from his father. I know that as a small boy I wanted my father to be a certain thing he was not. I wanted him to be a proud, silent, dignified father. When I was with other boys and he passed along the street, I wanted to feel a flow of pride. "There he is. That is my father."

But he wasn't such a one. He couldn't be. It seemed to me then that he was always showing off. Let's say someone in our town had got up a show. They were always doing it. The druggist would be in it, the shoe-store clerk, the horse doctor, and a lot of women and girls. My father would manage to get the chief comedy part. It was, let's say, a Civil War play and he was a comic Irish soldier. He had to do the most absurd things. They thought he was funny, but I didn't.

I thought he was terrible. I didn't see how mother could stand it. She even laughed with the others. Maybe I would have laughed if it hadn't been my father.

Or there was a parade, the Fourth of July or Decoration Day. He'd be in that, too, right at the front of it, as Grand Marshal or something, on a white horse hired from a livery stable.

He couldn't ride for shucks. He fell off the horse and everyone hooted with laughter, but he didn't care. He even seemed to like it. I remember once when he had done something ridiculous, and right out on Main Street, too. I was with some other boys and they were laughing and shouting at him and he was shouting back and having as good a time as they were. I ran down an alley back of some stores and there in the Presbyterian Church sheds I had a good long cry.

Or I would be in bed at night and father would come home a little lit up and bring some men with him. He was a man who was never alone. Before he went broke, running a harness shop, there

From *Memoirs of Sherwood Anderson*, edited by Ray Lewis White, The University of North Carolina Press, 1969. Reprinted by permission.

were always a lot of men loafing in the shop. He went broke, of course, because he gave too much credit. He couldn't refuse it and I thought he was a fool. I had got to hating him.

There'd be men I didn't think would want to be fooling around with him. There might even be the superintendent of our schools and a quiet man who ran the hardware store. Once I remember there was a white-haired man who was a cashier of the bank. It was a wonder to me they'd want to be seen with such a windbag. That's what I thought he was. I know now what it was that attracted them. It was because life in our town, as in all small towns, was at times pretty dull and he livened it up. He made them laugh. He could tell stories. He'd even get them to singing.

If they didn't come to our house they'd go off, say at night, to where there was a grassy place by a creek. They'd cook food there and drink beer and sit about listening to his stories.

He was always telling stories about himself. He'd say this or that wonderful thing had happened to him. It might be something that made him look like a fool. He didn't care.

If an Irishman came to our house, right away father would say he was Irish. He'd tell what county in Ireland he was born in. He'd tell things that happened there when he was a boy. He'd make it seem so real that, if I hadn't known he was born in southern Ohio, I'd have believed him myself.

If it was a Scotchman the same thing happened. He'd get a burr into his speech. Or he was a German or a Swede. He'd be anything the other man was. I think they all knew he was lying, but they seemed to like him just the same. As a boy that was what I couldn't understand.

And there was mother. How could she stand it? I wanted to ask but never did. She was not the kind you asked such questions.

I'd be upstairs in my bed, in my room above the porch, and father would be telling some of his tales. A lot of father's stories were about the Civil War. To hear him tell it he'd been in about every battle. He'd known Grant, Sherman, Sheridan and I don't know how many others. He'd been particularly intimate with General Grant so that when Grant went East to take charge of all the armies, he took father along.

"I was an orderly at headquarters and Sim Grant said to me, 'Irve,' he said, 'I'm going to take you along with me.' "

It seems he and Grant used to slip off sometimes and have a quiet drink together. That's what my father said. He'd tell about the day Lee surrendered and how, when the great moment came, they couldn't find Grant.

"You know," my father said, "about General Grant's book, his memoirs. You've read of how he said he had a headache and how, when he got word that Lee was ready to call it quits, he was suddenly and miraculously cured.

"Huh," said father. "He was in the woods with me.

"I was in there with my back against a tree. I was pretty well corned. I had got hold of a bottle of pretty good stuff.

"They were looking for Grant. He had got off his horse and come into the woods. He found me. He was covered with mud.

"I had the bottle in my hand. What'd I care? The war was over. I knew we had them licked."

My father said that he was the one who told Grant about Lee. An orderly riding by had told him, because the orderly knew how thick he was with Grant. Grant was embarrassed.

"But, Irve, look at me. I'm all covered with mud," he said to father.

And then, my father said, he and Grant decided to have a drink together. They took a couple of shots and then, because he didn't want Grant to show up potted before the immaculate Lee, he smashed the bottle against the tree.

"Sim Grant's dead now and I wouldn't want it to get out on him," my father said.

That's just one of the kind of things he'd tell. Of course the men knew he was lying, but they seemed to like it just the same.

When we got broke, down and out, do you think he ever brought anything home? Not he. If there wasn't anything to eat in the house, he'd go off visiting around at farmhouses. They all wanted him. Sometimes he'd stay away for weeks, mother working to keep us fed, and then home he'd come bringing, let's say, a ham. He'd got it from some farmer friend. He'd slap it on the table in the kitchen. "You bet I'm going to see that my kids have something to eat," he'd say, and mother would just stand smiling at him. She'd never say a word about all the weeks and months he'd been away, not leaving us a cent for food. Once I heard her speaking to a woman in our street. Maybe the woman had dared to sympathize with her. "Oh," she said, "it's all right. He isn't ever dull like most of the men in this street. Life is never dull when my man is about."

But often I was filled with bitterness, and sometimes I wished he wasn't my father. I'd even invent another man as my father. To protect my mother I'd make up stories of a secret marriage that for some strange reason never got known. As though some man, say the president of a railroad company or maybe a Congressman, had married my mother, thinking his wife was dead and then it turned out she wasn't.

So they had to hush it up but I got born just the same. I wasn't really the son of my father. Somewhere in the world there was a very dignified, quite wonderful man who was really my father. I even made myself half believe these fancies.

And then there came a certain night. He'd been off somewhere for two or three weeks. He found me alone in the house, reading by the kitchen table.

It had been raining and he was very wet. He sat and looked at me for a long time, not saying a word. I was startled, for there was on his face the saddest look I had ever seen. He sat for a time, his clothes dripping. Then he got up.

"Come on with me," he said.

I got up and went with him out of the house. I was filled with wonder but I wasn't afraid. We went along a dirt road that led down into a valley, about a mile out of town, where there was a pond. We walked in silence. The man who was always talking had stopped his talking.

I didn't know what was up and had the queer feeling that I was with a stranger. I don't know whether my father intended it so. I don't think he did.

The pond was quite large. It was still raining hard and there were flashes of lightning followed by thunder. We were on a grassy bank at the pond's edge when my father spoke, and in the darkness and rain his voice sounded strange.

"Take off your clothes," he said. Still filled with wonder, I began to undress. There was a flash of lightning and I saw that he was already naked.

Naked, we went into the pond. Taking my hand he pulled me in. It may be that I was too frightened, too full of a feeling of strangeness, to speak. Before that night my father had never seemed to pay any attention to me.

"And what is he up to now?" I kept asking myself. I did not swim very well, but he put my hand on his shoulder and struck out into the darkness.

He was a man with big shoulders, a powerful swimmer. In the darkness I could feel the movement of his muscles. We swam to the far edge of the pond and then back to where we had left our clothes. The rain continued and the wind blew. Sometimes my father swam on his back and when he did he took my hand in his large powerful one and moved it over so that it rested always on his shoulder. Sometimes there would be a flash of lightning and I could see his face quite clearly.

It was as it was earlier, in the kitchen, a face filled with sadness. There would be the momentary glimpse of his face and then again the darkness, the wind and the rain. In me there was a feeling I had never known before.

It was a feeling of closeness. It was something strange. It was as though there were only we two in the world. It was as though I had been jerked suddenly out of myself, out of my world of the school-boy, out of a world in which I was ashamed of my father.

He had become blood of my blood; he the strong swimmer and I the boy clinging to him in the darkness. We swam in silence and in silence we dressed in our wet clothes, and went home.

There was a lamp lighted in the kitchen and when we came in, the water dripping from us, there was my mother. She smiled at us. I remember that she called us "boys."

"What have you boys been up to," she asked, but my father did not answer. As he had begun the evening's experience with me in silence, so he ended it. He turned and looked at me. Then he went, I thought, with a new and strange dignity out of the room.

I climbed the stairs to my own room, undressed in the darkness and got into bed. I couldn't sleep and did not want to sleep. For the first time I knew that I was the son of my father. He was a story teller as I was to be. It may be that I even laughed a little softly there in the darkness. If I did, I laughed knowing that I would never again be wanting another father.

———

SHERWOOD ANDERSON (1876–1941) *achieved fame with the publication of* Winesburg, Ohio *(1919), a series of sketches and tales portraying, he wrote, "the truths that made the people grotesque." This chapter describing his father is from* Sherwood Anderson's Memoirs *(1939).*

1. *In this deceptively simple account, Anderson needs to manage tone with great skill. He must convince the reader of his early distaste, even hate for his father, and must then make convincing the change in attitudes that comes with the swimming scene at the end—all the while asking us to see beyond the boy's limitations of vision. We must share the boy's embarrassment at the undignified father even as we observe and value the imagination and vitality of the father, who has his own kind of dignity. Demonstrate how Anderson conveys these different attitudes by language and structure.*

2. *A great artist once declared that "art is a lie that tells the truth." How do the various examples of his father's "lies" help the writer to show his change in attitude toward what he later calls story telling? How does the language used in the swimming*

scene tend to confirm this change in attitudes?

3. *The writer appears to equate the discovery of his father with the discovery of an important fact about himself. What part of himself has been "discovered," and what attitude does the language of this discovery ask the reader to take?*

James Baldwin

NOTES OF A NATIVE SON

On the 29th of July, in 1943, my father died. On the same day, a few hours later, his last child was born. Over a month before this, while all our energies were concentrated in waiting for these events, there had been, in Detroit, one of the bloodiest race riots of the century. A few hours after my father's funeral, while he lay in state in the undertaker's chapel, a race riot broke out in Harlem. On the morning of the 3rd of August, we drove my father to the graveyard through a wilderness of smashed plate glass.

The day of my father's funeral had also been my nineteenth birthday. As we drove him to the graveyard, the spoils of injustice, anarchy, discontent, and hatred were all around us. It seemed to me that God himself had devised, to mark my father's end, the most sustained and brutally dissonant of codas. And it seemed to me, too, that the violence which rose all about us as my father left the world had been devised as a corrective for the pride of his eldest son. I had declined to believe in that apocalypse which had been central to my father's vision; very well, life seemed to be saying, here is something that will certainly pass for an apocalypse until the real thing comes along. I had inclined to be contemptuous of my father for the conditions of his life, for the conditions of our lives. When his life had ended I began to wonder about that life and also, in a new way, to be apprehensive about my own.

I had not known my father very well. We had got on badly, partly because we shared, in our different fashions, the vice of stubborn pride. When he was dead I realized that I had hardly ever spoken to him. When he had been dead a long time I began to wish I had. It seems to be typical of life in America, where opportunities, real and fancied, are thicker than anywhere else on the globe, that the second generation has no time to talk to the first. No one, including my father, seems to have known exactly how old he was, but his mother had been born during slavery. He was of the first generation of free men. He, along with thousands of other Negroes,

came North after 1919 and I was part of that generation which had
never seen the landscape of what Negroes sometimes call the Old
Country.

He had been born in New Orleans and had been a quite young
man there during the time that Louis Armstrong, a boy, was running errands for the dives and honky-tonks of what was always presented to me as one of the most wicked of cities—to this day, whenever I think of New Orleans, I also helplessly think of Sodom and
Gomorrah. My father never mentioned Louis Armstrong, except to
forbid us to play his records; but there was a picture of him on our
wall for a long time. One of my father's strong-willed female relatives
had placed it there and forbade my father to take it down. He
never did, but he eventually maneuvered her out of the house and
when, some years later, she was in trouble and near death, he refused
to do anything to help her.

He was, I think, very handsome. I gather this from photographs
and from my own memories of him, dressed in his Sunday best and
on his way to preach a sermon somewhere, when I was little.
Handsome, proud, and ingrown, "like a toe-nail," somebody said.
But he looked to me, as I grew older, like pictures I had seen of
African tribal chieftains: he really should have been naked, with
war-paint on and barbaric mementos, standing among spears. He
could be chilling in the pulpit and indescribably cruel in his personal life and he was certainly the most bitter man I have ever met;
yet it must be said that there was something else in him, buried in
him, which lent him his tremendous power and, even, a rather
crushing charm. It had something to do with his blackness, I think
—he was very black—with his blackness and his beauty, and with
the fact that he knew that he was black but did not know that he
was beautiful. He claimed to be proud of his blackness but it had
also been the cause of much humiliation and it had fixed bleak
boundaries to his life. He was not a young man when we were growing up and he had already suffered many kinds of ruin; in his out-
rageously demanding and protective way he loved his children, who
were black like him and menaced, like him; and all these things
sometimes showed in his face when he tried, never to my knowledge
with any success, to establish contact with any of us. When he
took one of his children on his knee to play, the child always became
fretful and began to cry; when he tried to help one of us with our
homework the absolutely unabating tension which emanated from
him caused our minds and our tongues to become paralyzed, so
that he, scarcely knowing why, flew into a rage and the child, not
knowing why, was punished. If it ever entered his head to bring a
surprise home for his children, it was, almost unfailingly, the wrong
surprise and even the big watermelons he often brought home on

his back in the summertime led to the most appalling scenes. I do
not remember, in all those years, that one of his children was ever
glad to see him come home. From what I was able to gather of his
early life, it seemed that this inability to establish contact with
other people had always marked him and had been one of the things
which had driven him out of New Orleans. There was something
in him, therefore, groping and tentative, which was never expressed
and which was buried with him. One saw it most clearly when he
was facing new people and hoping to impress them. But he never
did, not for long. We went from church to smaller and more im-
probable church, he found himself in less and less demand as a minister, and by the time he died none of his friends had come to see
him for a long time. He had lived and died in an intolerable bitterness of spirit and it frightened me, as we drove him to the graveyard through those unquiet, ruined streets, to see how powerful
and overflowing this bitterness could be and to realize that this
bitterness now was mine.

When he died I had been away from home for a little over a
year. In that year I had had time to become aware of the meaning
of all my father's bitter warnings, had discovered the secret of his
proudly pursed lips and rigid carriage: I had discovered the weight
of white people in the world. I saw that this had been for my
ancestors and now would be for me an awful thing to live with and
that the bitterness which had helped to kill my father could also kill
me.

He had been ill a long time—in the mind, as we now realized,
reliving instances of his fantastic intransigence in the new light of
his affliction and endeavoring to feel a sorrow for him which never,
quite, came true. We had not known that he was being eaten up by
paranoia, and the discovery that his cruelty, to our bodies and our
minds, had been one of the symptoms of his illness was not, then,
enough to enable us to forgive him. The younger children felt,
quite simply, relief that he would not be coming home anymore.
My mother's observation that it was he, after all, who had kept them
alive all these years meant nothing because the problems of keeping
children alive are not real for children. The older children felt, with
my father gone, that they could invite their friends to the house
without fear that their friends would be insulted or, as had sometimes happened with me, being told that their friends were in
league with the devil and intended to rob our family of everything
we owned. (I didn't fail to wonder, and it made me hate him, what
on earth we owned that anybody else would want.)

His illness was beyond all hope of healing before anyone realized
that he was ill. He had always been so strange and had lived, like a
prophet, in such unimaginably close communion with the Lord that

his long silences which were punctuated by moans and hallelujahs
and snatches of old songs while he sat at the living-room window
never seemed odd to us. It was not until he refused to eat because,
he said, his family was trying to poison him that my mother was
forced to accept as a fact what had, until then, been only an unwilling suspicion. When he was committed, it was discovered that he
had tuberculosis and, as it turned out, the disease of his mind
allowed the disease of his body to destroy him. For the doctors
could not force him to eat, either, and, though he was fed intra-
venously, it was clear from the beginning that there was no hope for
him.

In my mind's eye I could see him, sitting at the window, locked
up in his terrors; hating and fearing every living soul including his
children who had betrayed him, too, by reaching towards the world
which had despised him. There were nine of us. I began to wonder
what it could have felt like for such a man to have had nine children
whom he could barely feed. He used to make little jokes about our
poverty, which never, of course, seemed very funny to us; they could
not have seemed very funny to him, either, or else our all too feeble
response to them would never have caused such rages. He spent
great energy and achieved, to our chagrin, no small amount of success in keeping us away from the people who surrounded us, people who had all-night rent parties to which we listened when we
should have been sleeping, people who cursed and drank and
flashed razor blades on Lenox Avenue. He could not understand
why, if they had so much energy to spare, they could not use it to
make their lives better. He treated almost everybody on our block
with a most uncharitable asperity and neither they, nor, of course,
their children were slow to reciprocate.

The only white people who came to our house were welfare
workers and bill collectors. It was almost always my mother who
dealt with them, for my father's temper, which was at the mercy of
his pride, was never to be trusted. It was clear that he felt their very
presence in his home to be a violation: this was conveyed by his
carriage, almost ludicrously stiff, and by his voice, harsh and vin-
dictively polite. When I was around nine or ten I wrote a play
which was directed by a young, white schoolteacher, a woman, who
then took an interest in me, and gave me books to read and, in order
to corroborate my theatrical bent, decided to take me to see what she
somewhat tactlessly referred to as "real" plays. Theater-going was
forbidden in our house, but, with the really cruel intuitiveness of a
child, I suspected that the color of this woman's skin would carry
the day for me. When, at school, she suggested taking me to the
theater, I did not, as I might have done if she had been a Negro,
find a way of discouraging her, but agreed that she should pick me

up at my house one evening. I then, very cleverly, left all the rest
to my mother, who suggested to my father, as I knew she would,
that it would not be very nice to let such a kind woman make the
trip for nothing. Also, since it was a schoolteacher, I imagine that
my mother countered the idea of sin with the idea of "education,"
which word, even with my father, carried a kind of bitter weight.

Before the teacher came my father took me aside to ask *why* she
was coming, what *interest* she could possibly have in our house, in a
boy like me. I said I didn't know but I, too, suggested that it had
something to do with education. And I understood that my father
was waiting for me to say something—I didn't quite know what;
perhaps that I wanted his protection against this teacher and her
"education." I said none of these things and the teacher came and
we went out. It was clear, during the brief interview in our living
room, that my father was agreeing very much against his will and
that he would have refused permission if he had dared. The fact that
he did not dare caused me to despise him: I had no way of knowing
that he was facing in that living room a wholly unprecedented and
frightening situation.

Later, when my father had been laid off from his job, this
woman became very important to us. She was really a very sweet
and generous woman and went to a great deal of trouble to be of
help to us, particularly during one awful winter. My mother called
her by the highest name she knew: she said she was a "christian."
My father could scarcely disagree but during the four or five years
of our relatively close association he never trusted her and was
always trying to surprise in her open, Midwestern face the genuine,
cunningly hidden, and hideous motivation. In later years, particularly when it began to be clear that this "education" of mine was
going to lead me to perdition, he became more explicit and warned
me that my white friends in high school were not really my friends
and that I would see, when I was older, how white people would do
anything to keep a Negro down. Some of them could be nice, he
admitted, but none of them were to be trusted and most of them
were not even nice. The best thing was to have as little to do with
them as possible. I did not feel this way and I was certain, in my
innocence, that I never would.

But the year which preceded my father's death had made a great
change in my life. I had been living in New Jersey, working in
defense plants, working and living among southerners, white and
black. I knew about the south, of course, and about how southerners
treated Negroes and how they expected them to behave, but it
had never entered my mind that anyone would look at me and
expect *me* to behave that way. I learned in New Jersey that to be a
Negro meant, precisely, that one was never looked at but was simply

at the mercy of the reflexes the color of one's skin caused in other people. I acted in New Jersey as I had always acted, that is as though I thought a great deal of myself—I had to *act* that way—with results that were, simply, unbelievable. I had scarcely arrived before I had earned the enmity, which was extraordinarily ingenious, of all my superiors and nearly all my co-workers. In the beginning, to make matters worse, I simply did not know what was happening. I did not know what I had done, and I shortly began to wonder what *anyone* could possibly do, to bring about such unanimous, active, and unbearably vocal hostility. I knew about jim-crow but I had never experienced it. I went to the same self-service restaurant three times and stood with all the Princeton boys before the counter, waiting for a hamburger and coffee; it was always an extraordinarily long time before anything was set before me; but it was not until the fourth visit that I learned that, in fact, nothing had ever been set before me: I had simply picked something up. Negroes were not served there, I was told, and they had been waiting for me to realize that I was always the only Negro present. Once I was told this, I determined to go there all the time. But now they were ready for me and, though some dreadful scenes were subsequently enacted in that restaurant, I never ate there again.

It was the same story all over New Jersey, in bars, bowling alleys, diners, places to live. I was always being forced to leave, silently, or with mutual imprecations. I very shortly became notorious and children giggled behind me when I passed and their elders whispered or shouted—they really believed that I was mad. And it did begin to work on my mind, of course; I began to be afraid to go anywhere and to compensate for this I went places to which I really should not have gone and where, God knows, I had no desire to be. My reputation in town naturally enhanced my reputation at work and my working day became one long series of acrobatics designed to keep me out of trouble. I cannot say that these acrobatics succeeded. It began to seem that the machinery of the organization I worked for was turning over, day and night, with but one aim: to eject me. I was fired once, and contrived, with the aid of a friend from New York, to get back on the payroll; was fired again, and bounced back again. It took a while to fire me for the third time, but the third time took. There were no loopholes anywhere. There was not even any way of getting back inside the gates.

That year in New Jersey lives in my mind as though it were the year during which, having an unsuspected predilection for it, I first contracted some dread, chronic disease, the unfailing symptom of which is a kind of blind fever, a pounding in the skull and fire in the bowels. Once this disease is contracted, one can never be really carefree again, for the fever, without an instant's warning, can recur at any moment. It can wreck more important things than race relations. There is not a Negro alive who does not have this rage in his blood—one has the choice, merely, of living with it consciously or surrendering to it. As for me, this fever has recurred in me, and does, and will until the day I die.

My last night in New Jersey, a white friend from New York took me to the nearest big town, Trenton, to go to the movies and have a few drinks. As it turned out, he also saved me from, at the very least, a violent whipping. Almost every detail of that night stands out very clearly in my memory. I even remember the name of the movie we saw because its title impressed me as being so patly ironical. It was a movie about the German occupation of France, starring Maureen O'Hara and Charles Laughton and called *This Land Is Mine*. I remember the name of the diner we walked into when the movie ended: it was the "American Diner." When we walked in the counterman asked what we wanted and I remember answering with the casual sharpness which had become my habit: "We want a hamburger and a cup of coffee, what do you think we want?" I do not know why, after a year of such rebuffs, I so completely failed to anticipate his answer, which was, of course, "We don't serve Negroes here." This reply failed to discompose me, at least for the moment. I made some sardonic comment about the name of the diner and we walked out into the streets.

This was the time of what was called the "brown-out," when the lights in all American cities were very dim. When we re-entered the streets something happened to me which had the force of an optical illusion, or a nightmare. The streets were very crowded and I was facing north. People were moving in every direction but it seemed to me, in that instant, that all of the people I could see, and many more than that, were moving toward me, against me, and that everyone was white. I remember how their faces gleamed. And I felt, like a physical sensation, a *click* at the nape of my neck as though some interior string connecting my head to my body had been cut. I began to walk. I heard my friend call after me, but I ignored him. Heaven only knows what was going on in his mind, but he had the good sense not to touch me—I don't know what would have happened if he had—and to keep me in sight. I don't know what was going on in my mind, either; I certainly had no conscious plan. I wanted to do something to crush these white faces, which were crushing me. I walked for perhaps a block or two until I came to an enormous, glittering, and fashionable restaurant in which I knew not even the intercession of the Virgin would cause me to be served. I pushed through the doors and took the first vacant seat I saw, at a table for two, and waited.

I do not know how long I waited and I rather wonder, until

today, what I could possibly have looked like. Whatever I looked like, I frightened the waitress who shortly appeared, and the moment she appeared all of my fury flowed towards her. I hated her for her white face, and for her great, astounded, frightened eyes. I felt that if she found a black man so frightening I would make her fright worth-while.

She did not ask me what I wanted, but repeated, as though she had learned it somewhere, "We don't serve Negroes here." She did not say it with the blunt, derisive hostility to which I had grown so accustomed, but, rather, with a note of apology in her voice, and fear. This made me colder and more murderous than ever. I felt I had to do something with my hands. I wanted her to come close enough for me to get her neck between my hands.

So I pretended not to have understood her, hoping to draw her closer. And she did step a very short step closer, with her pencil poised incongruously over her pad, and repeated the formula: ". . . don't serve Negroes here."

Somehow, with the repetition of that phrase, which was already ringing in my head like a thousand bells of a nightmare, I realized that she would never come any closer and that I would have to strike from a distance. There was nothing on the table but an ordinary watermug half full of water, and I picked this up and hurled it with all my strength at her. She ducked and it missed her and shattered against the mirror behind the bar. And, with that sound, my frozen blood abruptly thawed, I returned from wherever I had been, I *saw*, for the first time, the restaurant, the people with their mouths open, already, as it seemed to me, rising as one man, and I realized what I had done, and where I was, and I was frightened. I rose and began running for the door. A round, potbellied man grabbed me by the nape of the neck just as I reached the doors and began to beat me about the face. I kicked him and got loose and ran into the streets. My friend whispered, *"Run!"* and I ran.

My friend stayed outside the restaurant long enough to misdirect my pursuers and the police, who arrived, he told me, at once. I do not know what I said to him when he came to my room that night. I could not have said much. I felt, in the oddest, most awful way, that I had somehow betrayed him. I lived it over and over and over again, the way one relives an automobile accident after it has happened and one finds oneself alone and safe. I could not get over two facts, both equally difficult for the imagination to grasp, and one was that I could have been murdered. But the other was that I had been ready to commit murder. I saw nothing very clearly but I did see this: that my life, my *real* life, was in danger, and not from anything other people might do but from the hatred I carried in my own heart.

I I · I had returned home around the second week in June—in great haste because it seemed that my father's death and my mother's confinement were both but a matter of hours. In the case of my mother, it soon became clear that she had simply made a miscalculation. This had always been her tendency and I don't believe that a single one of us arrived in the world, or has since arrived anywhere else, on time. But none of us dawdled so intolerably about the business of being born as did my baby sister. We sometimes amused ourselves, during those endless, stifling weeks, by picturing the baby sitting within in the safe, warm dark, bitterly regretting the necessity of becoming a part of our chaos and stubbornly putting it off as long as possible. I understood her perfectly and congratulated her on showing such good sense so soon. Death, however, sat as purposefully at my father's bedside as life stirred within my mother's womb and it was harder to understand why he so lingered in that long shadow. It seemed that he had bent, and for a long time, too, all of his energies towards dying. Now death was ready for him but my father held back.

All of Harlem, indeed, seemed to be infected by waiting. I had never before known it to be so violently still. Racial tensions throughout this country were exacerbated during the early years of the war, partly because the labor market brought together hundreds of thousands of ill-prepared people and partly because Negro soldiers, regardless of where they were born, received their military training in the south. What happened in defense plants and army camps had repercussions, naturally, in every Negro ghetto. The situation in Harlem had grown bad enough for clergymen, policemen, educators, politicians, and social workers to assert in one breath that there was no "crime wave" and to offer, in the very next breath, suggestions as to how to combat it. These suggestions always seemed to involve playgrounds, despite the fact that racial skirmishes were occurring in the playgrounds, too. Playground or not, crime wave or not, the Harlem police force had been augmented in March, and the unrest grew—perhaps, in fact, partly as a result of the ghetto's instinctive hatred of policemen. Perhaps the most revealing news item, out of the steady parade of reports of muggings, stabbings, shootings, assaults, gang wars, and accusations of police brutality, is the item concerning six Negro girls who set upon a white girl in the subway because, as they all too accurately put it, she was stepping on their toes. Indeed she was, all over the nation.

I had never before been so aware of policemen, on foot, on horseback, on corners, everywhere, always two by two. Nor had I ever been so aware of small knots of people. They were on stoops and on corners and in doorways, and what was striking about them, I think, was that they did not seem to be talking. Never, when I passed these groups, did the usual sound of a curse or a laugh ring out and neither did there seem to be any hum of gossip. There was certainly, on the other hand, occurring between them communication extraordinarily intense. Another thing that was striking was the unexpected diversity of the people who made up these groups. Usually for example, one would see a group of sharpies standing on the street corner, jiving the passing chicks; or a group of older men, usually, for some reason, in the vicinity of a barber shop, discussing baseball scores, or the numbers, or making rather chilling observations about women they had known. Women, in a general way, tended to be seen less often together—unless they were church women, or very young girls, or prostitutes met together for an unprofessional instant. But that summer I saw the strangest combinations: large, respectable, churchly matrons standing on the stoops or the corners with their hair tied up, together with a girl in sleazy satin whose face bore the marks of gin and the razor, or heavy-set, abrupt, no-nonsense older men, in company with the most disreputable and fanatical "race" men, or these same "race" men with the sharpies, or these sharpies with the churchly women. Seventh Day Adventists and Methodists and Spiritualists seemed to be hobnobbing with Holyrollers and they were all, alike, entangled with the most flagrant disbelievers; something heavy in their stance seemed to indicate that they had all, incredibly, seen a common vision, and on each face there seemed to be the same strange, bitter shadow.

The churchly women and the matter-of-fact, no-nonsense men had children in the Army. The sleazy girls they talked to had lovers there, the sharpies and the "race" men had friends and brothers there. It would have demanded an unquestioning patriotism, happily as uncommon in this country as it is undesirable, for these people not to have been disturbed by the bitter letters they received, by the newspaper stories they read, not to have been enraged by the posters, then to be found all over New York, which described the Japanese as "yellow-bellied Japs." It was only the "race" men, to be sure, who spoke ceaselessly of being revenged—how this vengeance was to be exacted was not clear—for the indignities and dangers suffered by Negro boys in uniform; but everybody felt a directionless, hopeless bitterness, as well as that panic which can scarcely be suppressed when one knows that a human being one loves is beyond one's reach, and in danger. This helplessness and this gnawing uneasiness does something, at length, to even the toughest mind. Perhaps the best way to sum all this up is to say that the people I knew felt, mainly, a peculiar kind of relief when they knew that their boys were being shipped out of the south, to do battle overseas. It was, perhaps, like feeling that the most dangerous part of a dangerous journey had been passed and that now, even if death should come, it would come with honor and without the complicity of their countrymen. Such a death would be, in short, a fact with which one could hope to live.

It was on the 28th of July, which I believe was a Wednesday, that I visited my father for the first time during his illness and for the last time in his life. The moment I saw him I knew why I·had put off this visit so long. I had told my mother that I did not want to see him because I hated him. But this was not true. It was only that I *had* hated him and I wanted to hold on to this hatred. I did not want to look on him as a ruin: it was not a ruin I had hated. I imagine that one of the reasons people cling to their hates so stubbornly is because they sense, once hate is gone, that they will be forced to deal with pain.

We traveled out to him, his older sister and myself, to what seemed to be the very end of a very Long Island. It was hot and dusty and we wrangled, my aunt and I, all the way out, over the fact that I had recently begun to smoke and, as she said, to give myself airs. But I knew that she wrangled with me because she could not bear to face the fact of her brother's dying. Neither could I endure the reality of her despair, her unstated bafflement as to what had happened to her brother's life, and her own. So we wrangled and I smoked and from time to time she fell into a heavy reverie. Covertly, I watched her face, which was the face of an old woman; it had fallen in, the eyes were sunken and lightless; soon she would be dying, too.

In my childhood—it had not been so long ago—I had thought her beautiful. She had been quick-witted and quick-moving and very generous with all the children and each of her visits had been an event. At one time one of my brothers and myself had thought of running away to live with her. Now she could no longer produce out of her handbag some unexpected and yet familiar delight. She made me feel pity and revulsion and fear. It was awful to realize that she no longer caused me to feel affection. The closer we came to the hospital the more querulous she became and at the same time, naturally, grew more dependent on me. Between pity and guilt and fear I began to feel that there was another me trapped in my skull like a jack-in-the-box who might escape my control at any moment and fill the air with screaming.

She began to cry the moment we entered the room and she saw him lying there, all shriveled and still, like a little black monkey. The great, gleaming apparatus which fed him and would have compelled him to be still even if he had been able to move brought to mind, not beneficence, but torture; the tubes entering his arm made me think of pictures I had seen when a child, of Gulliver, tied down by the pygmies on that island. My aunt wept and wept, there was a whistling sound in my father's throat; nothing was said; he could not speak. I wanted to take his hand, to say something. But I do not know what I could have said, even if he could have heard me. He was not really in that room with us, he had at last really embarked on his journey; and though my aunt told me that he said he was going to meet Jesus, I did not hear anything except that whistling in his throat. The doctor came back and we left, into that unbearable train again, and home. In the morning came the telegram saying that he was dead. Then the house was suddenly full of relatives, friends, hysteria, and confusion and I quickly left my mother and the children to the care of those impressive women, who, in Negro communities at least, automatically appear at times of bereavement armed with lotions, proverbs, and patience, and an ability to cook. I went downtown. By the time I returned, later the same day, my mother had been carried to the hospital and the baby had been born.

I I I • For my father's funeral I had nothing black to wear and this posed a nagging problem all day long. It was one of those problems, simple, or impossible of solution, to which the mind insanely clings in order to avoid the mind's real trouble. I spent most of that day at the downtown apartment of a girl I knew, celebrating my birthday with whiskey and wondering what to wear that night. When planning a birthday celebration one naturally does not expect that it will be up against competition from a funeral and this girl had anticipated taking me out that night, for a big dinner and a night club afterwards. Sometime during the course of that long day we decided that we would go out anyway, when my father's funeral service was over. I imagine *I* decided it, since, as the funeral hour approached, it became clearer and clearer to me that I would not know what to do with myself when it was over. The girl, stifling her very lively concern as to the possible effects of the whiskey on one of my father's chief mourners, concentrated on being conciliatory and practically helpful. She found a black shirt for me somewhere and ironed it and, dressed in the darkest pants and jacket I owned, and slightly drunk, I made my way to my father's funeral.

The chapel was full, but not packed, and very quiet. There were, mainly, my father's relatives, and his children, and here and there I saw faces I had not seen since childhood, the faces of my father's one-time friends. They were very dark and solemn now, seeming somehow to suggest that they had known all along that something like this would happen. Chief among the mourners was my aunt, who had quarreled with my father all his life; by which I do not mean to suggest that her mourning was insincere or that she had not loved him. I suppose that she was one of the few people in the world who had, and their incessant quarreling proved precisely the strength of the tie that bound them. The only other person in the world, as far as I knew, whose relationship to my father rivaled my aunt's in depth was my mother, who was not there.

It seemed to me, of course, that it was a very long funeral. But it was, if anything, a rather shorter funeral than most, nor, since there were no overwhelming, uncontrollable expressions of grief, could it be called—if I dare to use the word—successful. The minister who preached my father's funeral sermon was one of the few my father had still been seeing as he neared his end. He presented to us in his sermon a man whom none of us had ever seen—a man thoughtful, patient, and forbearing, a Christian inspiration to all who knew him, and a model for his children. And no doubt the children, in their disturbed and guilty state, were almost ready to believe this; he had been remote enough to be anything and, anyway, the shock of the incontrovertible, that it was really our father lying up there in that casket, prepared the mind for anything. His sister moaned and this grief-stricken moaning was taken as corroboration. The other faces held a dark, non-committal thoughtfulness. This was not the man they had known, but they had scarcely expected to be confronted with *him*; this was, in a sense deeper than questions of fact, the man they had not known, and the man they had not known may have been the real one. The real man, whoever he had been, had suffered and now he was dead: this was all that was sure and all that mattered now. Every man in the chapel hoped that when his hour came he, too, would be eulogized, which is to say forgiven, and that all of his lapses, greeds, errors, and strayings from the truth would be invested with coherence and looked upon with charity. This was perhaps the last thing human beings could give each other and it was what they demanded, after all, of the Lord. Only the Lord saw the midnight tears, only He was present when one of His children, moaning and wringing hands, paced up and down the room. When one slapped one's child in anger the recoil in the heart reverberated through heaven and became part of the pain of the universe. And when the children were hungry and sullen and distrustful and one watched them, daily, growing wilder, and further away, and running headlong into danger, it was the Lord who knew what the charged heart endured as the strap was laid to the backside; the Lord alone who knew what one *would* have said if one had had, like the Lord, the gift of the living word. It was the Lord who knew of the impossibility every parent in that room faced: how to prepare the child for the day when the child would be despised and how to *create* in the child—by what means?—a stronger antidote to this poison than one had found for oneself. The avenues, side streets, bars,

billiard halls, hospitals, police stations, and even the playgrounds
of Harlem—not to mention the houses of correction, the jails, and
the morgue—testified to the potency of the poison while remaining silent as to the efficacy of whatever antidote, irresistibly raising
the question of whether or not such an antidote existed; raising,
which was worse, the question of whether or not an antidote was
desirable; perhaps poison should be fought with poison. With these
several schisms in the mind and with more terrors in the heart than
could be named, it was better not to judge the man who had gone
down under an impossible burden. It was better to remember:
Thou knowest this man's fall; but thou knowest not his wrassling.

While the preacher talked and I watched the children—years of
changing their diapers, scrubbing them, slapping them, taking them
to school, and scolding them had had the perhaps inevitable result
of making me love them, though I am not sure I knew this then—
my mind was busily breaking out with a rash of disconnected impressions. Snatches of popular songs, indecent jokes, bits of books I
had read, movie sequences, faces, voices, political issues—I thought
I was going mad; all these impressions suspended, as it were, in the
solution of the faint nausea produced in me by the heat and liquor.
For a moment I had the impression that my alcoholic breath, inef-
ficiently disguised with chewing gum, filled the entire chapel.
Then someone began singing one of my father's favorite songs and,
abruptly, I was with him, sitting on his knee, in the hot, enormous,
crowded church which was the first church we attended. It was the
Abyssinia Baptist Church on 138th Street. We had not gone there
long. With this image, a host of others came. I had forgotten, in the
rage of my growing up, how proud my father had been of me when
I was little. Apparently, I had had a voice and my father had liked
to show me off before the members of the church. I had forgotten
what he had looked like when he was pleased but now I remembered that he had always been grinning with pleasure when my
solos ended. I even remembered certain expressions on his face
when he teased my mother—had he loved her? I would never know.
And when had it all begun to change? For now it seemed that he
had not always been cruel. I remembered being taken for a haircut
and scraping my knee on the footrest of the barber's chair and I
remembered my father's face as he soothed my crying and applied
the stinging iodine. Then I remembered our fights, fights which had
been of the worst possible kind because my technique had been
silence.

I remembered the one time in all our life together when we had
really spoken to each other.

It was on a Sunday and it must have been shortly before I left
home. We were walking, just the two of us, in our usual silence, to

or from church. I was in high school and had been doing a lot of writing and I was, at about this time, the editor of the high school magazine. But I had also been a Young Minister and had been preaching from the pulpit. Lately, I had been taking fewer engagements and preached as rarely as possible. It was said in the church, quite truthfully, that I was "cooling off."

My father asked me abruptly, "You'd rather write than preach, wouldn't you?"

I was astonished at his question—because it was a real question. I answered, "Yes."

That was all we said. It was awful to remember that that was all we had *ever* said.

The casket now was opened and the mourners were being led up the aisle to look for the last time on the deceased. The assumption was that the family was too overcome with grief to be allowed to make this journey alone and I watched while my aunt was led to the casket and, muffled in black, and shaking, led back to her seat. I disapproved of forcing the children to look on their dead father, considering that the shock of his death, or, more truthfully, the shock of death as a reality, was already a little more than a child could bear, but my judgment in this matter had been overruled and there they were, bewildered and frightened and very small, being led, one by one, to the casket. But there is also something very gallant about children at such moments. It has something to do with their silence and gravity and with the fact that one cannot help them. Their legs, somehow, seem *exposed*, so that it is at once incredible and terribly clear that their legs are all they have to hold them up.

I had not wanted to go to the casket myself and I certainly had not wished to be led there, but there was no way of avoiding either of these forms. One of the deacons led me up and I looked on my father's face. I cannot say that it looked like him at all. His blackness had been equivocated by powder and there was no suggestion in that casket of what his power had or could have been. He was simply an old man dead, and it was hard to believe that he had ever given anyone either joy or pain. Yet, his life filled that room. Further up the avenue his wife was holding his newborn child. Life and death so close together, and love and hatred, and right and wrong, said something to me which I did not want to hear concerning man, concerning the life of man.

After the funeral, while I was downtown desperately celebrating my birthday, a Negro soldier, in the lobby of the Hotel Braddock, got into a fight with a white policeman over a Negro girl. Negro girls, white policemen, in or out of uniform, and Negro males—in or out of uniform—were part of the furniture of the lobby of the

Hotel Braddock and this was certainly not the first time such an incident had occurred. It was destined, however, to receive an unprecedented publicity, for the fight between the policeman and the soldier ended with the shooting of the soldier. Rumor, flowing immediately to the streets outside, stated that the soldier had been shot in the back, an instantaneous and revealing invention, and that the soldier had died protecting a Negro woman. The facts were somewhat different—for example, the soldier had not been shot in the back, and was not dead, and the girl seems to have been as dubious a symbol of womanhood as her white counterpart in Georgia usually is, but no one was interested in the facts. They preferred the invention because this invention expressed and corroborated their hates and fears so perfectly. It is just as well to remember that people are always doing this. Perhaps many of those legends, including Christianity, to which the world clings began their conquest of the world with just some such concerted surrender to distortion. The effect, in Harlem, of this particular legend was like the effect of a lit match in a tin of gasoline. The mob gathered before the doors of the Hotel Braddock simply began to swell and to spread in every direction, and Harlem exploded.

The mob did not cross the ghetto lines. It would have been easy, for example, to have gone over Morningside Park on the west side or to have crossed the Grand Central railroad tracks at 125th Street on the east side, to wreak havoc in white neighborhoods. The mob seems to have been mainly interested in something more potent and real than the white face, that is, in white power, and the principal damage done during the riot of the summer of 1943 was to white business establishments in Harlem. It might have been a far bloodier story, of course, if, at the hour the riot began, these establishments had still been open. From the Hotel Braddock the mob fanned out, east and west along 125th Street, and for the entire length of Lenox, Seventh, and Eighth avenues. Along each of these avenues, and along each major side street—116th, 125th, 135th, and so on—bars, stores, pawnshops, restaurants, even little luncheonettes had been smashed open and entered and looted—looted, it might be added, with more haste than efficiency. The shelves really looked as though a bomb had struck them. Cans of beans and soup and dog food, along with toilet paper, corn flakes, sardines, and milk tumbled every which way, and abandoned cash registers and cases of beer leaned crazily out of the splintered windows and were strewn along the avenues. Sheets, blankets, and clothing of every description formed a kind of path, as though people had dropped them while running. I truly had not realized that Harlem *had* so many stores until I saw them all smashed open; the first time the word *wealth* ever entered my mind in relation to Harlem was when I saw it scattered in the streets. But one's first, incongruous impression of plenty was countered immediately by an impression of waste. None of this was doing anybody any good. It would have been better to have left the plate glass as it had been and the goods lying in the stores.

It would have been better, but it would also have been intolerable, for Harlem had needed something to smash. To smash something is the ghetto's chronic need. Most of the time it is the members of the ghetto who smash each other, and themselves. But as long as the ghetto walls are standing there will always come a moment when these outlets do not work. That summer, for example, it was not enough to get into a fight on Lenox Avenue, or curse out one's cronies in the barber shops. If ever, indeed, the violence which fills Harlem's churches, pool halls, and bars erupts outward in a more direct fashion, Harlem and its citizens are likely to vanish in an apocalyptic flood. That this is not likely to happen is due to a great many reasons, most hidden and powerful among them the Negro's real relation to the white American. This relation prohibits, simply, anything as uncomplicated and satisfactory as pure hatred. In order really to hate white people, one has to blot so much out of the mind—and the heart—that this hatred itself becomes an exhausting and self-destructive pose. But this does not mean, on the other hand, that love comes easily: the white world is too powerful, too complacent, too ready with gratuitous humiliation, and, above all, too ignorant and too innocent for that. One is absolutely forced to make perpetual qualifications and one's own reactions are always canceling each other out. It is this, really, which has driven so many people mad, both white and black. One is always in the position of having to decide between amputation and gangrene. Amputation is swift but time may prove that the amputation was not necessary—or one may delay the amputation too long. Gangrene is slow, but it is impossible to be sure that one is reading one's symptoms right. The idea of going through life as a cripple is more than one can bear, and equally unbearable is the risk of swelling up slowly, in agony, with poison. And the trouble, finally, is that the risks are real even if the choices do not exist.

"But as for me and my house," my father had said, "we will serve the Lord." I wondered, as we drove him to his resting place, what this line had meant for him. I had heard him preach it many times. I had preached it once myself, proudly giving it an interpretation different from my father's. Now the whole thing came back to me, as though my father and I were on our way to Sunday School and I were memorizing the golden text: *And if it seem evil unto you to serve the Lord, choose you this day whom you will serve; whether the gods which your fathers served that were on the other*

*side of the flood, or the gods of the Amorites, in whose land ye
dwell: but as for me and my house, we will serve the Lord.* I suspected in these familiar lines a meaning which had never been there
for me before. All of my father's texts and songs, which I had decided were meaningless, were arranged before me at his death like
empty bottles, waiting to hold the meaning which life would give
them for me. This was his legacy: nothing is ever escaped. That
bleakly memorable morning I hated the unbelievable streets and
the Negroes and whites who had, equally, made them that way.
But I knew that it was folly, as my father would have said, this bitterness was folly. It was necessary to hold on to the things that
mattered. The dead man mattered, the new life mattered; blackness
and whiteness did not matter; to believe that they did was to
acquiesce in one's own destruction. Hatred, which could destroy so
much, never failed to destroy the man who hated and this was an
immutable law.

It began to seem that one would have to hold in the mind forever two ideas which seemed to be in opposition. The first idea was
acceptance, the acceptance, totally without rancor, of life as it is,
and men as they are: in the light of this idea, it goes without saying
that injustice is a commonplace. But this did not mean that one
could be complacent, for the second idea was of equal power: that
one must never, in one's own life, accept these injustices as commonplace but must fight them with all one's strength. This fight
begins, however, in the heart and it now had been laid to my charge
to keep my own heart free of hatred and despair. This intimation
made my heart heavy and, now that my father was irrecoverable, I
wished that he had been beside me so that I could have searched his
face for the answers which only the future would give me now.

———

JAMES BALDWIN (1924–   ) *is the author of several novels, most
recently* Tell Me How Long the Train's Been Gone (1968), *and
many essays;* The Fire Next Time (1963) *and* Going to Meet the
Man (1965) *offer acute analyses of the American racial problem.
He is also writing the film adaptation of* The Autobiography of
Malcolm X. *This selection consists of the first three chapters of*
Notes of a Native Son (1955), *which gives, as autobiography, ma-
terial used for fiction in* Go Tell It on the Mountain (1953).

1. *Baldwin sees both his father and himself as they were years
   ago. He asks us to understand how his father appeared to him*

as a boy, as well as how the two of them appear to his mature judgment as a man. Choose one or two of the descriptive passages and show how both of these views of the father and son are conveyed by the language.

2. Even more obviously than Anderson, Baldwin seeks to understand his father in order to understand himself: "When his life had ended I began to wonder about that life and also, in a new way, to be apprehensive about my own." But Baldwin's need for understanding seems more urgent: "the bitterness which had helped to kill my father could also kill me." Compare Baldwin's tone with Anderson's, and demonstrate what it is in the language of each that causes the differences.

3. Consider the tone Baldwin uses to recount the incident in New Jersey that concludes the first chapter. How does the incident affect his and our understanding of and reaction to the father? In what ways does the incident help define the author's heritage of bitterness and make this heritage more threatening? Why, in the last sentence of this chapter, does Baldwin put the word "real" in italics? What is the tone and meaning of "my real life"?

4. Before he returns to the description of his father and the meaning of the hatred the boy had for him, Baldwin describes the "common vision" of the Harlem community. What is the tone of this description and how does it affect the reader? How does the placement of it affect our view of the hatred for the father and the wrangling with the father's sister?

5. What is the tone of the third paragraph of chapter three, the one describing the funeral? What is the effect of the word "successful" upon the reader's relationship to the author? How does the brief discussion of the "poison" of Harlem relate to the eulogy, and how does that discussion help keep us from making too simple a judgment of the father?

6. Baldwin speaks of the immense problem of controlling attitudes in this selection as he describes looking at the dead man in the casket: "Life and death so close together, and love and hatred, and right and wrong, said something to me which I did not want to hear concerning man, concerning the life of man." How does he make vivid and personal each of these sets of abstractions? What did they say to him that he did not want to hear? Why did he not want to hear them? How does his tone now hold these abstractions in balance, and show him able "to hold

in the mind forever two ideas which seemed to be in opposition"?

7. Although everything in this selection is infused by a frank awareness of race, Baldwin says in the next-to-last paragraph "*blackness and whiteness did not matter; to believe that they did was to acquiesce in one's own destruction.*" How has he sought to establish a relationship with his reader that will make this idea convincing? Has he succeeded in demonstrating this idea by controlling and ordering the account of his relationship to his father?

Dylan Thomas

A STORY

If you can call it a story. There's no real beginning or end and there's very little in the middle. It is all about a day's outing, by charabanc, to Porthcawl, which, of course, the charabanc never reached, and it happened when I was so high and much nicer.

I was staying at the time with my uncle and his wife. Although she was my aunt, I never thought of her as anything but the wife of my uncle, partly because he was so big and trumpeting and red-hairy and used to fill every inch of the hot little house like an old buffalo squeezed into an airing cupboard, and partly because she was so small and silk and quick and made no noise at all as she whisked about on padded paws, dusting the china dogs, feeding the buffalo, setting the mousetraps that never caught her; and once she sleaked out of the room, to squeak in a nook or nibble in the hayloft, you forgot she had ever been there.

But there he was, always, a steaming hulk of an uncle, his braces straining like hawsers, crammed behind the counter of the tiny shop at the front of the house, and breathing like a brass band; or guzzling and blustery in the kitchen over his gutsy supper, too big for everything except the great black boats of his boots. As he ate, the house grew smaller; he billowed out over the furniture, the loud check meadow of his waistcoat littered, as though after a picnic, with cigarette ends, peelings, cabbage stalks, birds' bones, gravy; and the forest fire of his hair crackled among the hooked hams from the ceiling. She was so small she could hit him only if she stood on a chair; and every Saturday night at half-past ten he would lift her up, under his arm, onto a chair, in the kitchen so that she could hit him on the head with whatever was handy, which was always a china dog. On Sundays, and when pickled, he sang high tenor, and had won many cups.

The first I heard of the annual outing was when I was sitting one evening on a bag of rice behind the counter, under one of my

From *Quite Early One Morning* by Dylan Thomas. Copyright 1954 by New Directions Publishing Corporation. Reprinted by permission of the publisher, New Directions Publishing Corporation.

uncle's stomachs, reading an advertisement for sheepdip, which was all there was to read. The shop was full of my uncle, and when Mr. Benjamin Franklyn, Mr. Weazley, Noah Bowen, and Will Sentry came in, I thought it would burst. It was like all being together in a drawer that smelled of cheese and turps, and twist tobacco and sweet biscuits and snuff and waistcoat. Mr. Benjamin Franklyn said that he had collected enough money for the charabanc and twenty cases of pale ale and a pound apiece over that he would distribute among the members of the outing when they first stopped for refreshment, and he was about sick and tired, he said, of being followed by Will Sentry.

"All day long, wherever I go," he said, "he's after me like a collie with one eye. I got a shadow of my own *and* a dog. I don't need no Tom, Dick or Harry pursuing me with his dirty muffler on."

Will Sentry blushed, and said, "It's only oily. I got a bicycle."

"A man has no privacy at all," Mr. Franklyn went on. "I tell you he sticks so close I'm afraid to go out the back in case I sit in his lap. It's a wonder to me," he said, "he don't follow me into bed at night."

"Wife won't let," Will Sentry said.

And that started Mr. Franklyn off again, and they tried to soothe him down by saying, "Don't you mind Will Sentry." "No harm in old Will." "He's only keeping an eye on the money, Benjie."

"Aren't I honest?" asked Mr. Franklyn in surprise. There was no answer for some time; then Noah Bowen said, "You know what the committee is. Ever since Bob the Fiddle they don't feel safe with a new treasurer."

"Do you think *I'm* going to drink the outing funds, like Bob the Fiddle did?" said Mr. Franklyn.

"You *might*," said my uncle, slowly.

"I resign," said Mr. Franklyn.

"Not with our money you won't," Will Sentry said.

"Who put the dynamite in the salmon pool?" said Mr. Weazley, but nobody took any notice of him. And, after a time, they all began to play cards in the thickening dusk of the hot, cheesy shop, and my uncle blew and bugled whenever he won, and Mr. Weazley grumbled like a dredger, and I fell to sleep on the gravy-scented mountain meadow of uncle's waistcoat.

On Sunday evening, after Bethesda, Mr. Franklyn walked into the kitchen where my uncle and I were eating sardines from the tin with spoons because it was Sunday and his wife would not let us play draughts. She was somewhere in the kitchen, too. Perhaps she was inside the grandmother clock, hanging from the weights and breathing. Then, a second later, the door opened again and Will Sentry edged into the room, twiddling his hard, round hat. He and Mr. Franklyn sat down on the settee, stiff and mothballed and black in their chapel and funeral suits.

"I brought the list," said Mr. Franklyn. "Every member fully paid. You ask Will Sentry."

My uncle put on his spectacles, wiped his whiskery mouth with a handkerchief big as a Union Jack, laid down his spoon of sardines, took Mr. Franklyn's list of names, removed the spectacles so that he could read, and then ticked the names off one by one.

"Enoch Davies. Aye. He's good with his fists. You never know. Little Gerwain. Very melodious bass. Mr. Cadwalladwr. That's right. He can tell opening time better than my watch. Mr. Weazley. Of course. He's been to Paris. Pity he suffers so much in the charabanc. Stopped us nine times last year between the Beehive and the Red Dragon. Noah Bowen. Ah, very peaceable. He's got a tongue like a turtledove. Never a argument with Noah Bowen. Jenkins Loughor. Keep him off economics. It cost us a plateglass window. And ten pints for the Sergeant. Mr. Jervis. Very tidy."

"He tried to put a pig in the charra," Will Sentry said.

"Live and let live," said my uncle.

Will Sentry blushed.

"Sinbad the Sailor's Arms. Got to keep in with him. Old O. Jones."

"Why old O. Jones?" said Will Sentry.

"Old O. Jones always goes," said my uncle.

I looked down at the kitchen table. The tin of sardines was gone. By Gee, I said to myself, Uncle's wife is quick as a flash.

"Cuthbert Johnny Fortnight. Now there's a card," said my uncle.

"He whistles after women," Will Sentry said.

"So do you," said Mr. Benjamin Franklyn, "in your mind."

My uncle at last approved the whole list, pausing only to say, when he came across one name, "If we weren't a Christian community, we'd chuck that Bob the Fiddle in the sea."

"We can do that in Porthcawl," said Mr. Franklyn, and soon after that he went, Will Sentry no more than an inch behind him, their Sunday-bright boots squeaking on the kitchen cobbles.

And then, suddenly, there was my uncle's wife standing in front of the dresser, with a china dog in one hand. By Gee, I said to myself again, did you ever see such a woman, if that's what she is. The lamps were not lit yet in the kitchen and she stood in a wood of shadows, with the plates on the dresser behind her shining— like pink and white eyes.

"If you go on that outing on Saturday, Mr. Thomas," she said to my uncle in her small, silk voice, "I'm going home to my mother's."

Holy Mo, I thought, she's got a mother. Now that's one old bald mouse of a hundred and five I won't be wanting to meet in a dark lane.

"It's me or the outing, Mr. Thomas."

I would have made my choice at once, but it was almost half a minute before my uncle said, "Well, then, Sarah, it's the outing, my love." He lifted her up, under his arm, onto a chair in the kitchen, and she hit him on the head with the china dog. Then he lifted her down again, and then I said good night.

For the rest of the week my uncle's wife whisked quiet and quick round the house with her darting duster, my uncle blew and bugled and swole, and I kept myself busy all the time being up to no good. And then at breakfast time on Saturday morning, the morning of the outing, I found a note on the kitchen table. It said, "There's some eggs in the pantry. Take your boots off before you go to bed." My uncle's wife had gone, as quick as a flash.

When my uncle saw the note, he tugged out the flag of his handkerchief and blew such a hubbub of trumpets that the plates on the dresser shook. "It's the same every year," he said. And then he looked at me. "But this year it's different. *You'll* have to come on the outing, too, and what the members will say I dare not think."

The charabanc drew up outside, and when the members of the outing saw my uncle and me squeeze out of the shop together, both of us cat-licked and brushed in our Sunday best, they snarled like a zoo.

"Are you bringing a *boy?*" asked Mr. Benjamin Franklyn as we climbed into the charabanc. He looked at me with horror.

"Boys is nasty," said Mr. Weazley.

"He hasn't paid his contributions," Will Sentry said.

"No room for boys. Boys get sick in charabancs."

"So do you, Enoch Davies," said my uncle.

"Might as well bring *women*."

The way they said it, women were worse than boys.

"Better than bringing grandfathers."

"Grandfathers is nasty, too," said Mr. Weazley.

"What can we do with him when we stop for refreshments?"

"I'm a grandfather," said Mr. Weazley.

"Twenty-six minutes to opening time," shouted an old man in a panama hat, not looking at a watch. They forgot me at once.

"Good old Mr. Cadwalladwr," they cried, and the charabanc started off down the village street.

A few cold women stood at their doorways, grimly watching us go. A very small boy waved goodbye, and his mother boxed his ears. It was a beautiful August morning.

We were out of the village, and over the bridge, and up the hill toward Steeplehat Wood when Mr. Franklyn, with his list of names in his hand, called out loud, "Where's old O. Jones?"

"Where's old O.?"

"We've left old O. behind."

"Cant go without old O."

And though Mr. Weazley hissed all the way, we turned and drove back to the village, where, outside the Prince of Wales, old O. Jones was waiting patiently and alone with a canvas bag.

"I didn't want to come at all," old O. Jones said as they hoisted him into the charabanc and clapped him on the back and pushed him on a seat and stuck a bottle in his hand, "but I always go." And over the bridge and up the hill and under the deep green wood and along the dusty road we wove, slow cows and ducks flying by, until "Stop the bus!" Mr. Weazley cried, "I left my teeth on the mantelpiece."

"Never you mind," they said, "you're not going to bite nobody," and they gave him a bottle with a straw.

"I might want to smile," he said.

"Not you," they said.

"What's the time, Mr. Cadwalladwr?"

"Twelve minutes to go," shouted back the old man in the panama, and they all began to curse him.

The charabanc pulled up outside the Mountain Sheep, a small, unhappy public house with a thatched roof like a wig with ringworm. From a flagpole by the Gents fluttered the flag of Siam. I knew it was the flag of Siam because of cigarette cards. The landlord stood at the door to welcome us, simpering like a wolf. He was a long, lean, black-fanged man with a greased love-curl and pouncing eyes. "What a beautiful August day!" he said, and touched his love-curl with a claw. That was the way he must have welcomed the Mountain Sheep before he ate it, I said to myself. The members rushed out, bleating, and into the bar.

"You keep an eye on the charra," my uncle said, "see nobody steals it now."

"There's nobody to steal it," I said, "except some cows," but my uncle was gustily blowing his bugle in the bar. I looked at the cows opposite, and they looked at me. There was nothing else for us to do. Forty-five minutes passed, like a very slow cloud. The sun shone down on the lonely road, the lost, unwanted boy, and the lake-eyed cows. In the dark bar they were so happy they were breaking glasses. A Shoni-Onion Breton man, with a beret and a necklace of onions, bicycled down the road and stopped at the door.

"*Quelle un grand matin, monsieur,*" * I said.

"There's French, boy bach!" he said.

I followed him down the passage, and peered into the bar. I could hardly recognize the members of the outing. They had all changed color. Beetroot, rhubarb and puce, they hollered and rollicked in that dark, damp hole like enormous ancient bad boys, and my uncle surged in the middle, all red whiskers and bellies. On the floor was broken glass and Mr. Weazley.

"Drinks all round," cried Bob the Fiddle, a small, absconding man with bright blue eyes and a plump smile.

"Who's been robbing the orphans?"

"Who sold his little babby to the gyppoes?"

"Trust old Bob, he'll let you down."

"You will have your little joke," said Bob the Fiddle, smiling like a razor, "but I forgive you, boys."

Out of the fug and babel I heard: "Where's old O. Jones?" "Where are you, old O.?" "He's in the kitchen cooking his dinner." "He never forgets his dinner time." "Good old O. Jones." "Come out and fight." "No, not now, later." "No, now when I'm in a temper." "Look at Will Sentry, he's proper snobbled." "Look at his willful feet." "Look at Mr. Weazley lording it on the floor."

Mr. Weazley got up, hissing like a gander. "That boy pushed me down deliberate," he said, pointing to me at the door, and I slunk away down the passage and out to the mild, good cows.

Time clouded over, the cows wondered, I threw a stone at them and they wandered wondering, away. Then out blew my uncle, ballooning, and one by one the members lumbered after him in a grizzle. They had drunk the Mountain Sheep dry. Mr. Weazley had won a string of onions that the Shoni-Onion man had raffled in the bar.

"What's the good of onions if you left your teeth on the mantelpiece?" he said. And when I looked through the back window of the thundering charabanc, I saw the pub grow smaller in the distance. And the flag of Siam, from the flagpole by the Gents, fluttered now at half mast.

The Blue Bull, the Dragon, the Star of Wales, the Twll in the Wall, the Sour Grapes, the Shepherd's Arms, the Bells of Aberdovey: I had nothing to do in the whole wild August world but remember the names where the outing stopped and keep an eye on the charabanc. And whenever it passed a public house, Mr. Weazley would cough like a billy goat and cry, "Stop the bus, I'm dying of breath." And back we would all have to go.

Closing time meant nothing to the members of that outing.

---

* "*Quelle un grand matin, monsieur.*" "What a fine morning, sir."

Behind locked doors, they hymned and rumpused all the beautiful afternoon. And, when a policeman entered the Druid's Tap by the back door, and found them all choral with beer, "Sssh!" said Noah Bowen, "the pub is shut."

"Where do you come from?" he said in his buttoned, blue voice.

They told him.

"I got a auntie there," the policeman said. And very soon he was singing "Asleep in the Deep."

Off we drove again at last, the charabanc bouncing with tenors and flagons, and came to a river that rushed along among willows.

"Water!" they shouted.

"Porthcawl!" sang my uncle.

"Where's the donkeys?" said Mr. Weazley.

And out they lurched, to paddle and whoop in the cool, white, winding water. Mr. Franklyn, trying to polka on the slippery stones, fell in twice. "Nothing is simple," he said with dignity as he oozed up the bank.

"It's cold!" they cried.

"It's lovely!"

"It's smooth as a moth's nose!"

"It's *better* than Porthcawl!"

And dusk came down warm and gentle on thirty wild, wet, pickled, splashing men without a care in the world at the end of the world in the west of Wales. And, "Who goes there?" called Will Sentry to a wild duck flying.

They stopped at the Hermit's Nest for a rum to keep out the cold. "I played for Aberavon in 1898," said a stranger to Enoch Davies.

"Liar," said Enoch Davies.

"I can show the photos," said the stranger.

"Forged," said Enoch Davies.

"And I'll show you my cap at home."

"Stolen."

"I got friends to prove it," the stranger said in a fury.

"Bribed," said Enoch Davies.

On the way home, through the simmering moonsplashed dark, old O. Jones began to cook his supper on a primus stove in the middle of the charabanc. Mr. Weazley coughed himself blue in the smoke. "Stop the bus!" he cried. "I'm dying of breath." We all climbed down into the moonlight. There was not a public house in sight. So they carried out the remaining cases, and the primus stove, and old O. Jones himself, and took them into a field, and sat down in a circle in the field and drank and sang while old O. Jones cooked sausage and mash and the moon flew above us. And there I drifted to sleep against my uncle's mountainous waistcoat, and, as I slept, "Who goes there?" called out Will Sentry to the flying moon.

———

DYLAN THOMAS (1914–1953) *is best known as a poet, though his poetic prose and fiction are becoming more widely known. The* Collected Poems *appeared in 1953;* Portrait of the Artist as a Young Dog *(1940) is an engaging autobiography;* "A Child's Christmas in Wales," *from a collection of prose pieces,* Quite Early One Morning, *has become a Christmas classic in Thomas' own recorded voice.* "A Story" *was originally published in 1953 in* The Listener.

1. *Uncle's wife and the grimly-watching cold women in the village see the drunken outing from a point of view we are not allowed to share. What is their attitude? What is the attitude the reader is asked to take?*

2. *What is the tone established by the structure of the first sentence of the story? How does Thomas reinforce this tone by other means (such as the kinds of details used, the arrangements of sounds, dialogue, characterization, etc.)?*

3. *The closing scenes show* "thirty wild, wet, pickled, splashing men without a care in the world at the end of the world in the west of Wales" *and the boy narrator drifting off to sleep* "against my uncle's mountainous waistcoat." *How does this harmonious, almost blissful conclusion tend to confirm the attitudes the language of the story has asked the reader to take toward the actions and characters, seen through the haze of memory?*

Part Two CONTROLLING

ANALYSIS: SCHOOLS AND INSTITUTIONS

In order to describe an institution clearly, a writer needs to be able to see it from both the inside and the outside. He must make clear to the reader the way it was, how it felt to be within the institution; at the same time he must evaluate it by standards different from those the institution professes. Otherwise the reader is likely to feel that he sees and knows more than the writer does about the topic, and so reject the writer's ideas and perspective. Thus, the selections in this section all show control over a double perspective:

> *And above all, I believed Bingo and Sim when they told me they were my benefactors. I see now, of course, that from Sim's point of view I was a good speculation.* —ORWELL

> *I have never met any one yet who could say he had been happy there [in an English private school]. Yet St. Wulfric's, where I went, was well run and vigorous, and did me good.* —CONNOLLY

> *The usual reason for this kind of song period is that the children are "broadened" while they learn something about music and singing. But what the children in fact learn about singing is to sing like everybody else. . . . Thus one of the first things a child with a good ear learns in elementary school is to be musically stupid.* —HENRY

> *Harvard College, as far as it educated at all, was a mild and liberal school, which sent young men into the world with all they needed to make respectable citizens, and something of what they wanted to make useful ones. Leaders of men it never tried to make. Its ideals were altogether different.* —ADAMS

> *And he would have been glad for a hand toward escape, though now, when Harvard is superimposed over Watts, though the Hoodlum is placed above my own reflection in the mirror,*

I suppose there truthfully could have been no escape. Harvard had become a ghostyard, empty. —SCOTT

We are in bondage to authority outside ourselves: most obviously—here in a great university it must be said—in bondage to the authority of books. —BROWN

The first problem in analyzing an institution is to find the most suitable way to make your reader understand the inside view, the way it was for you or for others who were really there. Detailed, concrete description, dialogue, and action will help make the situation clear and vivid; just as in the first section of this text, careful re-creation of character and scene provides the ground for analysis. At the same time that your reader is coming to understand this inside view of the institution, he will be responding to your tone. If your tone is under control, he is likely to share your feelings about what you describe. In fact, you yourself may only arrive at a clear sense of your own attitudes by the act of choosing the particular words that describe your subject clearly. (See the two drafts of a student paper in the appendix for an example of how this happens.)

But description is only half the job of analysis; evaluation of an institution asks you to bring an outside set of values to judge what you describe. The passages quoted just above tend to follow a pattern: "we (or they) felt the rules to be right because . . . , but I see now, from a new set of values, that other matters were really the important ones." Thus Orwell brings an entirely different version of economic and social ideals to bear upon assumptions in force at St. Cyprian's; Swift brings the whole weight of primitive Christianity to bear upon what he sees as a corrupt church; N. O. Brown, insisting upon the regenerative power of mysticism, warns his educated audience of the "bondage of books" and "dead authority." This collision between sets of values becomes the topic of these essays, the real reason the authors ask us to read. For finally, description and evaluation must be connected by a similar tone, one which says to the reader, this is why you should attend to my topic, this is what is important about my subject.

The selections in this section deal in different ways with the three problems considered here: What was it like in that institution? How do I see the institution now, from a different perspective? Why should I ask a reader to spend his time hearing what I have to say? Each selection provides some kind of answer to all three problems, as all good writing on this kind of subject must. Anyone writing a similar essay will find himself facing the same problems of con-

trolling tone. The search for solutions is likely to lead not only to more controlled writing, but to increased understanding of the self and past experience.

Towards the end of "Such, Such Were the Joys . . .", George Orwell gives an account of his fight with the school bully, Johnny Hall. This passage shows one direct way to deal with the problems of tone I have been discussing. Although a small part of an extended account of a school, the passage can stand by itself as an example of the sort of essay you may be asked to write.

The scene begins with a statement of the problem "Crossgates" (Orwell's name for St. Cyprian's) posed for him as a child, from the perspective of the grown man: "To survive, or at least to preserve any kind of independence, was essentially criminal, since it meant breaking rules which you yourself recognized." In order to demonstrate the truth of this, Orwell takes us back to the school as it was: "There was a boy named Johnny Hall who. . . ." The description of the bully not only brings his presence and nastiness vividly to our minds (he twists arms, wrings ears, etc.), but shows him as the embodiment of all that is valued at Crossgates. All elements of the community treasure him: "Bingo loved him," "Sim commended him," "He was followed about by a group of toadies who nicknamed him Strong Man."

The next paragraph continues the detailed account of the incident, and the physical action and concrete description bring us close to the event. When Orwell calls his decision to hit the bully when he was not expecting it "a terrible, wicked resolve," we know that he is using the standard of judgment at the school, not his mature evaluation. When we find out that the mature Orwell felt he had acted correctly as a child, we are not surprised; the tone of the earlier statement made it clear that the resolve was neither "terrible" nor "wicked," and only could be felt to be so by a guilty young boy misled by his teachers.

The following two paragraphs show the result of Orwell's action: a sort of general confusion at the violation of the school code, and no fight. The last two paragraphs analyze the whole affair, first from the point of view of the school boy ("Now, I had behaved wrongly, by my own code no less than his"), and then from the perspective of the grown man, wholly opposed to the values of the school ("The fact I hardly noticed was . . ." "It was perhaps twenty years before I saw . . ."). Orwell provides a double *perspective on the event by devoting a summary paragraph to each point of view, and stating explicitly, several times, from which perspective he is speaking in each paragraph.*

Throughout, Orwell has his eye on the reader, who is always about to ask why he should be concerned with someone else's childhood. The problem he faced as a child, Orwell makes clear, is one interesting in itself, but one with larger implications as well. His choice of words makes it clear that he is speaking at the same time of a problem familiar to everyone—the oppression of the weak by the strong. Johnny Hall is nicknamed Strong Man, the same title bestowed on military dictators by the press, and Orwell sees the bullying as an almost political fact: he "for some months oppressed me horribly." The analysis of the incident is even more expressly political in tone: "At the time I could not see beyond the moral dilemma that is presented to the weak in a world governed by the strong: Break the rules or perish." We should read his essay, Orwell tells us, because by speaking of his childhood he is presenting a particular example of a general problem, one in which everyone is interested.

While few of the other selections are as clear as "Such, Such Were the Joys . . ." in their control of tone, all of them must structure the reader's attitude in one way or another. In general, the arrangement of selections is parallel to that of the first section: the selections in turn become increasingly complex, and the ways in which they resolve the problem of tone become increasingly subtle.

George Orwell

"SUCH, SUCH WERE THE JOYS . . ."

Crossgates was an expensive and snobbish school which was in process of becoming more snobbish, and, I imagine, more expensive. The public school with which it had special connections was Harrow, but during my time an increasing proportion of the boys went on to Eton. Most of them were the children of rich parents, but on the whole they were the unaristocratic rich, the sort of people who live in huge shrubberied houses in Bournemouth or Richmond, and who have cars and butlers but not country estates. There were a few exotics among them—some South American boys, sons of Argentine beef barons, one or two Russians, and even a Siamese prince, or someone who was described as a prince.

Sim had two great ambitions. One was to attract titled boys to the school, and the other was to train up pupils to win scholarships at public schools, above all Eton. He did, towards the end of my time, succeed in getting hold of two boys with real English titles. One of them, I remember, was a wretched little creature, almost an albino, peering upwards out of weak eyes, with a long nose at the end of which a dewdrop always seemed to be trembling. Sim always gave these boys their titles when mentioning them to a third person, and for their first few days he actually addressed them to their faces as "Lord So-and-so." Needless to say he found ways of drawing attention to them when any visitor was being shown round the school. Once, I remember, the little fair-haired boy had a choking fit at dinner, and a stream of snot ran out of his nose onto his plate in a way horrible to see. Any lesser person would have been called a dirty little beast and ordered out of the room instantly: but Sim and Bingo laughed it off in a "boys will be boys" spirit.

All the very rich boys were more or less undisguisedly favoured. The school still had a faint suggestion of the Victorian "private academy" with its "parlour boarders," and when I later read about that kind of school in Thackeray I immediately saw the resemblance. The rich boys had milk and biscuits in the middle of the morning, they were given riding lessons once or twice a week, Bingo mothered them and called them by their Christian names, and above all they were never caned. Apart from the South Americans, whose parents were safely distant, I doubt whether Sim ever caned any boy whose father's income was much above £2,000 a year. But he was sometimes willing to sacrifice financial profit to scholastic prestige. Occasionally, by special arrangement, he would take at greatly reduced fees some boy who seemed likely to win scholarships and thus bring credit on the school. It was on these terms that I was at Crossgates myself: otherwise my parents could not have afforded to send me to so expensive a school.

I did not at first understand that I was being taken at reduced fees; it was only when I was about eleven that Bingo and Sim began throwing the fact in my teeth. For my first two or three years I went through the ordinary educational mill: then, soon after I had started Greek (one started Latin at eight, Greek at ten), I moved into the scholarship class, which was taught, so far as classics went, largely by Sim himself. Over a period of two or three years the scholarship boys were crammed with learning as cynically as a goose is crammed for Christmas. And with what learning! This business of making a gifted boy's career depend on a competitive examination, taken when he is only twelve or thirteen, is an evil thing at best, but there do appear to be preparatory schools which send scholars to Eton, Winchester, etc., without teaching them to see everything in terms of marks. At Crossgates the whole process was frankly a preparation for a sort of confidence trick. Your job was to learn exactly those things that would give an examiner the impression that you knew more than you did know, and as far as possible to avoid burdening your brain with anything else. Subjects which lacked examination-value, such as geography, were almost completely neglected, mathematics was also neglected if you were a "classical," science was not taught in any form—indeed it was so despised that even an interest in natural history was discouraged— and the books you were encouraged to read in your spare time were chosen with one eye on the "English Paper." Latin and Greek, the main scholarship subjects, were what counted, but even these were deliberately taught in a flashy, unsound way. We never, for example, read right through even a single book of a Greek or Latin author: we merely read short passages which were picked out because they were the kind of thing likely to be set as an "unseen translation." During the last year or so before we went up for our scholarships, most of our time was spent in simply working our way through the scholarship papers of previous years. Sim had sheaves of these in his possession, from every one of the major public schools. But the greatest outrage of all was the teaching of history.

There was in those days a piece of nonsense called the Harrow History Prize, an annual competition for which many preparatory schools entered. At Crossgates we mugged up every paper that had been set since the competition started. They were the kind of stupid question that is answered by rapping out a name or a quotation. Who plundered the Begams? Who was beheaded in an open boat? Who caught the Whigs bathing and ran away with their clothes? Almost all our historical teaching was on this level. History was a series of unrelated unintelligible but—in some way that was never explained to us—important facts with resounding phrases tied to them. Disraeli brought peace with honour. Clive was astonished at his moderation. Pitt called in the New World to redress the balance of the Old. And the dates, and the mnemonic devices! (Did you know, for example, that the initial letters of "A black Negress was my aunt: there's her house behind the barn" are also the initial letters of the battles in the Wars of the Roses?) Bingo, who "took" the higher forms in history, revelled in this kind of thing. I recall positive orgies of dates, with the keener boys leaping up and down in their places in their eagerness to shout out the right answers, and at the same time not feeling the faintest interest in the meaning of the mysterious events they were naming.

"1587?"

"Massacre of St. Bartholomew!"

"1707?"

"Death of Aurangzeeb!"

"1713?"

"Treaty of Utrecht!"

"1773?"

"The Boston Tea Party!"

"1520?"

"Oh, Mum, please, Mum—"

"Please, Mum, please, Mum! Let me tell him, Mum!"

"Well; 1520?"

"Field of the Cloth of Gold!"

And so on.

But history and such secondary subjects were not bad fun. It was in "classics" that the real strain came. Looking back, I realise that I then worked harder than I have ever done since, and yet at the time it never seemed possible to make quite the effort that was demanded of one. We would sit round the long shiny table, made of some very pale-coloured, hard wood, with Sim goading, threatening, exhorting, sometimes joking, very occasionally praising, but always prodding, prodding away at one's mind to keep it up to the right pitch of concentration, as one might keep a sleepy person awake by sticking pins into him.

"Go on, you little slacker! Go on, you idle, worthless little boy! The whole trouble with you is that you're bone and horn idle. You eat too much, that's why. You wolf down enormous meals, and then when you come here you're half asleep. Go on, now, put your back into it. You're not *thinking*. Your brain doesn't sweat."

He would tap away at one's skull with his silver pencil, which, in my memory, seems to have been about the size of a banana, and which certainly was heavy enough to raise a bump: or he would pull the short hairs round one's ears, or, occasionally, reach out under the table and kick one's shin. On some days nothing seemed to go right, and then it would be: "All right, then, I know what you want. You've been asking for it the whole morning. Come along, you useless little slacker. Come into the study." And then whack, whack, whack, whack, and back one would come, red-wealed and smarting—in later years Sim had abandoned his riding crop in favour of a thin rattan cane which hurt very much more—to settle down to work again. This did not happen very often, but I do remember, more than once being led out of the room in the middle of a Latin sentence, receiving a beating and then going straight ahead with the same sentence, just like that. It is a mistake to think such methods do not work. They work very well for their special purpose. Indeed, I doubt whether classical education ever has been or can be successfully carried on without corporal punishment. The boys themselves believed in its efficacy. There was a boy named Beacham, with no brains to speak of, but evidently in acute need of a scholarship. Sim was flogging him towards the goal as one might do with a foundered horse. He went up for a scholarship at Uppingham, came back with a consciousness of having done badly, and a day or two later received a severe beating for idleness. "I wish I'd had that caning before I went up for the exam," he said sadly—a remark which I felt to be contemptible, but which I perfectly well understood.

The boys of the scholarship class were not all treated alike. If a boy were the son of rich parents to whom the saving of fees was not all-important, Sim would goad him along in a comparatively fatherly way, with jokes and digs in the ribs and perhaps an occasional tap with the pencil, but no hair-pulling and no caning. It was the poor but "clever" boys who suffered. Our brains were a goldmine in which he had sunk money, and the dividends must be squeezed out of us. Long before I had grasped the nature of my financial relationship with Sim, I had been made to understand that I was not on the same footing as most of the other boys. In effect there were three castes in the school. There was the minority with an aristocratic or millionaire background, there were the children of the ordinary suburban rich, who made up the bulk of the school, and there were a few underlings like myself, the sons of clergymen, Indian civil servants, struggling widows and the like. These poorer ones were discouraged from going in for "extras" such as shooting and carpentry, and were humiliated over clothes and petty possessions. I never, for instance, succeeded in getting a cricket bat of my own, because "your parents wouldn't be able to afford it." This phrase pursued me throughout my schooldays. At Crossgates we were not allowed to keep the money we brought back with us, but had to "give it in" on the first day of term, and then from time to time were allowed to spend it under supervision. I and similarly placed boys were always choked off from buying expensive toys like model aeroplanes, even if the necessary money stood to our credit. Bingo, in particular, seemed to aim consciously at inculcating a humble outlook in the poorer boys. "Do you think that's the sort of thing a boy like you should buy?" I remember her saying to somebody—and she said this in front of the whole school; "You know you're not going to grow up with money, don't you? Your people aren't rich. You must learn to be sensible. Don't get above yourself!" There was also the weekly pocket-money, which we took out in sweets, dispensed by Bingo from a large table. The millionaires had sixpence a week, but the normal sum was threepence. I and one or two others were only allowed twopence. My parents had not given instructions to this effect, and the saving of a penny a week could not conceivably have made any difference to them: it was a mark of status. Worse yet was the detail of the birthday cakes. It was usual for each boy, on his birthday, to have a large iced cake with candles, which was shared out at tea between the whole school. It was provided as a matter of routine and went on his parents' bill. I never had such a cake, though my parents would have paid for it readily enough. Year after year, never daring to ask, I would miserably hope that this year a cake would appear. Once or twice I even rashly pretended to my companions that this time I *was* going to have a cake. Then came teatime, and no cake, which did not make me more popular.

Very early it was impressed upon me that I had no chance of a decent future unless I won a scholarship at a public school. Either I won my scholarship, or I must leave school at fourteen and become, in Sim's favourite phrase "a little office-boy at forty pounds a year." In my circumstances it was natural that I should believe this. Indeed, it was universally taken for granted at Crossgates that u less you went to a "good" public school (and only about fifteen schools came under this heading) you were ruined for life. It is not easy to convey to a grown-up person the sense of strain, of nerving oneself for some terrible, all-deciding combat, as the date of the examination crept nearer—eleven years old, twelve years old, then thirteen, the fatal year itself! Over a period of about two years, I do not think there was ever a day when "the exam," as I called it, was quite out of my waking thoughts. In my prayers it figured invariably: and whenever I got the bigger portion of a wishbone, or picked up a horseshoe, or bowed seven times to the new moon, or succeeded in passing through a wishing-gate without touching the sides, then the wish I earned by doing so went on "the exam" as a matter of course. And yet curiously enough I was also tormented by an almost irresistible impulse *not* to work. There were days when my heart sickened at the labours ahead of me, and I stood stupid as an animal before the most elementary difficulties. In the holidays, also, I could not work. Some of the scholarship boys received extra tuition from a certain Mr. Batchelor, a likeable, very hairy man who wore shaggy suits and lived in a typical bachelor's "den"— booklined walls, overwhelming stench of tobacco—somewhere in the town. During the holidays Mr. Batchelor used to send us extracts from Latin authors to translate, and we were supposed to send back a wad of work once a week. Somehow I could not do it. The empty paper and the black Latin dictionary lying on the table, the consciousness of a plain duty shirked, poisoned my leisure, but somehow I could not start, and by the end of the holidays I would only have sent Mr. Batchelor fifty or a hundred lines. Undoubtedly part of the reason was that Sim and his cane were far away. But in term time, also, I would go through periods of idleness and stupidity when I would sink deeper and deeper into disgrace and even achieve a sort of feeble defiance, fully conscious of my guilt and yet unable or unwilling—I could not be sure which—to do any better. Then Bingo or Sim would send for me, and this time it would not even be a caning.

Bingo would search me with her baleful eyes. (What colour were those eyes, I wonder? I remember them as green, but actually no human being has green eyes. Perhaps they were hazel.) She would start off in her peculiar, wheedling, bullying style, which never failed to get right through one's guard and score a hit on one's better nature.

"I don't think it's awfully decent of you to behave like this, is it? Do you think it's quite playing the game by your mother and father to go on idling your time away, week after week, month. after month? Do you *want* to throw all your chances away? You know your people aren't rich, don't you? You know they can't afford the same things as other boys' parents. How are they to send you to a public school if you don't win a scholarship? I know how proud your mother is of you. Do you *want* to let her down?"

"I don't think he wants to go to a public school any longer,"

Sim would say, addressing himself to Bingo with a pretence that I was not there. "I think he's given up that idea. He wants to be a little office-boy at forty pounds a year."

The horrible sensation of tears—a swelling in the breast, a tickling behind the nose—would already have assailed me. Bingo would bring out her ace of trumps:

"And do you think it's quite fair to *us*, the way you're behaving? After all we've done for you? You *do* know what we've done for you, don't you?" Her eyes would pierce deep into me, and though she never said it straight out, I did know. "We've had you here all these years—we even had you here for a week in the holidays so that Mr. Batchelor could coach you. We don't *want* to have to send you away, you know, but we can't keep a boy here just to eat up our food, term after term. *I* don't think it's very straight, the way you're behaving. Do you?"

I never had any answer except a miserable "No, Mum," or "Yes, Mum" as the case might be. Evidently it was *not* straight, the way I was behaving. And at some point or other the unwanted tear would always force its way out of the corner of my eye, roll down my nose, and splash.

Bingo never said in plain words that I was a non-paying pupil, no doubt because vague phrases like "all we've done for you" had a deeper emotional appeal. Sim, who did not aspire to be loved by his pupils, put it more brutally, though, as was usual with him, in pompous language. "You are living on my bounty" was his favourite phrase in this context. At least once I listened to these words between blows of the cane. I must say that these scenes were not frequent, and except on one occasion they did not take place in the presence of other boys. In public I was reminded that I was poor and that my parents "wouldn't be able to afford" this or that, but I was not actually reminded of my dependent position. It was a final unanswerable argument, to be brought forth like an instrument of torture when my work became exceptionally bad.

To grasp the effect of this kind of thing on a child of ten or twelve, one has to remember that the child has little sense of proportion or probability. A child may be a mass of egoism and rebelliousness, but it has not accumulated experience to give it confidence in its own judgements. On the whole it will accept what it is told, and it will believe in the most fantastic way in the knowledge and power of the adults surrounding it. Here is an example.

I have said that at Crossgates we were not allowed to keep our own money. However, it was possible to hold back a shilling or two, and sometimes I used furtively to buy sweets which I kept hidden in the loose ivy on the playing-field wall. One day when I had been sent on an errand I went into a sweetshop a mile or more from the school and bought some chocolates. As I came out of the shop I saw on the opposite pavement a small sharp-faced man who seemed to be staring very hard at my school cap. Instantly a horrible fear went through me. There could be no doubt as to who the man was. He was a spy placed there by Sim! I turned away unconcernedly, and then, as though my legs were doing it of their own accord, broke into a clumsy run. But when I got round the next corner I forced myself to walk again, for to run was a sign of guilt, and obviously there would be other spies posted here and there about the town. All that day and the next I waited for the summons to the study, and was surprised when it did not come. It did not seem to me strange that the headmaster of a private school should dispose of an army of informers, and I did not even imagine that he would have to pay them. I assumed that any adult, inside the school or outside, would collaborate voluntarily in preventing us from breaking the rules. Sim was all-powerful, and it was natural that his agents should be everywhere. When this episode happened I do not think I can have been less than twelve years old.

I hated Bingo and Sim, with a sort of shamefaced, remorseful hatred, but it did not occur to me to doubt their judgement. When they told me that I must either win a public school scholarship or become an office-boy at fourteen, I believed that those were the unavoidable alternatives before me. And above all, I believed Bingo and Sim when they told me they were my benefactors. I see now, of course, that from Sim's point of view I was a good speculation. He sank money in me, and he looked to get it back in the form of prestige. If I had "gone off," as promising boys sometimes do, I imagine that he would have got rid of me swiftly. As it was I won him two scholarships when the time came, and no doubt he made full use of them in his prospectuses. But it is difficult for a child to realise that a school is primarily a commercial venture. A child believes that the school exists to educate and that the schoolmaster disciplines him either for his own good, or from a love of bullying. Sim and Bingo had chosen to befriend me, and their friendship included canings, reproaches and humiliations, which were good for me and saved me from an office stool. That was their version, and I believed in it. It was therefore clear that I owed them a vast debt of gratitude. But I was *not* grateful, as I very well knew. On the contrary, I hated both of them. I could not control my subjective feelings, and I could not conceal them from myself. But it is wicked, is it not, to hate your benefactors? So I was taught, and so I believed. A child accepts the codes of behaviour that are presented to it, even when it breaks them: From the age of eight, or even earlier, the consciousness of sin was never far away from me. If I contrived to seem callous and defiant, it was only a thin cover over a mass of shame and dismay. All through my boyhood I had a profound conviction that I was no good, that I was wasting my time, wrecking my talents, behaving with monstrous folly and wickedness and ingratitude—and all this, it seemed, was inescapable, because I lived among laws which were absolute, like the law of gravity, but which it was not possible for me to keep.

No one can look back on his schooldays and say with truth that they were altogether unhappy.

I have good memories of Crossgates, among a horde of bad ones. Sometimes on summer afternoons there were wonderful expeditions across the Downs, or to Beachy Head, where one bathed dangerously among the chalk boulders and came home covered with cuts. And there were still more wonderful midsummer evenings when, as a special treat, we were not driven off to bed as usual but allowed to wander about the grounds in the long twilight, ending up with a plunge into the swimming bath at about nine o'clock. There was the joy of waking early on summer mornings and getting in an hour's undisturbed reading (Ian Hay, Thackeray, Kipling and H. G. Wells were the favourite authors of my boyhood) in the sunlit, sleeping dormitory. There was also cricket, which I was no good at but with which I conducted a sort of hopeless love affair up to the age of about eighteen. And there was the pleasure of keeping caterpillars—the silky green and purple puss-moth, the ghostly green poplar-hawk, the privet hawk, large as one's third finger, specimens of which could be illicitly purchased for sixpence at a shop in the town—and, when one could escape long enough from the master who was "taking the walk," there was the excitement of dredging the dew-ponds on the Downs for enormous newts with orange-coloured bellies. This business of being out for a walk, coming across something of fascinating interest and then being dragged away from it by a yell from the master, like a dog jerked onwards by the leash, is an important feature of school life, and helps to build up the conviction, so strong in many children, that the things you most want to do are always unattainable.

Very occasionally, perhaps once during each summer, it was possible to escape altogether from the barrack-like atmosphere of school, when Brown, the second master, was permitted to take one or two boys for an afternoon of butterfly hunting on a common a few miles away. Brown was a man with white hair and a red face like a strawberry, who was good at natural history, making models and plaster casts, operating magic lanterns, and things of that kind. He and Mr. Batchelor were the only adults in any way connected with the school whom I did not either dislike or fear. Once he took me into his room and showed me in confidence a plated, pearl-handled revolver—his "six-shooter," he called it—which he kept in a box under his bed. And oh, the joy of those occasional expeditions! The ride of two or three miles on a lonely little branch line, the afternoon of charging to and fro with large green nets, the beauty of the enormous dragon flies which hovered over the tops of the grasses, the sinister killing-bottle with its sickly smell, and then tea in the parlour of a pub with large slices of pale-coloured cake! The essence of it was in the railway journey, which seemed to put magic distances between yourself and school.

Bingo, characteristically, disapproved of these expeditions, though not actually forbidding them. "And have you been catching *little butterflies?*" she would say with a vicious sneer when one got back, making her voice as babyish as possible. From her point of view, natural history ("bug-hunting" she would probably have called it) was a babyish pursuit which a boy should be laughed out of as early as possible. Moreover it was somehow faintly plebeian, it was traditionally associated with boys who wore spectacles and were no good at games, it did not help you to pass exams, and above all it smelt of science and therefore seemed to menace classical education. It needed a considerable moral effort to accept Brown's invitation. How I dreaded that sneer of *little butterflies!* Brown, however, who had been at the school since its early days, had built up a certain independence for himself: he seemed able to handle Sim, and ignored Bingo a good deal. If it ever happened that both of them were away, Brown acted as deputy headmaster, and on those occasions, instead of reading the appointed lesson for the day at morning chapel, he would read us stories from the Apocrypha.

Most of the good memories of my childhood, and up to the age of about twenty, are in some way connected with animals. So far as Crossgates goes, it also seems, when I look back, that all my good memories are of summer. In winter your nose ran continually, your fingers were too numb to button your shirt (this was an especial misery on Sundays, when we wore Eton collars), and there was the daily nightmare of football—the cold, the mud, the hideous greasy ball that came whizzing at one's face, the gouging knees and trampling boots of the bigger boys. Part of the trouble was that in winter, after the age of about ten, I was seldom in good health, at any rate during term time. I had defective bronchial tubes and a lesion in one lung which was not discovered till many years later. Hence I not only had a chronic cough, but running was a torment to me. In those days, however, "wheeziness," or "chestiness," as it was called, was either diagnosed as imagination or was looked on as essentially a moral disorder, caused by overeating. "You wheeze like a concertina," Sim would say disapprovingly as he stood be-

hind my chair; "You're perpetually stuffing yourself with food,
that's why." My cough was referred to as a "stomach cough," which
made it sound both disgusting and reprehensible. The cure for it
was hard running, which, if you kept it up long enough, ultimately
"cleared your chest."

It is curious, the degree—I will not say of actual hardship, but
of squalor and neglect, that was taken for granted in upper-class
schools of that period. Almost as in the days of Thackeray, it
seemed natural that a little boy of eight or ten should be a miserable, snotty-nosed creature, his face almost permanently dirty, his
hands chapped, his nails bitten, his handkerchief a sodden horror,
his bottom frequently blue with bruises. It was partly the prospect
of actual physical discomfort that made the thought of going back
to school lie in one's breast like a lump of lead during the last few
days of the holidays. A characteristic memory of Crossgates is the
astonishing hardness of one's bed on the first night of term. Since
this was an expensive school, I took a social step upwards by attending it, and yet the standard of comfort was in every way far lower
than in my own home, or indeed, than it would have been in a pros-
perous working-class home. One only had a hot bath once a week,
for instance. The food was not only bad, it was also insufficient.
Never before or since have I seen butter or jam scraped on bread so
thinly. I do not think I can be imaging the fact that we were underfed, when I remember the lengths we would go in order to steal
food. On a number of occasions I remember creeping down at two
or three o'clock in the morning through what seemed like miles of
pitch-dark stairways and passages—barefooted, stopping to listen
after each step, paralysed with about equal fear of Sim, ghosts and
burglars—to steal stale bread from the pantry. The assistant masters
had their meals with us, but they had somewhat better food, and if
one got half a chance it was usual to steal left-over scraps of bacon
rind or fried potato when their plates were removed.

As usual, I did not see the sound commercial reason for this
under-feeding. On the whole I accepted Sim's view that a boy's
appetite is a sort of morbid growth which should be kept in check
as much as possible. A maxim often repeated to us at Crossgates was
that it is healthy to get up from a meal feeling as hungry as when
you sat down. Only a generation earlier than this it had been common for school dinners to start off with a slab of unsweetened suet
pudding, which, it was frankly said, "broke the boys' appetites."
But the under-feeding was probably less flagrant at preparatory
schools, where a boy was wholly dependent on the official diet,
than at public schools, where he was allowed—indeed, expected
—to buy extra food for himself. At some schools, he would literally
not have had enough to eat unless he had bought regular supplies

of eggs, sausages, sardines, etc.; and his parents had to allow him money for this purpose. At Eton, for instance, at any rate in College, a boy was given no solid meal after mid-day dinner. For his afternoon tea he was given only tea and bread and butter, and at eight o'clock he was given a miserable supper of soup or fried fish, or more often bread and cheese, with water to drink. Sim went down to see his eldest son at Eton and came back in snobbish ecstasies over the luxury in which the boys lived. "They give them fried fish for supper!" he exclaimed, beaming all over his chubby face. "There's no school like it in the world." Fried fish! The habitual supper of the poorest of the working class! At very cheap boarding-schools it was no doubt worse. A very early memory of mine is of seeing the boarders at a grammar school—the sons, probably, of farmers and shopkeepers—being fed on boiled lights.

Whoever writes about his childhood must beware of exaggeration and self-pity. I do not want to claim that I was a martyr or that Crossgates was a sort of Dotheboys Hall. But I should be falsifying my own memories if I did not record that they are largely memories of disgust. The overcrowded, underfed, underwashed life that we led *was* disgusting, as I recall it. If I shut my eyes and say "school," it is of course the physical surroundings that first come back to me: the flat playing-field with its cricket pavilion and the little shed by the rifle range, the draughty dormitories, the dusty splintery passages, the square of asphalt in front of the gymnasium, the raw-looking pinewood chapel at the back. And at almost every point some filthy detail obtrudes itself. For example, there were the pewter bowls out of which we had our porridge. They had overhanging rims, and under the rims there were accumulations of sour porridge, which could be flaked off in long strips. The porridge itself, too, contained more lumps, hairs and unexplained black things than one would have thought possible, unless someone were putting them there on purpose. It was never safe to start on that porridge without investigating it first. And there was the slimy water of the plunge bath—it was twelve or fifteen feet long, the whole school was supposed to go into it every morning, and I doubt whether the water was changed at all frequently—and the always-damp towels with their cheesy smell: and, on occasional visits in the winter, the murky sea-water of the local Baths, which came straight in from the beach and on which I once saw floating a human turd. And the sweaty smell of the changing-room with its greasy basins, and, giving on this, the row of filthy, dilapidated lavatories, which had no fastenings of any kind on the doors, so that whenever you were sitting there someone was sure to come crashing in. It is not easy for me to think of my school days without seeming to breath in a whiff of something cold and evil-smelling—a sort of compound of sweaty stockings, dirty towels, faecal smells blowing along corridors, forks with old food between the prongs, neck-of-mutton stew, and the banging doors of the lavatories and the echoing chamberpots in the dormitories.

It is true that I am by nature not gregarious, and the W.C. and dirty-handkerchief side of life is necessarily more obtrusive when great numbers of human beings are crushed together in small space. It is just as bad in an army, and worse, no doubt, in a prison. Besides, boyhood is the age of disgust. After one has learned to differentiate, and before one has become hardened—between seven and eighteen, say—one seems always to be walking the tightrope over a cesspool. Yet I do not think I exaggerate the squalor of school life, when I remember how health and cleanliness were neglected, in spite of the hoo-ha about fresh air and cold water and keeping in hard training. It was common to remain constipated for days together. Indeed, one was hardly encouraged to keep one's bowels open, since the aperients tolerated were Castor Oil or another almost equally horrible drink called Liquorice Powder. One was supposed to go into the plunge bath every morning, but some boys shirked it for days on end, simply making themselves scarce when the bell sounded, or else slipping along the edge of the bath among the crowd, and then wetting their hair with a little dirty water off the floor. A little boy of eight or nine will not necessarily keep himself clean unless there is someone to see that he does it. There was a new boy named Hazel, a pretty, mother's darling of a boy, who came a little before I left. The first thing I noticed about him was the beautiful pearly whiteness of his teeth. By the end of that term his teeth were an extraordinary shade of green. During all that time, apparently, no one had taken sufficient interest in him to see that he brushed them.

But of course the differences between home and school were more than physical. That bump on the hard mattress, on the first night of term, used to give me a feeling of abrupt awakening, a feeling of: "This is reality, this is what you are up against." Your home might be far from perfect, but at least it was a place ruled by love rather than by fear, where you did not have to be perpetually on your guard against the people surrounding you. At eight years old you were suddenly taken out of this warm nest and flung into a world of force and fraud and secrecy, like a goldfish into a tank full of pike. Against no matter what degree of bullying you had no redress. You could only have defended yourself by sneaking, which, except in a few rigidly defined circumstances, was the unforgivable sin. To write home and ask your parents to take you away would have been even less thinkable, since to do so would have been to admit yourself unhappy and unpopular, which a boy will never do. Boys are Erewhonians: they think that misfortune is disgraceful and must be concealed at all costs. It might perhaps have been considered permissible to complain to your parents about bad food, or an injustified caning, or some other ill-treatment inflicted by masters and not by boys. The fact that Sim never beat the richer boys suggests that such complaints were made occasionally. But in my own peculiar circumstances I could never have asked my parents to intervene on my behalf. Even before I understood about the reduced fees, I grasped that they were in some way under an obligation to Sim, and therefore could not protect me against him. I have mentioned already that throughout my time at Crossgates I never had a cricket bat of my own. I had been told this was because "your parents couldn't afford it." One day in the holidays, by some casual remark, it came out that they had provided ten shillings to buy me one: yet no cricket bat appeared. I did not protest to my parents, let alone raise the subject with Sim. How could I? I was dependent on him, and the ten shillings was merely a fragment of what I owed him. I realise now, of course, that it is immensely unlikely that Sim had simply stuck to the money. No doubt the matter had slipped his memory. But the point is that I assumed that he had stuck to it, and that he had a right to do so if he chose.

How difficult it is for a child to have any real independence of attitude could be seen in our behaviour towards Bingo. I think it would be true to say that every boy in the school hated and feared her. Yet we all fawned on her in the most abject way, and the top layer of our feelings towards her was a sort of guilt-stricken loyalty. Bingo, although the discipline of the school depended more on her than on Sim, hardly pretended to dispense justice. She was frankly capricious. An act which might get you a caning one day, might next day be laughed off as a boyish prank, or even commended because it "showed you had guts." There were days when everyone cowered before those deepset, accusing eyes, and there were days when she was like a flirtatious queen surrounded by courtier-lovers, laughing and joking, scattering largesse, or the promise of largesse ("And if you win the Harrow History Prize I'll give you a new case for your camera!"), and occasionally even packing three or four favoured boys into her Ford car and carrying them off to a teashop in town, where they were allowed to buy coffee and cakes. Bingo was inextricably mixed up in my mind with Queen Elizabeth, whose relations with Leicester and Essex and Raleigh were intelligible to me from a very early age. A word we all constantly used in speaking of Bingo was "favour." "I'm in good favour," we would say, or "I'm in bad favour." Except for the handful of wealthy or titled boys, no one was permanently in good favour, but on the other hand even the outcasts had patches of it from time to time. Thus, although my memories of Bingo are mostly hostile, I also remember considerable periods when I basked under her smiles, when she called me "old chap" and used my Christian name, and allowed me to frequent her private library, where I first made acquaintance with *Vanity Fair*. The high-water mark of good favour was to be invited to serve at table on Sunday nights when Bingo and Sim had guests to dinner. In clearing away, of course, one had a chance to finish off the scraps, but one also got a servile pleasure from standing behind the seated guests and darting deferentially forward when something was wanted. Whenever one had the chance to suck up, one did suck up, and at the first smile one's hatred turned into a sort of cringing love. I was always tremendously proud when I succeeded in making Bingo laugh. I have even, at her command, written *vers d'occasion*, comic verses to celebrate memorable events in the life of the school.

I am anxious to make it clear that I was not a rebel, except by force of circumstances. I accepted the codes that I found in being. Once, towards the end of my time, I even sneaked to Brown about a suspected case of homosexuality. I did not know very well what homosexuality was, but I knew that it happened and was bad, and that this was one of the contexts in which it was proper to sneak. Brown told me I was "a good fellow," which made me feel horribly ashamed. Before Bingo one seemed as helpless as a snake before a snake-charmer. She had a hardly varying vocabulary of praise and abuse, a whole series of set phrases, each of which promptly called forth the appropriate response. There was "*Buck* up, old chap!", which inspired one to paroxysms of energy; there was "Don't *be* such a fool!" (or, "It's path*e*tic, isn't it?"), which made one feel a born idiot; and there was "It isn't very straight of you, is it?", which always brought one to the brink of tears. And yet all the while, at the middle of one's heart, there seemed to stand an incorruptible inner self who knew that whatever one did—whether one laughed or snivelled or went into frenzies of gratitude for small favours—one's only true feeling was hatred.

The various codes which were presented to you at Crossgates —religious, moral, social and intellectual—contradicted one another if you worked out their implications. The essential conflict was between the tradition of nineteenth-century asceticism and the actually existing luxury and snobbery of the pre-1914 age. On the one side were low-church Bible Christianity, sex puritanism, insistence on hard work, respect for academic distinction, disapproval of self-indulgence: on the other, contempt for "braininess" and worship of games, contempt for foreigners and the working class, an almost neurotic dread of poverty, and, above all, the assumption not only that money and privilege are the things that matter, but that it is better to inherit them than to have to work for them. Broadly, you were bidden to be at once a Christian and a social success, which is impossible. At the time I did not perceive that the various ideals which were set before us cancelled out. I merely saw that they were all, or nearly all, unattainable, so far as I was concerned, since they all depended not only on what you did but on what you *were*.

Very early, at the age of only ten or eleven, I reached the conclusion—no one told me this, but on the other hand I did not simply make it up out of my own head: somehow it was in the air I breathed—that you were no good unless you had £100,000. I had perhaps fixed on this particular sum as a result of reading Thackeray. The interest on £100,000 a year (I was in favour of a safe 4 per cent), would be £4,000, and this seemed to me the minimum income that you must possess if you were to belong to the real top crust, the people in the country houses. But it was clear that I could never find my way into that paradise, to which you did not really belong unless you were born into it. You could only *make* money, if at all, by a mysterious operation called "going into the City," and when you came out of the City, having won your £100,000, you were fat and old. But the truly enviable thing about the top-notchers was that they were rich while young. For people like me, the ambitious middle class, the examination passers, only a bleak, laborious kind of success was possible. You clambered upwards on a ladder of scholarships into the Home Civil Service or the Indian Civil Service, or possibly you became a barrister. And if at any point you "slacked" or "went off" and missed one of the rungs in the ladder, you became "a little office boy at forty pounds a year." But even if you climbed to the highest niche that was open to you, you could still only be an underling, a hanger-on of the people who really counted.

Even if I had not learned this from Sim and Bingo, I would have learned it from the other boys. Looking back, it is astonishing how intimately, intelligently snobbish we all were, how knowledgeable about names and addresses, how swift to detect small differences in accents and manners and the cut of clothes. There were some boys who seemed to drop money from their pores even in the bleak misery of the middle of a winter term. At the beginning and end of the term, especially, there was naively snobbish chatter about Switzerland, and Scotland with its ghillies and grouse moors, and "my uncle's yacht," and "our place in the country," and "my pony" and "my pater's touring car." There never was, I suppose, in the history of the world a time when the sheer vulgar fatness of wealth, without any kind of aristocratic elegance to redeem it, was so obtrusive as in those years before 1914. It was the age when crazy millionaires in curly top hats and lavender waistcoats gave champagne parties in rococo houseboats on the Thames, the age of diabolo and hobble skirts, the age of the "knut" in his grey bowler and cutaway coat, the age of *The Merry Widow*, Saki's novels, *Peter Pan* and *Where the Rainbow Ends*, the age when people talked about chocs and cigs and ripping and topping and heavenly, when they went for divvy weekends at Brighton and had scrumptious teas at the Troc. From the whole decade before 1914, there seems to breathe forth a smell of the more vulgar, un-grown-up kinds of luxury, a smell of brilliantine and crème de menthe and soft-centred chocolates—an atmosphere, as it were, of eating everlasting strawberry ices on green lawns to the tune of the Eton Boating Song. The extraordinary thing was the way in which everyone took it for granted that this oozing, bulging wealth of the English upper and upper-middle classes would last for ever, and was part of the order of things. After 1918 it was never quite the same again. Snobbishness and expensive habits came back, certainly, but they were self-conscious and on the defensive. Before the war the worship of money was entirely unreflecting and untroubled by any pang of conscience. The goodness of money was as unmistakable as the goodness of health or beauty, and a glittering car, a title or a horde of servants was mixed up in people's minds with the idea of actual moral virtue.

At Crossgates, in term time, the general bareness of life enforced a certain democracy, but any mention of the holidays, and the consequent competitive swanking about cars and butlers and country houses, promptly called class distinctions into being. The school was pervaded by a curious cult of Scotland, which brought out the fundamental contradiction in our standard of values. Bingo claimed Scottish ancestry, and she favoured the Scottish boys, encouraging them to wear kilts in their ancestral tartan instead of the school uniform, and even christened her youngest child by a Gaelic name. Ostensibly we were supposed to admire the Scots because they were "grim" and "dour" ("stern" was perhaps the key word), and irresistible on the field of battle. In the big schoolroom there was a steel engraving of the charge of the Scots Greys at Waterloo, all looking as though they enjoyed every moment of it. Our picture of Scotland was made up of burns, braes, kilts, sporrans, claymores, bagpipes, and the like, all somehow mixed up with the invigorating effects of porridge, Protestantism and a cold climate. But underlying this was something quite different. The real reason for the cult of Scotland was that only very rich people could spend their summers there. And the pretended belief in Scottish superiority was a cover for the bad conscience of the occupying English, who had pushed the Highland peasantry off their farms to make way for the deer forests, and then compensated them by turning them into servants. Bingo's face always beamed with innocent snobbishness when she spoke of Scotland. Occasionally she even attempted a trace of Scottish accent. Scotland was a private paradise which a few initiates could talk about and make outsiders feel small.

"You going to Scotland this hols?"

"Rather! We go every year."

"My pater's giving me a new gun for the twelfth. There's jolly good black game where we go. Get out, Smith! What are you listening for? You've never been in Scotland. I bet you don't know what a black-cock looks like."

Following on this, imitations of the cry of a black-cock, of the roaring of a stag, of the accent of "our ghillies," etc., etc.

And the questionings that new boys of doubtful social origin were sometimes put through—questionings quite surprising in their mean-minded particularity, when one reflects that the inquisitors were only twelve or thirteen!

"How much a year has your pater got? What part of London do you live in? Is that Knightsbridge or Kensington? How many bathrooms has your house got? How many servants do your people keep? Have you got a butler? Well, then, have you got a cook? Where do you get your clothes made? How many shows did you go to in the hols? How much money did you bring back with you?" etc., etc.

I have seen a little new boy, hardly older than eight, desperately lying his way through such a catechism:

"Have your people got a car?"

"Yes."

"What sort of car?"

"Daimler."

"How many horse-power?"

(Pause, and leap in the dark.) "Fifteen."

"What kind of lights?"

The little boy is bewildered.

"What kind of lights? Electric or acetylene?"

(A longer pause, and another leap in the dark.) "Acetylene."

"Coo! He says his pater's car's got acetylene lamps. They went out years ago. It must be as old as the hills."

"Rot! He's making it up. He hasn't got a car. He's just a navvy. Your pater's a navvy."

And so on.

By the social standards that prevailed about me, I was no good, and could not be any good. But all the different kinds of virtue seemed to be mysteriously interconnected and to belong to much the same people. It was not only money that mattered: there were also strength, beauty, charm, athleticism and something called "guts" or "character," which in reality meant the power to impose your will on others. I did not possess any of these qualities. At games, for instance, I was hopeless. I was a fairly good swimmer and not altogether contemptible at cricket, but these had no prestige value, because boys only attach importance to a game if it requires strength and courage. What counted was football, at which I was a funk. I loathed the game, and since I could see no pleasure or use-fulness in it, it was very difficult for me to show courage at it. Football, it seemed to me, is not really played for the pleasure of kicking a ball about, but is a species of fighting. The lovers of foot-ball are large, boisterous, nobbly boys who are good at knocking down and trampling on slightly smaller boys. That was the pattern of school life—a continuous triumph of the strong over the weak. Virtue consisted in winning: it consisted in being bigger, stronger, handsomer, richer, more popular, more elegant, more unscrupu-lous than other people—in dominating them, bullying them, mak-ing them suffer pain, making them look foolish, getting the better of them in every way. Life was hierarchical and whatever happened was right. There was the strong, who deserved to win and always did win, and there were the weak, who deserved to lose and always did lose, everlastingly.

I did not question the prevailing standards, because so far as I could see there were no others. How could the rich, the strong, the elegant, the fashionable, the powerful, be in the wrong? It was their world, and the rules they made for it must be the right ones. And yet from a very early age I was aware of the impossibility of any *subjective* conformity. Always at the centre of my heart the inner self seemed to be awake, pointing out the difference between the moral obligation and the psychological *fact*. It was the same in all matters, worldly or other-worldly. Take religion, for instance. You were supposed to love God, and I did not question this. Till the age of about fourteen I believed in God, and believed that the accounts given of him were true. But I was well aware that I did not love him. On the contrary, I hated him, just as I hated Jesus and the Hebrew patriarchs. If I had sympathetic feelings towards any char-acter in the Old Testament, it was towards such people as Cain, Jezebel, Haman, Agag, Sisera: in the New Testament my friends, if any, were Ananias, Caiaphas, Judas and Pontius Pilate. But the whole business of religion seemed to be strewn with psychological impossibilities. The Prayer Book told you, for example, to love God and fear him: but how could you love someone whom you feared? With your private affections it was the same. What you *ought* to feel was usually clear enough, but the appropriate emotion could not be commanded. Obviously it was my duty to feel grateful towards Bingo and Sim; but I was not grateful. It was equally clear that one ought to love one's father, but I knew very well that I merely disliked my own father, whom I had barely seen before I was eight and who appeared to me simply as a gruff-voiced elderly man forever saying "Don't." It was not that one did not want to possess the right qualities or feel the correct emotions, but that one could not. The good and the possible never seemed to coincide.

There was a line of verse that I came across, not actually while I was at Crossgates, but a year or two later, and which seemed to strike a sort of leaden echo in my heart. It was: "The armies of unalterable law." I understood to perfection what it meant to be Lucifer, defeated and justly defeated, with no possibility of revenge. The schoolmasters with their canes, the millionaires with their Scottish castles, the athletes with their curly hair—these were the armies of the unalterable law. It was not easy, at that date, to realise that in fact it *was* alterable. And according to that law I was damned. I had no money, I was weak, I was ugly, I was unpopular, I had a chronic cough, I was cowardly, I smelt. This picture, I should add, was not altogether fanciful. I was an unattractive boy. Crossgates soon made me so, even if I had not been so before. But a child's belief of its own shortcomings is not much influenced by facts. I believed, for example, that I "smelt," but this was based simply on general probability. It was notorious that disagreeable people smelt, and therefore presumably I did so too. Again, until after I had left school for good I continued to believe that I was preternaturally ugly. It was what my schoolfellows had told me, and I had no other authority to refer to. The conviction that it was *not possible* for me to be a success went deep enough to influence my actions till far into adult life. Until I was about thirty I always planned my life on the assumption not only that any major undertaking was bound to fail, but that I could only expect to live a few years longer.

But this sense of guilt and inevitable failure was balanced by something else: that is, the instinct to survive. Even a creature that is weak, ugly, cowardly, smelly and in no way justifiable still wants to stay alive and be happy after its own fashion. I could not invert the existing scale of values, or turn myself into a success, but I could accept my failure and make the best of it. I could resign myself to being what I was, and then endeavour to survive on those terms.

To survive, or at least to preserve any kind of independence, was essentially criminal, since it meant breaking rules which you yourself recognized. There was a boy named Johnny Hall who for some months oppressed me horribly. He was a big, powerful, coarsely handsome boy with a very red face and curly black hair, who was for ever twisting somebody's arm, wringing somebody's ear, flogging somebody with a riding crop (he was a member of the Sixth Form), or performing prodigies of activity on the football field. Bingo loved him (hence the fact that he was habitually called by his Christian name), and Sim commended him as a boy who "had character" and could "keep order." He was followed about by a group of toadies who nicknamed him Strong Man.

One day, when we were taking off our overcoats in the changing-room, Hall picked on me for some reason. I "answered him back," whereupon he gripped my wrist, twisted it round, and bent my forearm back upon itself in a hideously painful way. I remember his handsome, jeering red face bearing down upon mine. He was, I think, older than I, besides being enormously stronger. As he let go of me a terrible, wicked resolve formed itself in my heart. I would get back on him by hitting him when he did not expect it. It was a strategic moment, for the master who had been "taking" the walk would be coming back almost immediately, and then there could be no fight. I let perhaps a minute go by, walked up to Hall with the most harmless air I could assume, and then, getting the weight of my body behind it, smashed my fist into his face. He was flung backwards by the blow and some blood ran out of his mouth. His always sanguine face turned almost black with rage. Then he turned away to rinse his mouth at the washing-basins.

"*All right!*" he said to me between his teeth as the master led us away.

For days after this he followed me about, challenging me to fight. Although terrified out of my wits, I steadily refused to fight. I said that the blow in the face had served him right, and there was an end of it. Curiously enough he did not simply fall upon me then and there, which public opinion would probably have supported him in doing. So gradually the matter tailed off, and there was no fight.

Now, I had behaved wrongly, by my own code no less than his. To hit him unawares was wrong. But to refuse to fight afterwards, knowing that if we fought he would beat me—that was far worse: it was cowardly. If I had refused because I disapproved of fighting, or because I genuinely felt the matter to be closed, it would have been all right; but I had refused merely because I was afraid. Even my revenge was made empty by that fact. I had struck the blow in a moment of mindless violence, deliberately not looking far ahead and merely determined to get my own back for once and damn the consequences. I had had time to realise that what I did was wrong, but it was the kind of crime from which you could get some satisfaction. Now all was nullified. There had been a sort of courage in the first act, but my subsequent cowardice had wiped it out.

The fact I hardly noticed was that although Hall formally challenged me to fight, he did not actually attack me. Indeed, after receiving that one blow he never oppressed me again. It was perhaps twenty years before I saw the significance of this. At the time I could not see beyond the moral dilemma that is presented to the weak in a world governed by the strong: Break the rules, or perish. I did not see that in that case the weak have the right to make a different set of rules for themselves; because, even if such an idea had occurred to me, there was no one in my environment who could have confirmed me in it. I lived in a world of boys, gregarious animals, questioning nothing, accepting the law of the stronger and avenging their own humiliations by passing them down to someone smaller. My situation was that of countless other boys, and if potentially I was more of a rebel than most, it was only because, by boyish standards, I was a poorer specimen. But I never did rebel intellectually, only emotionally. I had nothing to help me except my dumb selfishness, my inability—not, indeed, to despise myself, but to *dislike* myself—my instinct to survive.

It was about a year after I hit Johnny Hall in the face that I left Crossgates for ever. It was the end of a winter term. With a sense of coming out from darkness into sunlight I put on my Old Boy's tie as we dressed for the journey. I well remember the feeling of that brand-new silk tie round my neck, a feeling of emancipation, as though the tie had been at once a badge of manhood and an amulet against Bingo's voice and Sim's cane. I was escaping from bondage. It was not that I expected, or even intended, to be any more successful at a public school than I had been at Crossgates. But still, I was escaping. I knew that at a public school there would be more privacy, more neglect, more chance to be idle and self-indulgent and degenerate. For years past I had been resolved—unconsciously at first, but consciously later on—that when once my scholarship was won I would "slack off" and cram no longer. This resolve, by the way, was so fully carried out that between the ages of thirteen and twenty-two or -three I hardly ever did a stroke of avoidable work.

Bingo shook hands to say good-bye. She even gave me my Christian name for the occasion. But there was a sort of patronage, almost a sneer, in her face and in her voice. The tone in which she said good-bye was nearly the tone in which she had been used to say *little butterflies*. I had won two scholarships, but I was a failure, because success was measured not by what you did but by what you *were*. I was "not a good type of boy and could bring no credit on the school. I did not possess character or courage or health or strength or money, or even good manners, the power to look like a gentleman."

"Good-bye," Bingo's parting smile seemed to say; "it's not worth quarrelling now. You haven't made much of a success of your time at Crossgates, have you? And I don't suppose you'll get on awfully well at a public school either. We made a mistake, really, in wasting our time and money on you. This kind of education hasn't much to offer to a boy with your background and outlook. Oh, don't think we don't understand you! We know all about those ideas you have at the back of your head, we know you disbelieve in everything we've taught you, and we know you aren't in the least grateful for all we've done for you. But there's no use in bringing it all up now. We aren't responsible for you any longer, and we shan't be seeing you again. Let's just admit that you're one of our failures and part without ill-feeling. And so, good-bye."

That at least was what I read into her face. And yet how happy I was, that winter morning, as the train bore me away with the gleaming new silk tie round my neck! The world was opening before me, just a little, like a grey sky which exhibits a narrow crack of blue. A public school would be better fun than Crossgates but at bottom equally alien. In a world where the prime necessities were money, titled relatives, athleticism, tailor-made clothes, neatly brushed hair, a charming smile, I was no good. All I had gained was a breathing-space. A little quietude, a little self-indulgence, a little respite from cramming—and then, ruin. What kind of ruin I did not know: perhaps the colonies or an office stool, perhaps prison or an early death. But first a year or two in which one could "slack off" and get the benefit of one's sins, like Doctor Faustus. It is the advantage of being thirteen that you cannot only live in the moment, but do so with full consciousness, foreseeing the future and yet not caring about it. Next term I was going to Wellington. I had also won a scholarship at Eton. but was uncertain whether there would be a vacancy, and I was going to Wellington first. At Eton you had a room to yourself—a room which might even have a fire in it. At Wellington you had your own cubicle, and could make cocoa in the evenings. The privacy of it, the grown-upness! And there would be libraries to hang about in, and summer afternoons when you could shirk games and mooch about the countryside alone, with no master driving you along. Meanwhile there were the holidays. There was the .22 rifle that I had bought the previous holidays (the Crackshot, it was called, costing twenty-two and sixpence), and Christmas was coming next week. There were also the pleasures of overeating. I thought of some particularly voluptuous cream buns which could be bought for twopence each at a shop in our town. (This was 1916, and food-rationing had not yet started.) Even the detail that my journey-money had been slightly miscalculated, leaving about a

shilling over—enough for an unforeseen cup of coffee and a cake
or two somewhere on the way—was enough to fill me with bliss.
There was time for a bit of happiness before the future closed in
upon me. But I did know that the future was dark. Failure, failure,
failure—failure behind me, failure ahead of me—that was by far
the deepest conviction that I carried away.

———

GEORGE ORWELL (1903–1950) *achieved success with* Animal Farm
(1946), *a short satire on Soviet Russian history, but remains best
known for the grim political vision of* 1984 (1949). *However,
throughout the 1940's he had been one of England's leading es-
sayists and journalists, and had become known for his writings on
social, political, and literary matters. At his death he was called
"the conscience of his generation"; later generations continue to
value his clarity of vision, his refusal to accept slogans or cant, his
reliance on common sense decency and honesty. Orwell (a pen name
for Eric Blair) attended St. Cyprian's ("Crossgates") from 1911 to
1916, accepted a scholarship to Eton, then declined an opportunity
to attend Cambridge to go to Burma as a colonial policeman. The
severity of the attack on English institutions in "Such, Such Were
the Joys" has led to its being banned from an English edition of
Orwell's essays, and may in part explain his refusal to go to Cambridge.*

*The ironic title is taken from the second stanza of William
Blake's "The Echoing Green," one of his "Songs of Innocence":*

> Old John, with white hair,
> Does laugh away care,
> Sitting under the oak,
> Among the old folk.
> They laugh at our play,
> And soon they all say:
> "Such, such were the joys
> When we all, girls and boys,
> In our youth time were seen
> On the Echoing Green."

1. *Reread the discussion of the "Johnny Hall" passage in the
   preface to this section. Find another passage which demonstrates Orwell's ability to recreate a scene vividly, then to examine it according to both schoolboy and adult standards.*

Analyze the passage you have chosen.

2. Choose a paragraph which vividly renders a scene, such as the one beginning "He would tap away at one's skull. . . ." Look closely at the kinds of nouns (skull, bump, short hairs around one's ears, shin, etc.) and the kinds of verbs (tap, raise a bump, pull, kick, whack—repeated four times!, etc.). In the paragraph you have chosen, what kinds of nouns and verbs are used? Do they tend toward precision or generality? What tone do they establish and how?

3. How does Orwell convey to us the "memories of disgust"? When he says "at almost every point some filthy detail obtrudes itself" what is he telling us about his craft and intention as a writer?

4. Choose one of the significant abstract terms in this essay (snobbishness, rebellion, the incorruptible inner self, the contradictory codes at the school, for example) and show how Orwell defines the term for the reader.

5. As you write about your own "institution," refer back to some of the ways Orwell combines his adult perspective and value system with sharply remembered detailed scenes. To what degree do your own words convey the actual experience you describe? What is the meaning of the description? What abstractions of interest emerge from the details? Have you defined them for the reader? How have you related details to meaning?

Cyril Connolly

WHITE SAMITE

The new school my parents chose for me was on the coast. At first I was miserable there and cried night after night. My mother cried too at sending me, and I have often wondered if that incubator of persecution mania, the English private school, is worth the money that is spent on it, or the tears its pupils shed. At an early age small boys are subjected to brutal partings and long separations which undermine their love for their parents, before the natural period of conflict, and are encouraged to look down on them without knowing why. To owners of private schools they are a business like any other, to masters a refuge for incompetence, in fact a private school has all the faults of a public school, without any of its compensations, without tradition, freedom, historical beauty, good teaching, or communication between pupil and teacher. It is one of the few tortures confined to the ruling classes and from which the workers are free. I have never met anybody yet who could say he had been happy there.

Yet St. Wulfric's, where I went, was well run and vigorous, and did me good. We called the headmistress Flip and the headmaster Sambo. Flip, around whom the school revolved, was able, ambitious, temperamental, and energetic. She wanted it to be a success, to have more boys, to attract the sons of peers and to send them all to Eton. She was an able instructress in French and History, and we learnt with her as fast as fear could teach us. Sambo was a cold, business-like and dutiful consort. The morale of the school was high, and every year it won a shooting trophy and the Harrow History Prize from all the other preparatory schools. Inside the chapel was a chaplain, inside the gym a drill-sergeant, and there were a virid swimming-pool, a cadet corps, carpenter's shop and riding class.

The school was typical of England before the war; it was worldly and worshipped success, political and social; through Spartan, the death-rate was low, for it was well run, and based on that stoicism which characterized the English governing class, and which has since

From *Enemies of Promise* by Cyril Connolly, The Macmillan Company, 1938. Copyright © 1938, 1948, 1966 by Cyril Connolly. Reprinted with the author's permission through International Famous Agency, Inc.

been under-estimated. "Character, character, character," was the message which emerged when we rattled the radiators, or the fence round the playing fields, and it reverberated from the rifles in the armory, the bullets on the miniature range, the saw in the carpenter's shop, and the hoofs of the ponies on their trot to the Downs.

> Not once or twice in our rough island's story
> The path of duty was the way to glory

was what we had to learn, and there were other sacred messages from Kipling or Newbolt.

Muscle-bound with character the alumni of St. Wulfric's would pass on to the best public schools, cleaning up houses with doubtful tone, reporting their best friends for homosexuality and seeing them expelled, winning athletic distinctions—for the house rather than themselves, for the school rather than the house, and prizes and scholarships and shooting competitions as well—and then find their vocation in India, Burma, Nigeria, and the Sudan, administering, with Roman justice, the natives for whom the final profligate overflow of Wulfrician character had been all the time predestined.

After I had spent one or two terms at St. Wulfric's, blue with cold, haunting the radiators and the lavatories, and waking up every morning with the accumulated misery of the mornings before, the war broke out. My parents had gone to live in London in Brompton Square, and the holidays had become an oasis after St. Wulfric's austerity. In the big room at the top of the house with my grandfather's sea chest and the animal books by Ernest Thompson Seton, a fire and the view of the sea-green limes of the Brompton Oratory, or in the rosewood drawing-room with its vine-clad balcony, I could be happy. The square abounded with looper caterpillars, tight in the shallow earth wriggled the pupae of the privet moth (in those that did not wriggle the ichneumon was at work). On Sundays people made jokes about not going to church, but went, and the churches disgorged their top-hatted congregations into the Park, from whence they strolled back, myself in an Eton jacket moving in an Anglo-Irish phalanx, and imagining I was Charles Hawtrey, through gates and squares and crescents aromatic with Sunday luncheons, the roast beef, the boredom, the security of 1913. At night my fear of the dark was still acute. I had to have night-lights, and I had a terror of anything "going out"—I could not bear a dying fire or a guttering candle, or even a clock to run down—it seemed a kind of death-agony.

The rest of my time at St. Wulfric's was spent on a war-time basis. The school throve; its *raison d'être* apparent in the Roll of Honour. Old boys came down in uniform, and retired generals lectured to the corps, while the boys stuck flags into maps, gave

Woodbines to the wounded soldiers, and learned to knit; doing without more and more, as Flip's organizing genius found its expression.

The master who took me in hand was Mr. Ellis. He was gruff and peppery with an egg-shaped bald head. He and Mr. Potter, the high-priest of the shooting trophies, were professional teachers, the rest makeshifts thrown up by the war. Ellis was pro-German; the Germans deserved to win the war, he thought, because of their superior efficiency. The boys respected his point of view; to them, a German victory would have seemed natural, a chastisement on England for neglecting duty and discipline, and not listening to "Lest we forget." He made me enthusiastic over algebra, and as my enthusiasm grew I became good at it.

From that moment Daddy Ellis befriended me. He called me Tim Connolly and built up a personality for me as the Irish Rebel, treating me as an intelligent and humorous person, an opponent to respect. When the Germans conquered our decadent country through their discipline and the superiority of general staff I should be one of the first elements to be shot.

My new personality appealed to me. I changed my handwriting and way of doing my hair, jumped first instead of last into the plunge-bath, played football better, and became an exhibit, the gay, generous, rebellious Irishman, with a whiff of Kipling's McTurk. Flip also admired the transformation and began to introduce me to parents as "our dangerous Irishman," "our little rebel." At that time I used to keep a favour chart in which, week by week, I would graph my position at her court. I remember my joy as the upward curve continued, and as I began to make friends, win prizes, enjoy riding, and succeed at trying to be funny again. The favour charts I kept for several terms; one began at the top and then went downwards as term wore on, and tempers.

When angry, Flip would slap our faces, in front of the school, or pull the hair behind our ears, till we cried. She would make satirical remarks at meals that pierced like a rapier, and then put us through interviews in which we bellowed with repentance—"It wasn't very straight of you, was it, Tim? Don't you *want* to do me credit— don't you *want* to have character—or do you simply not care what I think of you as long as you can get a few cheap laughs from your friends and shirk all responsibility?" On all the boys who went through this Elizabeth and Essex relationship she had a remarkable effect, hotting them up like little Alfa-Romeos for the Brooklands of life.

The only thing that would bring our favour back (for, woman-like, Flip treated the very being-out-of-favour as a crime in itself, punishing us for the timid looks and underdog manner by which we showed it) was a visit from parents, and many a letter was sent off begging for their aid. I was restored, after a low period during which I had been compared, before the whole school, to the tribe of Reuben because "unstable as water thou shalt not excel," by an enquiry from Lord Meath, the founder of Empire Day. Sometimes we could get back by clinging to friends who were still "in favour." It might drag them down, or it might bring us up, and the unhappiness of these little boys forced to choose between dropping a friend in his disgrace or risking disgrace themselves was affecting.

I had two friends whose "favour" was as uncertain as my own, George Orwell, and Cecil Beaton. I was a stage rebel, Orwell a true one. Tall, pale, with his flaccid cheeks, and a matter-of-fact, supercilious voice, he was one of those boys who seem born old. He was incapable of courtship, and when his favour went, it went for ever. He saw through St. Wulfric's, despised Sambo and hated Flip, but was valuable to them as scholarship fodder. We often walked together over the downs in our green jerseys and corduroy breeches, discussing literature, and we both won, in consecutive years, the inevitable "Harrow History Prize." There was another prize for having the "best list" of books taken out of the library during the term, the kind which might have been only invented to create intellectual snobs, and to satiate boys with the world's culture at a time when they were too young to understand it. The books were given out in the evening by Flip herself, and a way by which it was sometimes possible to get back into "favour" was by taking out or returning one which caught her eye. Old boys who came down enquired, "What sort of favour are you in?" and letters to those who had gone on ended up, "I am (touch wood) still in good favour"—"I shall have to do something, I'm losing favour"—or "I am in the most awful favour"; unjust as this feminine tyranny seemed at the time it was a valuable foretaste of the world outside; even the nickname Flip suggested some primitive goddess of fortune. Thus, although I won the prize through heading my list with "Carlyle's *French Revolution*"—and Orwell won it next, we were caught at last with two volumes of *Sinister Street*, and our favour sunk to zero.

We both wrote poetry. At sunset, or late at night, in the dark, I would be visited by the Muse. In an ecstasy of flushing and shivering, the tears welling up as I wrote, I would put down some lines to the Night Wind. The next morning they would be copied out. Although the process of composition seemed an authentic visitation, the result was an imitation of Stevenson or Longfellow, or my favourite, Robert W. Service. I would compare them with Orwell's, being critical of his, while he was polite about mine, and we would separate feeling ashamed of each other.

The remarkable thing about Orwell was that he alone among the boys was an intellectual, and not a parrot, for he thought for himself, read Shaw and Samuel Butler, and rejected not only St. Wulfric's, but the war, the Empire, Kipling, Sussex, and Character. I remember a moment under a fig-tree in one of the inland boulevards of the seaside town, Orwell striding beside me, and saying in his flat, ageless voice: "You know, Connolly, there's only one remedy for all diseases." I felt the usual guilty tremor when sex was mentioned and hazarded, "You mean going to the lavatory?" "No —I mean Death!" He was not a romantic, he had no use for the blandishments of the drill sergeant who made us feel character was identical with boxing, nor for the threats of the chaplain with his grizzled cheektufts, and his gospel of a Jesus of character, who detested immorality and swearing as much as he loved the Allies. "Of course, you realize, Connolly," said Orwell, "that, whoever wins this war, we shall emerge a second-rate nation."

Orwell proved to me that there existed an alternative to character, Intelligence. Beaton showed me another, Sensibility. He had a charming, dreamy face, enormous blue eyes with long lashes, and wore his hair in a fringe. His voice was slow, affected, and creamy. He was not good at games or work, but he escaped persecution through good manners, and a baffling independence. We used to mow the lawn together behind an old pony, sit eating the gooseberries in the kitchen garden, or pretend to polish brass in the chapel; from Orwell I learnt about literature, from Cecil I learnt about art. He occupied his spare time drawing and painting and his holidays in going to the theater.

On Saturday nights, when the school was entertained in the big schoolroom by such talent as the place could offer, when Mr. Potter had shown lantern slides of *Scrooge*, or Mr. Smedley, dressed up like a pirate at a P. & O. gala, had mouthed out what he called "Poethry" there would be a hush, and Cecil would step forward and sing, "If you were the only girl in the World, and I was the only boy." His voice was small but true, and when he sang these sentimental songs, imitating Violet Loraine or Beatrice Lillie, the eighty-odd Wulfricans felt there could be no other boy in the world for them, the beetling chaplain forgot hell-fire and masturbation, the Irish drill-sergeant his bayonet practice, the staff refrained from disapproving, and for a moment the whole structure of character and duty tottered, the principles of hanging on, muddling through, and building empires were called into question.

On other Saturday nights gramophone records were played; when we came to "I have a song to sing O, sing me your song O"

I would open a book which I had bought in the Charing Cross Road, at the prepared place and read:

> Far out at sea when the evening's dusk is falling you may often observe a dark-coloured bird with white under-plumage flit by just above the waves—another and another make their appearance, and you soon find out that a party of Manx Shearwaters have paid your vessel a passing call. They are nocturnal birds for the most part, spending the hours of daylight in their burrows, and coming out in the gloom to speed across the frowning waters in quest of food. There is something very exciting about the appearance of this singular bird. The noisy gulls which have been playing about all day drop slowly astern as the sun nears the west; the parties of Razorbills and Guillemots and Puffins have sped away to their distant breeding colonies; and the wide waste of waters seems unusually destitute and dreary as the night approaches, and the evening breeze fluttering in the sails, and through the rigging, is the only sound that breaks the oppressive stillness. But the hour of the Manx Shearwater's ghostly revelry has come, he holds high carnival over the waste of gray waters, flitting about in most erratic manner in his wild impetuous course, following the curve of every wave, dipping down into the hollows, where he is almost invisible, and then mounting the foamy crests, where you catch a brief glimpse of his hurried movements.

The combination of the music with this passage was intoxicating. The two blended into an experience of isolation and flight which induced the sacred shiver. The classroom disappeared, I was alone on the dark seas, there was a hush, a religious moment of suspense, and the Manx shearwaters appeared, held their high carnival, etc., and vanished. Then, the schoolroom where each boy sat by his desk, his few possessions inside, his charted ink channels on top, returned to focus. This experience, which I repeated like a drug, every Saturday, was typical of the period. For those were the days when literature meant the romantic escape, the purple patch; when nobody who taught it would have questioned the absolute beauty of such a line as "clothed in white Samite, mystic, wonderful!" We were still in the full Tennysonian afterglow and our beliefs, if the muse of St. Wulfric's could have voiced them, would have been somewhat as follows.

"There is a natural tradition in English poetry, my dear Tim, Chaucer begat Spenser, Spenser begat Shakespeare, Shakespeare begat Milton, Milton begat Keats, Coleridge, Shelley, Wordsworth, and they begat Tennyson, who begat Longfellow, Stevenson, Kipling, Quiller-Couch and Sir Henry Newbolt. There are a few bad boys we do not speak about—Donne, Dryden, Pope, Blake, Byron, Browning, Fitzgerald, who wrote *The Rubá'iyát of Omar Khayyám*, and Oscar Wilde, who was a criminal degenerate. Chaucer is mediæval but coarse, Spenser is the poet's poet, Shakespeare you will remember from your performance as the witch ('aroint thee, wretch, the rumpfed runion cried her husbands to Aleppo gone the master of the tiger, but in a sieve I'll thither sail and like a rat without a tail I'll do I'll do and I'll do'). Precisely. Milton was a great poet, he wrote *L'Allegro*, *Il Penseroso* and *Paradise Lost*; Keats wrote *The Ode to a Nightingale*; and Tennyson wrote *The Lady of Shalott*—and what else? *Morte d'Arthur*, *Locksley Hall*, *In Memoriam*, *Break, Break, Break*, and *Crossing the Bar*. Longfellow wrote *Hiawatha*, Stevenson *Under the Wide and Starry Sky*, Kipling *Sussex* and *If* and *Gunga Din*, Quiller-Couch is a Good Influence and *Drake's Drum* and *Lyra Heroica* are by Sir Henry Newbolt.

"There are other good poems, *Chevy Chase*, *John Gilpin*, *The Armada*, *The Ancient Mariner*, *Grayselegy*. A poem is good either because it is funny (Ingoldsby Legends, Bab Ballads) or because it makes you want to cry. Some funny poems make you want to cry (the Jumblies, the Dong with a Luminous Nose); that is because you are not a healthy little boy. You need more Character. The best poems have the most beautiful lines in them; these lines can be detached, they are purple patches, and Useful in Examinations. Gray's *Elegy* is almost all Purple Patch and so is the *Ode to a Nightingale*, especially

> Magic casements, opening on the foam
> Of perilous seas, in faëry lands forlorn.

When you come to a purple patch you can tell it by an alarm clock going off, you feel a cold shiver, a lump in the throat, your eyes fill with tears and your hair stands on end. You can get these sensations for yourself when you write poems like your *Ode on the Death of Lord Kitchener* or *To the Night Wind*.

"Nobody wrote so many purple patches as Tennyson, and he had character too (*Bury the Great Duke*, *Charge of the Light Brigade*, *The Revenge*). Kipling is the only great poet alive to-day. Poetry is romantic, purple—a help in time of trouble—or else it is clever and funny, like Calverley—or has Character. (Life is real, Life is earnest, And the grave is NOT its goal.) It is also something to be ashamed of, like sex, and (except with the chaplain) religion."

My experience with the Manx shearwater fulfilled these conditions. It was prose, so could not become poetry and truly purple, till heightened by music. It was romantic; something out of the

ordinary, remote, and false, for in real life I should hate tossing
about the Hebrides in a small boat—and escapist, since I imagined
myself away from my present surroundings, alone on the northern
waters, and yet not alone, a Manx shearwater, playing with others
of my kind. The twilight was "my" time of day (the time I felt most
the poetical thrill), the waste of grey waters my weepy Celtic spiritual home. Because poetry was associated with emotional excess,
night and unhappiness, I felt disgusted with it by day, as by a
friend in whom, when drunk, one has unwisely confided, and I
never exhibited the Manx shearwater even to Orwell.

It will be seen that the thread running through this autobiography is an analysis of romanticism, that romanticism in decline
under whose shadow we grew up. Romanticism I would call the
refusal to face certain truths about the world and ourselves, and the
consequences of that refusal. It is a refusal which can be both splendid and necessary, this pretence that truth is beauty and beauty
truth, that love is stronger than death, the soul immortal, and the
body divine, but in the hundred years that have gone by since the
romantic revival we have had too much of it. By the twentieth
century its best work has been done and those of us who thought
we were angels or devils have had a long struggle to free ourselves
from such ideology. We have been the dupe of words and ideas,
we have been unable to know when we are well off, we have expected too much from life, too many treats, and we have precipi-
tated crises to satisfy the appetite for sensation acquired in
childhood; the womb world of the hot bath and the celluloid duck
has been too near us. The romantic's artillery is always bracketing
over the target of reality, falling short into cynicism, or overreach-
ing it into sentimental optimism, so that, whatever the achievements of romanticism in the past, to be a romantic to-day, knowing
what we know about the nature of man and his place in the universe,
is the mark of a wilful astigmatism, a confession of cowardice and
immaturity.

———

*CYRIL CONNOLLY (1903–   ) was a schoolmate of George Orwell
at St. Cyprian's and Eton; unlike Orwell, he went on to Oxford
before entering journalism and fiction writing. Throughout the
1940's, he edited* Horizon, *and his published novels include* The
Rock Pool *(1935),* The Unquiet Grave *(1944),* The Condemned
Playground *(1945),* Ideas and Places *(1953). This description of St.
Cyprian's comes from* Enemies of Promise *(1938). When Orwell
heard the book was out, he wrote Connolly of his eagerness to*

read it:

> It will interest me very much to see whether the impressions
> you retain are anything like my own. Of course you were in every
> way much more of a success at school than I, and my own posi-
> tion was complicated and in fact dominated by the fact that I
> had much less money than most of the people about me, but as
> far as externals go we had very much the same experience from
> 1912 to 1921. . . . I'm always meaning one of these days to
> write a book about St Cyprian's. I've always held that the public
> schools aren't so bad, but people are wrecked by those filthy
> private schools long before they get to public school age.*

By 1945, however, Orwell's antagonism to Connolly and the
class attitudes he embodied superseded the school friendship. This
was clearly demonstrated in a review of The Unquiet Grave where
Orwell made an attack upon "Palinurus" (Connolly's pen name).

> "Palinurus" is the easily penetrable pseudonym of a well-
> known literary critic, but even without knowing his identity one
> could infer that the writer of this book is about forty, is inclined
> to stoutness, has lived much in continental Europe, and has never
> done any real work. . . . With his background of classical cul-
> ture, religious scepticism, travel, leisure, country houses, and
> civilised meals, "Palinurus" naturally contemplates the modern
> world without enthusiasm and even, at moments, with sheer
> aristocratic disdain: but also—and this is the peculiar mark of
> our age—with self-accusation . . . the author wants his com-
> forts and privileges, and is ashamed of wanting them: he feels
> he has a right to them, and yet feels certain that they are
> doomed to disappear. **

1. Connolly tells us he "was a stage rebel, Orwell a true one."
    Find passages which reveal Connolly's attitude toward St.
    Cyprian's and analyze the tone. Are the contradictions implied
    by "stage rebel" present in these passages? Compare these pas-
    sages with parallel ones by Orwell; is Connolly's statement born
    out by the comparison?
2. What attitude did Orwell's essay ask his readers to take toward
    the school? What attitude does Connolly ask for? In what ways
    are they different? the same? Choose specific sentences from
    each which call for these attitudes, and analyze them to show

* *The Collected Essays, Journalism and Letters of George Orwell*, ed. Sonia
Orwell and Ian Angus (N.Y.: Harcourt, Brace & World, Inc., 1968), I, 362–363. Re-
printed by permission of the publisher.
** *Ibid;* III, 318–319.

what words and structures each writer chose to carry out his intentions.

3. *Three major abstractions dominate this account: "character," "intelligence," and "sensibility." Whom does Connolly associate with each of these terms? How does he define the terms, and what attitude does he take towards each? Which does he respect most? What is the difference between the "literature" he learned about from Orwell and the "art" he learned from Beaton? Which has to do with the romanticism he satirizes at the end of the essay?*

4. *Which description of St. Cyprian's, Orwell's or Connolly's, seems to reveal more? Which writer seems to have seen more and seen more clearly? Analyze specific passages to explain your response.*

Jules Henry

AMERICAN SCHOOLROOMS: LEARNING
THE NIGHTMARE

School is an institution for drilling children in cultural orientations. Educators have attempted to free the school from drill, but have failed because they have always chosen the most obvious "enemy" to attack. Furthermore, with every enemy destroyed, new ones are installed among the old fortifications that are the enduring contradictory maze of the culture. Educators think that when they have made arithmetic or spelling into a game; made it unnecessary for children to "sit up straight"; defined the relation between teacher and children as democratic; and introduced plants, fish, and hamsters into schoolrooms, they have settled the problem of drill. They are mistaken.

The paradox of the human condition is expressed more in education than elsewhere in human culture, because learning to learn has been and continues to be *Homo sapiens'* most formidable evolutionary task. Although it is true that mammals, as compared to birds and fishes, have to learn so much that it is difficult to say by the time we get to chimpanzees which behavior is inborn and which is learned, the learning task has become so enormous for man that today, education, along with survival, constitutes a major preoccupation. In all the fighting over education we are simply saying that after a million years of struggling to become human, we are not yet satisfied that we have mastered the fundamental human task, learning.

Another learning problem inherent in the human condition is this: We must conserve culture while changing it, we must always be *more* sure of surviving than of adapting. Whenever a new idea appears, our first concern as *animals* must be that it does not kill us; then, and only then, can we look at it from other points of view. In general, primitive people solved this problem simply by walling their children off from new possibilities by educational methods that, largely through fear, so narrowed the perceptual sphere that nontraditional ways of viewing the world became unthinkable.

From the *Columbia University Forum*, Spring 1963. Reprinted by permission of the author.

The function of education has never been to free the mind and the spirit of man, but to bind them. To the end that the mind and spirit of his children should never escape, *Homo sapiens* has wanted acquiescence, not originality, from his offspring. It is natural that this should be so, for where every man is unique there is no society, and where there is no society there can be no man. Contemporary American educators think they want creative children, yet it is an open question as to what they expect these children to create. If all through school the young were provoked to question the Ten Commandments, the sanctity of revealed religion, the foundations of patriotism, the profit motive, the two-party system, monogamy, the laws of incest, and so on, we would have more creativity than we could handle. In teaching our children to accept fundamentals of social relationships and religious beliefs without question we follow the ancient highways of the human race.

American classrooms, like educational institutions anywhere, express the values, preoccupations, and fears found in the culture as a whole. School has no choice; it must train the children to fit the culture as it is. School can give training in skills; it cannot teach creativity. Since the creativity that *is* encouraged—as in science and mathematics, for example—will always be that which satisfies the cultural drives at the time, all the American school can do is nurture that creativity when it appears.

Creative intellect is mysterious, devious, and irritating. An intellectually creative child may fail in social studies, for example, simply because he cannot understand the stupidities he is taught to believe as "fact." He may even end up agreeing with his teachers that he is "stupid" in social studies. He will not be encouraged to play among new social systems, values, and relationships, if for no other reason than that the social studies teachers will perceive such a child as a poor student. Furthermore, such a child will simply be unable to fathom the absurdities that seem transparent *truth* to the teacher. What idiot believes in the "law of supply and demand," for example? But the children who do, tend to *become* idiots; and learning to be an idiot is part of growing up! Or, as Camus put it, learning to be *absurd*. Thus the intellectually creative child who finds it impossible to learn to think the absurd the truth, who finds it difficult to accept absurdity as a way of life, usually comes to think himself stupid.

Schools have therefore never been places for the stimulation of young minds; they are the central conserving force of the culture, and if we observe them closely they will tell us much about the cultural pattern that binds us.

Much of what I am now going to say pivots on the inordinate

capacity of a human being to learn more than one thing at a time.
A child writing the word "August" on the board, for example, is
not only learning the word "August," but also how to hold the
chalk without making it squeak, how to write clearly, how to keep
going even though the class is tittering at his slowness, how to
appraise the glances of the children in order to know whether he is
doing it right or wrong. If a classroom can be compared to a communications system—a flow of messages between teacher (trans-
mitter) and pupils (receivers)—it is instructive to recall another
characteristic of communications systems applicable to classrooms:
their inherent tendency to generate *noise. Noise*, in communications theory, applies to all those random fluctuations of the system
that cannot be controlled, the sounds that are not part of the message. The striking thing about the child is that along with his
"messages about spelling" he learns all the noise in the system also.
But—and mark this well—it is *not* primarily the message (the
spelling) that constitutes the most important subject matter to be
learned, but the noise! The most significant cultural learnings—
primarily the cultural drives—are communicated as *noise*. Let us
see the system operate in some of the contemporary suburban
classrooms my students and I studied over a period of six years.

It is March 17 and the children are singing songs from
Ireland and her neighbors. The teacher plays on the piano,
while the children sing. While some children sing, a number
of them hunt in the index, find a song belonging to one of
Ireland's neighbors, and raise their hands in order that they
may be called on to name the next song. The singing is of
that pitchless quality always heard in elementary school
classrooms. The teacher sometimes sings through a song
first, in her off-key, weakishly husky voice.

The usual reason for this kind of song period is that the children are "broadened" while they learn something about music and
singing. But what the children in fact learn about singing is to sing
like everybody else. (This phenomenon—the standard, elementary
school pitchlessness of the English-speaking world—was impressive
enough for D. H. Lawrence to mention it in *Lady Chatterley's
Lover.* The difficulty in achieving true pitch is so pervasive among
us that missionaries carry it with them to distant jungles, teaching
the natives to sing hymns off key. Hence on Sundays we would hear
our Pilagá Indian friends, all of them excellent musicians in the
Pilagá scale, carefully copy the missionaries by singing Anglican
hymns, translated into Pilagá, off key exactly as sharp or as flat as
the missionaries sang.) Thus one of the first things a child with a
good ear learns in elementary school is to be musically stupid; he

learns to doubt or to scorn his innate musical capacities.

But possibly more important than this is the use to which teacher and pupils put the lesson in ways not related at all to singing or to Ireland and her neighbors. To the teacher this was an opportunity to let the children somehow share the social aspects of the lesson with her. The consequence was distraction from singing as the children hunted in the index, and the net result was to activate the children's drives toward competition, achievement, and dominance. In this way the song period was scarcely a lesson in singing, but rather one in extorting the maximal benefit for the Self from *any* situation.

The first lesson a child has to learn when he comes to school is that lessons are not what they seem. He must then forget this and act as if they were. This is the first step toward "school mental health"; it is also the first step in becoming absurd. The second lesson is to put the teachers' and students' criteria in place of his own. The child must learn that the proper way to sing is tunelessly and not the way he hears the music; that the proper way to paint is the way the teacher says, not the way he sees it; that the proper attitude is not pleasure, but competitive horror at the success of his classmates, and so on. And these lessons must be so internalized that he will fight his parents if they object. The early schooling process is not successful unless it has produced in the child an acquiescence in its criteria, unless the child *wants* to think the way school has taught him to think. What we see in kindergarten and the early years of school is the pathetic surrender of babies. How could it be otherwise?

Now nothing so saps self-confidence as alienation from the Self. It would follow that school, the chief agent in the process, must try to provide the children with "ego support," for culture tries to remedy the ills it creates. Hence the effort to give children recognition in our schools. Hence the conversion of the songfest into an exercise in Self-realization. That anything essential was nurtured in this way is an open question, for the kind of individuality that was recognized as the children picked titles out of the index was mechanical, without a creative dimension, and under the strict control of the teacher. In short, the school metamorphoses the child, giving it the kind of Self the school can manage, and then proceeds to minister to the Self it has made.

We can see this at work in another example:

> The observer is just entering her fifth-grade classroom for the observation period. The teacher says, "Which one of you nice, polite boys would like to take [the observer's] coat and hang it up?" From the waving hands, it would

seem that all would like to claim the honor. The teacher chooses one child, who takes the observer's coat. . . . The teacher conducted the arithmetic lessons mostly by asking, "Who would like to tell the answer to the next problem?" This question was followed by the usual large and agitated forest of hands, with apparently much competition to answer.

What strike us here are the precision with which the teacher was able to mobilize the potentialities in the boys for the proper social behavior, and the speed with which they responded. The large number of waving hands proves that most of the boys have already become absurd; but they have no choice. Suppose they sat there frozen?

A skilled teacher sets up many situations in such a way that *a negative attitude can be construed only as treason*. The function of questions like, "Which one of you nice, polite boys would like to take [the observer's] coat and hang it up?" is to bind the children into absurdity—to compel them to acknowledge that absurdity is existence, to acknowledge that it is better to exist absurd than not to exist at all. The reader will have observed that the question is not put, "Who *has* the answer to the next problem?" but, "Who *would like to tell*" it. What at one time in our culture was phrased as a challenge to skill in arithmetic, becomes here an invitation to group participation. The essential issue is that *nothing is but what it is made to be by the alchemy of the system*.

In a society where competition for the basic cultural goods is a pivot of action, people cannot be taught to love one another. It thus becomes necessary for the school to teach children how to hate, and without appearing to do so, for our culture cannot tolerate the idea that babes should hate each other. How does the school accomplish this ambiguity? Obviously through fostering competition itself, as we can see in an incident from a fifth-grade arithmetic lesson.

Boris had trouble reducing 12/16 to the lowest terms, and could only get as far as 6/8. The teacher asked him quietly if that was as far as he could reduce it. She suggested he "think." Much heaving up and down and waving of hands by the other children, all frantic to correct him. Boris pretty unhappy, probably mentally paralyzed. The teacher, quiet, patient, ignores the others and concentrates with look and voice on Boris. After a minute or two, she turns to the class and says, "Well, who can tell Boris what the number is?" A forest of hands appears, and the teacher calls Peggy. Peggy says that four may be divided into the numerator and the denominator.

Boris's failure has made it possible for Peggy to succeed; his misery is the occasion for her rejoicing. This is the standard condition of the contemporary American elementary school. To a Zuñi, Hopi, or Dakota Indian, Peggy's performance would seem cruel beyond belief, for competition, the wringing of success from somebody's failure, is a form of torture foreign to those noncompetitive cultures. Yet Peggy's action seems natural to us; and so it is. How else would you run our world?

Looked at from Boris's point of view, the nightmare at the blackboard was, perhaps, a lesson in controlling himself so that he would not fly shrieking from the room under enormous public pressure. Such experiences force every man reared in our culture, over and over again, night in, night out, even at the pinnacle of success, to dream not of success, but of failure. In school the external nightmare is internalized for life. Boris was not learning arithmetic only; he was learning the *essential nightmare also. To be successful in our culture one must learn to dream of failure.*

When we say that "culture teaches drives and values" we do not state the case quite precisely. We should say, rather, that culture (and especially the school) provides the occasions in which drives and values are *experienced in events* that strike us with *overwhelming and constant force.* To say that culture "teaches" puts the matter too mildly. Actually culture invades and infests the mind as an obsession. If it does not, it will be powerless to withstand the impact of critical differences, to fly in the face of contradiction, to so engulf the mind that the world is seen only as the culture decrees it shall be seen, to compel a person to be absurd. The central emotion in obsession is fear, and the central obsession in education is fear of failure. In school, one becomes absurd through being afraid; but paradoxically, *only by remaining absurd can one feel free from fear.*

Let us see how absurdity is reinforced: consider this spelling lesson in a fourth-grade class.

The children are to play "spelling baseball," and they have lined up to be chosen for the two teams. There is much noise, but the teacher quiets it. She has selected a boy and a girl and sent them to the front of the room as team captains to choose their teams. As the boy and girl pick the children to form their teams, each child takes a seat in orderly succession around the room. Apparently they know the game well. Now Tom, who has not yet been chosen, tries to call attention to himself in order to be chosen. Dick shifts his position to be more in the direct line of vision of the choosers, so that he may not be overlooked. He

seems quite anxious. Jane, Tom, Dick, and one girl whose
name the observer does not know are the last to be chosen.
The teacher even has to remind the choosers that Dick and
Jane have not been chosen. . . .

The teacher now gives out words for the children to
spell, and they write them on the board. [Each word is a
pitched ball, and each correctly spelled word is a base hit.
The children move around the room from base to base as
their teammates spell the words correctly.] The outs seem
to increase in frequency as each side gets near the children
chosen last. The children have great difficulty spelling "August." As they make mistakes, those in the seats say, "No!"
The teacher says, "Man on third." As a child at the board
stops and thinks, the teacher says, "There's a time limit;
you can't take too long, honey." At last, after many children
fail on "August" one child gets it right and returns, grinning with pleasure, to her seat. . . . The motivation level
in this game seems terrific. All the children seem to watch
the board, to know what's right and wrong, and seem quite
keyed up. There is no lagging in moving from base to base.
The child who is now writing "Thursday" stops to think
after the first letter, and the children snicker. He stops after
another letter. More snickers. He gets the word wrong. There
are frequent signs of joy from the children when their side is
right.

"Spelling baseball" is an effort to take the "weariness, the
fever, and the fret" out of spelling by absurdly transforming it into
a competitive game. Children are usually good competitors, though
they may never become good spellers; and although they may never
learn to *spell* success, they know what it *is*, how to go after it, and
how it feels not to have it. A competitive game is indicated when
children are failing, because the drive to succeed in the *game* may
carry them to victory over the subject matter. But once a spelling
lesson is cast in the form of a game of baseball a great variety of
noise enters the system; because the sounds of *baseball* (the baseball "messages") cannot but be *noise* in a system intended to com-
municate *spelling*. If we reflect that one could not settle a baseball
game by converting it into a spelling lesson, we see that baseball
is bizarrely irrelevant to spelling. If we reflect further that a child
who is a poor speller might yet be a magnificent ballplayer, we are
even further impressed that learning spelling through baseball is
learning by absurd association.

In making spelling into a baseball game one drags into the classroom whatever associations a child may have to the impersonal

sorting process of kid baseball, but there are differences between the baseball world and the "spelling baseball" world also. One's failure is paraded before the class minute upon minute, until, when the worst spellers are the only ones left, the conspicuousness of the failures has been enormously increased. Thus the *noise* from baseball is amplified by a *noise* factor specific to the classroom.

It should not be imagined that I "object" to all of this, for in the first place I am aware of the indispensable social functions of the spelling game, and in the second place, I can see that the rendering of failure conspicuous cannot but intensify the quality of the essential nightmare, and thus render an important service to the culture. Without nightmares human culture has never been possible. Without hatred competition cannot take place except in games.

The unremitting effort by the system to bring the cultural drives to a fierce pitch must ultimately turn the children against one another; and though they cannot punch one another in the nose or pull one another's hair in class, they can vent some of their hostility in carping criticism of one another's work. Carping criticism, painfully evident in almost any American classroom, is viciously destructive of the early tillage of those creative impulses we say we cherish.

Listen to a fifth-grade class: The children are taking turns reading stories they have made up. Charlie's is called *The Unknown Guest*.

"One dark, dreary night, on a hill a house stood. This house was forbidden territory for Bill and Joe, but they were going in anyway. The door creaked, squealed, slammed. A voice warned them to go home. They went upstairs. A stair cracked. They entered a room. A voice said they might as well stay and find out now; and their father came out. He laughed and they laughed, but they never forgot their adventure together."

Teacher: Are there any words that give you the mood of the story?

Lucy: He could have made the sentences a little better. . . .

Teacher: Let's come back to Lucy's comment. What about his sentences?

Gert: They were too short. [Charlie and Jeanne have a discussion about the position of the word "stood" in the first sentence.]

Teacher: Wait a minute; some people are forgetting their manners. . . .

Jeff: About the room: the boys went up the stairs and

one "cracked," then they were in the room. Did they fall through the stairs, or what?

The teacher suggests Charlie make that a little clearer. . . .

Teacher: We still haven't decided about the short sentences. Perhaps they make the story more spooky and mysterious.

Gwynne: I wish he had read with more expression instead of all at one time.

Rachel: Not enough expression.

Teacher: Charlie, they want a little more expression from you. I guess we've given you enough suggestions for one time. [Charlie does not raise his head, which is bent over his desk as if studying a paper.] Charlie! I guess we've given you enough suggestions for one time, Charlie, haven't we?

If American children fail while one of their number succeeds, they carp. And why not? We must not let our own "inner Borises" befog our thinking. A competitive culture endures by tearing people down. Why blame the children for doing it?

The contemporary school is not all horrors; it has its gentler aspects as well. Nearing a conclusion, let us examine impulse release and affection as they appear in many suburban classrooms.

Impulse is the root of life, and its release in the right amount, time, and place is a primary concern of culture. Nowadays the problem of impulse release takes on a special character because of the epoch's commitment to "letting down the bars." This being the case, teachers have a task unique in the history of education: the fostering of impulse release rather than the installation of controls. Everywhere controls are breaking down, and firmness with impulse is no part of contemporary pedagogy of "the normal child." Rather, impulse release, phrased as "spontaneity," "life adjustment," "democracy," "permissiveness," and "mothering," has become a central doctrine of education. It persists despite tough-minded critics from the Eastern Seaboard who concentrate on curriculum. The teachers know better; the real, the persisting, subject matter is *noise*.

How can the teacher release children's emotions without unchaining chaos? How can she permit so much *noise* and not lose the message? Were they alive, the teachers I had in P.S. 10 and P.S. 186 in New York City, who insisted on absolute silence, would say that chaos does prevail in many modern classrooms and that the message *is* lost. But lest old-fashioned readers argue that the social structure has fallen apart, I will point out what does *not* happen: The children do not fight or wrestle, run around the room, throw things, sing loudly, or whistle. The boys do not attack the girls or vice versa. Children do not run in and out of the room. They do not make the teacher's life miserable. All this occurs when the social structure *is* torn down, but in the average suburban classrooms we studied, it never quite happens. Why not? Here are some excerpts from an interview with a second-grade teacher I'll call Mrs. Olan.

> In the one-room schoolhouse in which I first taught, the children came from calm homes. There was no worry about war, and there was no TV or radio. Children of today know more about what is going on; they are better informed. So you can't hold a strict rein on them.
>
> Children need to enjoy school and like it. They also need their work to be done; it's not all play. You must get them to accept responsibility and to do work on their own.

To the question, "What would you say is your own particular way of keeping order in the classroom?" Mrs. Olan says:

> Well, I would say I try to get that at the beginning of the year by getting this bond of affection and a relationship between the children and me. And we do that with stories; and I play games *with* them—don't just teach them how to play. It's what you get from living together comfortably. We have "share" times. . . . These are the things that contribute toward discipline. Another thing in discipline—it took me a long time to learn it, too: I thought I was the boss, but I learned that even with a child, if you speak to him as you would to a neighbor or a friend you get a better response than if you say, "Johnny, do this or that."

Mrs. Olan has a creed: Love is the path to discipline through permissiveness; and school is a continuation of family life, in which the values of sharing and democracy lead to comfortable living and ultimately to discipline. She continues:

> With primary children the teacher is a mother during the day; they have to be able to bring their problems to you. They get love and affection at home, and I see no reason not to give it in school.

To Mrs. Olan, mother of a 21-year-old son, second-grade children are pussy-cats. When asked, "Do you think the children tend to be quieter if the teacher is affectionate?" she says:

> If a teacher has a well-modulated voice and a pleasing

disposition, her children are more relaxed and quiet. Children are like kittens: If kittens have a full stomach and lie in the sun they purr. If the atmosphere is such that the children are more comfortable, they are quiet. It is comfortable living that makes the quiet child. When you are shouting at them and they're shouting back at you, it isn't comfortable living.

It is clear to the observer that Mrs. Olan is no "boss," but lodges responsibility in the children. She clarifies the matter further:

It means a great deal to them to give them their own direction. When problems do come up in the room we talk them over and discuss what is the right thing to do when this or that happens. Usually you get pretty good answers. They are a lot harder on themselves than I would be; so if any punishment comes along like not going to an assembly you have group pressure.

As the interviewer was leaving, Mrs. Olan remarked, "My children don't rate as high [on achievement tests] as other children. I don't push, and that's because I believe in comfortable living." *Noise* has indeed become subject matter.

In such classrooms the contemporary training for impulse release and fun is clear. There the children are not in uniform, but in the jerkins and gossamer of *The Midsummer Night's Dream*; it is a sweet drilling without pain. Since impulse and release and fun are a major requirement of the classroom, and since they must be contained within the four walls, the instrument of containment can only be affection. The teacher must therefore become a parent, for it is a parent above all who deals with the impulses of the child.

It is hard for us to see, since we consider most people inherently replaceable, that there is anything remarkable in a parent-figure like a teacher showering the symbols of affection on a child for a year and then letting him walk out of her life. However, this is almost unheard of outside the stream of Western civilization; and even in the West it is not common. As a matter of fact, the existence of *children* willing to accept such demonstrations is in itself an interesting phenomenon, based probably on the obsolescence of the two-parent family. (Today our children *do not have enough parents*, because parents are unable to do all that has to be done *by* parents nowadays.) The fact that a teacher can be demonstrative without inflicting deep wounds on *herself* implies a character structure having strong brakes on involvement. Her expressions of tenderness, then, must imply "so far and no farther"; and over the years, children must come to recognize this. If this were not so, children would have to be dragged shrieking from grade to grade and teachers would flee teaching, for the mutual attachment would be so deep that its annual severing would be too much for either to bear. And so this noise, too, teaches two lessons important to today's culture. From regular replacement-in-affection children learn that the affection-giving figure, the teacher, is replaceable also, and so they are drilled in uninvolvement. Meanwhile, they learn that the symbols of affectivity can be used ambiguously, and that they are not binding—that they can be scattered upon the world without commitment.

Again, the reader should not imagine that I am "against" affectionate classrooms. They are a necessary adjunct to contemporary childhood and to the socialization of parenthood (the "three-parent family") at this stage of our culture. Meanwhile, the dialectic of culture suggests that there is some probability that when love like this enters by the door, learning leaves by the transom.

What, then, is the central issue? The central issue is *love of knowledge* for its own sake, not as the creature of drive, exploited largely for survival and for prestige. Creative cultures have loved the "beautiful person"—meditative, intellectual, and exalted. As for the individual, the history of great civilizations reveals little except that creativity has had an obstinate way of emerging only in a few, and that it has never appeared in the mass of the people. Loving the beautiful person more, we may alter this.

The contemporary school is a place where children are drilled in very general cultural orientations, and where subject matter becomes to a very considerable extent the instrument for instilling them. Because school deals with masses of children, it can manage only by reducing children all to a common definition. Naturally that definition is determined by the cultural preoccupations and so school creates the *essential nightmare* that drives people away from something (in our case, failure) and toward something (success). Today our children, instead of loving knowledge, become embroiled in the nightmare.

———

JULES HENRY (1904–   ) *is professor of anthropology and sociology at Washington University in St. Louis. His published work includes studies of South American Indians and North American nursery schools. In his preface to* Culture Against Man *(1963), Dr. Henry speaks of the effect of careful rewriting (for six years) of his manuscript:*

Probably one must write a book about his society in order to really understand what change is, in society and in one's self. Something else happens when one writes a book about which he feels deeply: he becomes a creature of his book, for as he pours ideas and emotion into it the process shapes him, so that he can never be the same again. Writing clarifies positions and commits one's soul—often far beyond what one ever imagined possible. In order to remain placid and uncommitted, I would say, never write a book that has deep meaning for you.

This essay first appeared in the Columbia University Forum, Spring, 1963, and is adapted by the author from Culture Against Man.

1. What does Henry mean by "bind" when he says, "The function of education has never been to free the mind and the spirit of man, but to bind them"? Define the following phrases Henry uses to express this idea as he particularizes it in modern schools: "the essential nightmare," "one must learn to dream of failure," "only by remaining absurd can one feel free from fear," "noise has indeed become subject matter."

2. What is the basis of the opposition Henry describes between creativity, or "loving knowledge," and the function and process of the schools? To what degree does Henry's description apply to the St. Cyprian's described by Orwell and Connolly? To what degree does the description apply to your own schooling?

3. As a distinguished social scientist, Henry is careful to claim his position as a neutral observer: "It should not be imagined that I 'object' to all of this"; "the reader should not imagine that I am 'against' affectionate classrooms," etc. But in his preface he says "writing clarifies positions and commits one's soul," and denies being "placid and uncommitted." How does the tone of the essay clarify these seeming contradictions?

Johnie Scott

THE COMING OF THE HOODLUM

The coming of the Hoodlum was not an entirely unpremeditated affair. Characters within characters took part: Harvard, Watts, and I. It was in the form of a journey, a traveling from the teeming black heart of Los Angeles, Watts, to the pulse of America's intellectual showplace, Harvard: a journey that took only a year in which to begin the gradual eroding away of all former attitudes toward life: an experience that carried its pilgrim beyond his concepts of educational, racial, and social attitudes, that was to find at the culmination of that eventual year's passage a new, albeit embittered and disenchanted, man where before there had been but a child of promise.

At the war's end, the Hoodlum was born: 1948, in Cheyenne County Memorial Hospital. The month of May, of May and sunshine, of a world finally breathing again, of the ending of the spilling of blood on the land, on the birth of a new generation, on the coming of the nuclear bomb, and the passing of a collective hysteria that had produced the bloodiest holocaust in mortal history.

The war's end had found his father, our father, father of the Hoodlum, a soldier awaiting his leave orders, a Negro who had left the South after a painful youth of his own: a son who had to leave school in the fifth grade, the Old South, deepest Louisiana, picking cotton so that a family might survive: a son of sharecroppers and former slaves, a man who longed to be free, free of the bonds all Southern Negroes felt, free to work where he loved—he got his leave orders, his discharge, honorably, all the returning heroes of the war got honorable discharges and all war veterans were called heroes. From Cheyenne to the South to Los Angeles: from the war to the Old South to the West: from death to birth to chance: but then, all men felt a new promise in the air—children were being born, I was born, the Hoodlum was born, the War Babies all were born. Not born into happiness, but into hope, some of the hope to be disillusioned, some of the hope to be fulfilled: the growing years

Reprinted by permission of The World Publishing Company from *From the Ashes* edited by Budd Schulberg. An NAL book. Copyright © 1967 by The New American Library, Inc.

of the child born in a country hospital were to be spent in the teeming ghetto of black folk, Southern emigrants, a dozen dialects, to be
known as Watts: its old name, the name of history, was Mudtown.

When Father first brought me to Watts, he had found work in
an airplane plant: North American Aircraft: the Korean war, a newer
war, going on, the old veterans now sheetmetal workers and engi-
neers while younger men went on to die: Negroes flooding Los
Angeles and other western towns, in search of these jobs that took
Negroes. He had been fortunate, had saved his money, had bought
a small wooden frame house: worked night shifts and, come the
light of day, was out in the streets looking for more work, more
money, had to have it, the family was growing larger: soon there
were two children, three children, four, then five, then six.

In the meanwhile, the wooden structure caught fire and burned
completely down. His dreams burned down with it—we moved into
the housing projects, the old Jordan Downs Housing Projects.
Roaches carpeted the floor at night, a black floor that moved up and
down and around the walls, if one woke in the middle of the night
to see this shifting blackness in the blackness moving inevitably a
scream would escape the lips: we learned to live with them, however; in time man learns to adjust to anything, anyone, any fear,
even the fear of insects, the fear of filth: that is, if man wants to
live.

Those years in the "old" projects, for newer ones were built late
in the 1950's, were changing years, full of growth as Watts grew
and the city grew. Negroes continued to come into Los Angeles,
Negroes continued to look for those jobs in the West: some, my
father, were laid off, others were hired, then fired, more came in
their place: it was a cycle, as complete a cycle as one could hope.
The ghetto had become more than roaches, or buildings that stank
both day and night, more than the oppressive summer heat that
left us rasping for breath along with the flies that zipped in and out
of the houses—the ghetto had become the people. It was the people: their wishes, their dreams, their forgotten homes, their hopes,
starved and starving hopes, and the coming of the bitterness. In this
world, a world of darkness, churches were built. Into this world was
I born, a half-complete angel.

Those years saw the scars come, scars from fights. Fights that
took in neighbors, roaches, broken bottles, brickbats, saw gangs
chase people blocks, saw men hop fences six feet tall in one bound,
saw bricks barely miss bashing skulls in, saw knives, saw the erec-
tion of the churches, saw the night, and the darkness, and the unlit
streets: these were the lightless streets, streets that saw bar-b-que
joints like Page's on 103rd and Grape, that saw a person's mother
get her purse snatched at night if she walked home without a stick

in her hand: to become a man and know that there is not that much happiness in the world: to know that you can cry because you have grown old in such a short span of time.

You see police beat people on the streets, in their cars; you hear the mothers cursing the police, calling them "White Crackers!"; you wonder in confusion, What are these words? and then you see the skins: all the white skins clothed in black, all the shiny badges: association of forms, the white skins become the black uniforms, Police, and the voices, the curses, the People—your People, dark as you, fathers and mothers, friends.

And just as suddenly, your consciousness expands. Poverty is not just withered bodies, flesh lost in weeks of hunger, but something else; as an inner Presence, poverty is far greater and menacing. The Spirit of Christmas To Come leading Scrooge before a dead Tiny Tim. Or, something else; more personal—The Poverty had led *you* back in time to your childhood. All of the voices were the voices of friends—a comradery within Watts.

To have a father carried from his home, you the Watcher and the child, away for questioning: you wonder and you see, the handcuffs, memories of the police on television handcuffing the bad guys: the Law and the wrong-doing: again, white versus colored: if the beginning of racism didn't set in by then, it only took the isolation to come, isolation from the white world: the streets and Us against the markets, the cars, the dealers, the other world, Them. We learned, fought off fear against, the white boys, going to the Opera on public school excursions: seeking culture, and found it— found it one's own balled hand smashing against a face you would never see because you had never seen it: smashing out against a blind prejudice: the orphan if you were taken for what you were: wanting to be loved, but in the middle of an unnamed world, alone. I ran out of the house crying, but ran into my neighbors: out in their yards, listening—there never was privacy in a housing project.

But somehow, out of wanting a place into which I could withdraw, I found a refuge in books: I would read, would go to the old library by myself, seven years old: a walk that took me past savage dogs, saw me running by some of the yards with rotting wood fences: on into the quiet, the book: would read of a Round Table, and could see myself in a land where honor was upheld, where men were as free as their pride would carry them.

Would it matter that our Hoodlum could look back on those years and think of how he stood on streetcorners like everyone else; that taunts flowed as swiftly from his mouth when someone could be seen carrying books home from school, or going to the library to do some homework? He didn't think so. That is why, during those years, the beginning of a cleavage began to be felt within himself:

a strange and troubling turmoil, born out of the chaos that refused to be shaped in the image of education: a world that refused any sort of understanding, brutal and brutalized, the feelings of the rejected: a time when life came to a standstill for him as he surveyed the great emptiness of his own heart, dissatisfied with the answers streets would whisper into his ears—no less dissatisfied with the chalkboards of the schools, where numbers remained numbers and never became a thought more: while his thoughts sank into memories, wishes.

A cleavage was born that would be nourished by the bitter spirit of the ghetto even though our Hoodlum tried to hide this tear from the eyes of all: include Mother and Father, who soon were to break apart as so many of the neighbors had broken apart: who soon were to become numbers that remained numbers, statistics in the files of the divorce courts and the long rows of Vital Statistics in the news-papers. The pulse of the nation beat swiftly, but not as swiftly as that young heart racing even further into the Hell that was to come. It was a Hell that would see blood flow, his own, and those dear to him—a Hell that would see disputes rise, a family divide against itself and send each member out flying into the streets of that world. Was it any wonder that he sought refuge in books? Was it any wonder that his spirit grew ever more divided? There existed truth, it could be found in the world if only he became a part of it. All that could be found in books were dreams, high and full of mystery. But he wanted dreams.

And so he entered school, the alienated. Alienated out of his own frustration, that longing to resolve the incoherent patterns of a world in which all intemperate attitudes might survive: from ultra-racism to Uncle Tomism, from the fear of God to the police-fearing pimps and petty racketeers. His own resolution was simply to sur-vive: to survive and laugh, for it was sheerly by being able to laugh that the horrors could be compromised, that sanity could be main-tained. Mayors and governors entered office and then left office. Nothing changed.

What was Watts like?

The year the Hoodlum (we can forget that name, he was no hoodlum, but his friends were, even though they shared his feelings, what made him different?) was elected president of the student body at his junior high school many things happened: inter-school council meetings were held, speeches given, a girl found raped in a classroom during a lunch break, the accent given to good oral hygiene, a seventh-grade girl stabbing her math teacher seventeen times with a butcher-knife because he called her "stupid." But he survived, as the class dwindled in number from 750 to 550, but on the day of graduation this was said:

> Lives of great men all remind us
> We can make our lives sublime;
> And, departing, leave behind us
> Footprints on the sands of Time.

I *apologize*, Mr. Longfellow.

> Leave Markham knowing you left
> Far more than mere footprints,
> Leave Markham knowing you helped
> Begin a brighter future for us all.

From seventh grade to ninth grade, from 750 to 550, from small children to wide-eyed adolescents. But, three days later, they had all matured: 250 were left, the "largest incoming class in Jordan's history," or so it went according to the head counselor: the following years would see larger classes, to be sure, more babies were born each year, illegitimacy and wedlock both strove to rise higher even as people married younger and lives broke up faster. Had the Hoodlum changed in this time?

Yes. He had learned to feel. He had learned that there was no love in this world. He had learned, three years later, as 97 men and women walked across an auditorium stage to receive diplomas, that of the forgotten and the fallen, of those empty 153 "other" diplomas that were not given, there could be no crying. They had not asked for remorse. Even now, they sat in the audience, among the spectators, silent when the speeches were given, laughing when the clowns tripped over their gowns, crying as a brother finally made it, gone when it was over: gone as surely as Death leaves when faced with an attitude of toughness. For the Hoodlum had grown a shell of toughness, that resisted both the hate of the streets, and the love that he tried, wanted, to release. It would have been futile for him to relate these emotions.

Instead, the toughness grew harder, making communication with him all but impossible. But of what, from where, had this bitterness come? Surely not from the mere presence of failure, from the odor of death! One would have thought that the scene of dying hardened one to the facts of life, but this was a different sort of hardening: you went out for sports, wrote on the school paper, became active in student government, studied diligently. Then, you were the biggest prankster in class, the loudest mouth, the silent antagonist of affairs between student and teacher: when in the streets these conflicts were magnified, distorted, the image of truth was purposely turned inside out, hoping to make the true false in order to make things for oneself more bearable. Inside the soul, the pressure was mounting: the days of waiting in outer offices on dis-

ciplinary actions, of hearing teachers pass the rumor that you were
a "smart-alecky" kid that could think quickly when it came time for
assignments but even more quickly when it came time to lie. You
went home with him, saw his mother as she went through her daily
motions, trying to make a bearable existence out of living, playing
the blues. B. B. King, Blind Lemon Jefferson, Billie Holiday,
Charles Brown, the old Lowell Fulsom: sounds from his home and
from the streets, no longer from Page and Page's Bar-B-Que Pit, it
had burned down in the years before. Nothing had been built there,
but then, what had ever been built there. Only roasted meat had
been sold, and ice cream on hot summer afternoons, and the sound
of music where there would only have been the oppressive stillness
of one's own thoughts brooding.

At one time, like most of his friends, the Hoodlum hated school,
hated Jordan High especially for what it had done to him: *nothing*.
That was the reason for all hatred toward the school: his class read
no better than sixth-graders and this showed in its average grade-
point: 1.8, the equal of the bottom fifth of the intellectual cracker
barrel. His hatred did not last long, a break came, the big break in
his life—accepted into Harvard College, the acme of the East, the
springboard of Presidents and businessmen; most of all, the place
from which decent homes came: *homes* like they didn't exist in his
world. Had he been a brilliant student to be admitted? Not if his
grades were looked at—3.03. Had he exceptionally high college
board scores? Not especially—1096. What had he done in school to
earn entrance into a Harvard class which claimed an average I.Q. of
128, was selective enough to pick 1,200 people from over 6,000
applicants from the best schools and training institutes in the
world?

Nothing, nothing except survive those years of his childhood.
Nothing, nothing except remember what those years were, except
make it his purpose to somehow do something about it. Nothing,
nothing save start out on a career that soon would see him thrown
into an even graver crisis: to decide between one's environment,
one's home, and the atmosphere of Academia.

Not too many survived that regimen our Hoodlum went
through. He had a friend, a member of the 99th percentile, as sensitive and as introspective as anyone, *a human being like we all are*,
who never got past the tenth grade. That friend came to class one
day, (a science course handled by a man who doubled as a gym
teacher in the high school) with a cigar, puffing away as conspicu-
ously as he could. Asked to put it out, he replied, "No. Not if you
have to be my teacher. Not if I have to stay here and 'learn' like
everyone else. Because I care. I care enough to not give a damn
whether you kick me out of school or not." And he was kicked out.

Like so many others were kicked out. For reasons of caring. For reasons of wanting something that was neither at home nor in the school. For reasons that still exist in every school even now. For want of a true friend. For want of love. For reasons incomprehensible to used textbooks and second-rate equipment, reasons that surpassed inadequate school facilities.

It is very simple. Have a sister and have her an unwed mother. Close your eyes, blush with secret shame, hide the secret, live on as though nothing happened. Bury that scar with the other scars. And then, at an airport, pose for pictures as the first Negro to enter Harvard with her and your other sisters. With teachers that did not know her but looked away when looked to for answers why: the pictures were taken, the plane took off, and you sat on the plane remembering the past: "I'm surprised you aren't going to Pomona or Whittier College, or somewhere like that! You could have been something but you talked too much. You could have done something with your life. *I thought you were different from the rest!*"

It is not easy to make a happy world when your diet has been tragedy. The tragedy of having to see how much hate, and being hated, of ignorance, and being unknown, of wanting, and being unwanted, the sheer tragedy of being a human in this world. A stigma if you dare to care: the withdrawing into your soul; the thought of another way of life. The ghetto has a way of reaching into your life just when you think you have climbed to the top of the mountain, and bringing everything crashing down. Sisyphus pushing a rock to the top of the mountain, seeing it roll to the bottom again. Laughing while accepting his fate, walking down again to begin over: this, in the real world, was not a myth or a treatise on why not to take death over a half-emptied bottle of sleeping pills: pill-taking had begun far earlier for so many of us, of Them, of the Others who were not on that jet flying across the country to Cambridge in search of a new life as well as an education. But what was education?

It was not so easily defined. It couldn't be: not if, in the process, one knows that only in rebelling against a system that consciously seeks to stifle the creative instinct one rises to the fore, is regarded by one's equals in that environment as a leader that will never be seen or known or heard over airwaves as the representative. Representative! Of what, and then—why? Why, if being representative meant having as one's constituents aged and aging whores, homosexual preachers whose antics sooner or later hit the presses and, when they did, made an even greater mockery of the Church; what if one's constituents were little half-clothed kids who would never be more than half-clothed throughout life, if they got to be any older, they threw away instinctively the protective shell of insulated education for the more existentialist proposition of freedom Now, or Never! Representative of friends and enemies, of those who had not learned their "ABC's" until the seventh grade, who, when they left school, still read at fourth- and fifth-grade levels yet who could, when asked, make the fastest dollar simply by jacking up a car, taking all four tires, the battery, and selling them at dirt-cheap prices to small garages in and around the neighborhood. You stayed penniless those years not because you had no father, or because your mother was on welfare: you were penniless because you were afraid, afraid of being killed out there on the streets, ashamed of being ashamed if you were caught. You remembered bullets, had seen guns pointed and heard them fired at human beings in your world, had seen men die in the streets and it was not called War by the press.

But you got off that plane. With two suitcases, a shaving kit, an open-flight back home for Christmas, and the determination to be something you had only seen in books. A man in love with his dreams. Was it any wonder, then, that the Hoodlum found it so easy to read Herman Hesse's *Steppenwolf?*:

> I cannot understand or share these joys, though they are within my reach, for which thousands of others strive. On the other hand, what happens to me in my rare hours of bliss, what for me is bliss and life and ecstasy and exaltation, the world in general seeks at most in its imagination; in life it finds it absurd. And in fact, if the world is right, if this music of the cafes, these mass enjoyments and Americanized men who are pleased with so little are right, then I am wrong, I am crazy. I am in truth the Steppenwolf that I often call myself; that beast astray who finds neither home nor joy nor nourishment in a world that is strange and incomprehensible to him.

For him, for that Hoodlum, it had been with a near-attitude of revenge that he had walked into the offices of Jordan High, when he had shown each one the letters of acceptance from different schools, had shown them all and had announced his intentions of attending Harvard: and then had come home, had sat with friends who were both awe-stricken and now, in the face of this turn of events, respectful: a distance was growing between the Hoodlum and his world, a distance that soon was to become as marked as that cleavage within his own soul, the division between the ugliness of reality and the bliss of his own imaginations, his wildest dreams for the future. Unless a person fights back with all he has and believes in, the social and academic world of the school system in the ghetto will crush him. But, the fight within our Hoodlum became distorted—transfigured; it was now a short-lived revenge. And, in this especial, bitter cup of emptiness, of tightly wound despair, he knew his own truth—he had found no solace in a sneering attitude, only wanting again to let them know that there existed within each man such a temper of life that, with its own drive, it could surmount the obstacles, it could climb the mountain.

It *had* to climb the mountain for it was the fear of dying lonely, without a soul around, that pushed, that inspired the fearful drive: strange, but during the summer which preceded the Harvard adventure, there was no inkling really of what was to come up, of what the intellectual challenge would be: nor, of how the Harvard *Crimson* would run articles on the stiff competition the freshmen offered upperclassmen in studies, of the new vitality in the class, of its expanding representation of the masses, nor of how his mind would look once he left, a year later. All of that was forgotten, just as all thoughts of the future were forgotten: put aside, the attention was given to parties held in honor of him, held in honor of his achievements, to the beaches where he went to sit and stare at the sand, the sound of the waters flooding into his ears, his mind, his eyes closed. The scent of new life was like a long hungered-for resurrection of the spirit—the total mood was one of enjoyment within the Now, within the real senses of the present, for time had come to a standstill and all that the eye could conceive and comprehend was there before it. Much plainer than the nose of Cyrano's face. But then, that nose caused Cyrano no end of grief, it was the cause of his blushings, his stammerings when faced with the reality of his existence. Eugene O'Neill had said that "stammering is the native eloquence of us fog people." And this tonguetied Hoodlum tried to break out of that habit, as fiercely as he had been reared to break habits.

He sought out his father, going into the heart of south Los Angeles, for reasons why he should continue to live, though that purpose was hidden under another guise: he was worried about the pregnancy of his sister, her being left stranded in the world after bravely venturing out on her own to sample it, her rude shock at being discovered without knowledge of refuges within herself so that she was left marooned on a sea of leering faces. For three hours that conversation lasted. It spoke of the draft, of what the Army had meant to him as he sought out purpose in life. It spoke of how lonely a man can be who has no home to call his own, no family to call his own: though his children come to see him, he is not theirs, not like "Ozzie and Harriet and David and Rickey," not like singing stars or glamour queens divorcing one husband and picking up another one. As his father said, "I wouldn't marry a woman for her money. She'd have to be a little more than pretty, too. She'd have to understand some of the facts about life."

But the Hoodlum did not want to understand some of the facts of life. He wanted to see where there was some justification for these facts, and so the conversation ended as suddenly as it had begun, for the mind of the man had closed and it trailed off again.

His eyes opened again and he was in Boston. He was in Harvard Square, in the Old Commons, the day bright and the opening of school still three days off. Thoughts reeled in of childhood and growing up. The sight of Mama waving good-bye. My sisters laughing. Irvin's crooked grin concealing his devilish heart. Mr. Anderson and Mrs. Trotter, former high school teachers and friends. Both of them, standing there beneath the plane, so small and yet, so BIG. Watts was just as big as they were. Where was everybody? But then, he wasn't lost. He was in Harvard Square, away from ties he had always hated. He had begun to wonder why he was here, who he was, most of all, why Harvard had let someone with the mark of the ghetto, with the sign of the outcast, into its ivied walls. It was as though Cain had slipped unawares into the Garden of Eden again, but this was a Cain that did not know what his crime was, nor where he was, but only that he did not belong here: neither Harvard, nor Watts would ever be personal worlds for him, and yet they were, because he lived within them.

Now there had been those along the way who sought to look after him. People like Christopher Wadsworth, Senior Advisor at Harvard, and Dr. Dana Cotton, member of the Admissions staff. To him, all of eighteen years old, much of what he saw and felt inspired fear: fear as the voices of the past came into his ears, voices that had predicted failure along the route toward self, voices that never stopped singing in his ear: the voices of the Serpent, the man who wore so much clothing until his body could not be seen and yet who, with but a single question, three words, could disrupt all of his life. *Who are you?* The fear was not of Harvard, but of Watts: a much stronger force than books. He could sit down in dining halls, he could talk with any of a number of people, he could try to study. And then, his sister's face floated across the pages. Here, and then gone. But he could not articulate. He only stammered before the judges, his advisors, these kindly men who sat in on him when he came to them for help: for a help that could not be named, a help that welled up from the bottom of his being, a need that had been there for so long until it was becoming painfully obvious that there could be no life inside of that world. No life was in education if that life had to be shared with the voices of a dead past—a past of Death, whose presence never failed to make itself felt. A presence so overpowering as to draw tears when he sat in his room, isolated, and played the muted trumpet of Miles Davis, played "It Never Entered My Mind," and then turned his gaze outward, into Harvard Yard, into tradition, and history, into all that he had ever read of as a young child striving to find values in life: and could not see because he was blind.

Hello, Mr. Wadsworth, I understand you want to see me?

Yes, I do. How are things here at Harvard for you?

Oh. They're all right, I guess.

Like the way they've been treating you here?

Yes. Everything's all right, I guess. It's an all right place. It hasn't done anything wrong to me I can think of.

Guess it's kind of different from Watts, eh?

Yes. It is a little different from Watts.

How's that?

Well, it ain't anything you can put your finger on. It's like, well, it's like this is a new life, a different place, with different people. It's the kind of thing I expected (seeing surprise on his face), so I don't feel out of place in the sense of running into prejudice.

But then, conversations always ran through those currents for him: he sought to express the difference. It would have been easy to say that he *felt* two different people within him, but he was afraid that someone might overhear and call him crazy. For expressing fears. But this wasn't the simple case, it went much deeper, much further, than an alienation from Harvard society.

Ghettos are built within the mind, and in one part of the Hoodlum's mind he was *black*, which meant apart from all that is white and stands for white, which meant the faces and opinions of his former friends, those that now were in Watts, behind him and yet in front of him, in front of his face as he sat and talked with Wadsworth: while there was its opposite, that part which had seen the humanity of all men because it had seen the humanity within itself, and known that love could be if only men dedicated their minds to liberation. But to express this was difficult. He would slow down in his speech, some of his Cambridge comrades noticed an overly drawn-out drawl, while at the same time injecting a hatred of white society, a hatred that carried itself into his living quarters. There, walking in late at night from drunken sprees, he found his two white roommates listening to Bach, Mozart.

What is this Mozart *shit?* he would holler, and then, striding to the record player, place atop it jazz albums that were freedom songs: the songs of protest, that spoke out against all the injustices, that were in themselves reflective of the black position, of the position of Watts and black life as it had to reach out for breath in an all-white, and all-dominated superstructure largely unknown to it. A super-society that was predicated upon a foundation of books, of knowledge: the same books that had fed the Hoodlum's soul at night when he was a child. His mind would roll back: there was Dale and

Jack and J. C., finally reading *Baldwin* after I've been through King
Arthur and so much more of other things until it's almost pitiful.
But then, he would be glad at the same time, glad to see the hunger
for truth in the faces of others. He had begun to wonder to himself
about the possibility of communication amongst peers. That Christmas of 1964, he sat in an old garage in Watts, talking with some of
his former childmates, deep in the depth of Harvard and what
Veritas might mean for Us.

That's right! They have got so much to read, to see, to
understand! IT'S LIKE THEY GOT THE POWER AND THEY
DON'T REALLY KNOW IT BUT AS LONG AS WE SIT HERE TALKING
ABOUT IT INSTEAD OF GETTING UP AND DOING SOMETHING
WE GONNA ALWAYS BE ON THE BOTTOM, FELLAS! Yes, he had
styled himself a revolutionary. He had majored in African
History, would sortie and frequent with the foreign ex-
change-students. Much of what they said and much of their
humor he couldn't understand. But he could sense their
own feeling of desolation in this great community, a sense
of aloneness that was very much within him, too, and as
homing devices are attracted to one another, he came to
know of those customs. But he was also a Negro, a fact he
couldn't, didn't, escape from: he did sort out other Negroes
on the campus and together they formed a group which
centered its interests, aspirations, on a black culture: the
scene was established for a black dialogue, meetings were
called in which other Negroes of the freshman class discussed
racial sorespots on the Cantabrigian scene. Then, though no
resolutions were ever reached, they always ended the meetings with firm declarations on the strength of black peoples,
of their right to survive, of their pride in themselves as future leaders, and on the beauty of the black woman, a beauty
that could not be marred in its sensuality—not even by the
stated four-hundred-year rape of Prospero.

That was a year of many changes. From revolutionary, the Hoodlum went to mystic. His religion had become one of Godhood,
though it concerned no Christian God. He found himself in his
room again many nights, questioning his belief in life. Am I a Muslim? Can I, do I, I know that in *some* ways I hate white people,
but then there are some that are all right! I can't be a Muslim!
But that doesn't make me an Uncle Tom! It was a term that had
come to be feared, as many people were becoming aware of the yet-
carpetbagging ghost of Uncle Tom stealing in and out of the nights
with caches of cash while whites walked away smiling, thinking
communication had been established with *comprehensible* Negroes.

But nothing is so reprehensible as an Uncle Tom, or the smug face of the white collar that tells of working for everything he's ever gotten in life. As if life wasn't a struggle in the ghetto, but rather, a mere question of survival! What was the difference? What had Harvard become that he thought like this? He lay on his bed into the waking hours, looking at the sun flood the room, the bed, the body, his mind: standing up, he would shiver with the first cold, and then, smile almost ritualistically. To think that I can be here anyway, be here and be mad and be free! Walking into the Co-Op, he bought records, books, gloves, paper, pencil, letterheads, anything he could buy: he charged it willfully, beyond his allowance, wanted to break himself completely, knew that destruction loomed just ahead but rushed on pell-mell.

There was a continued interest in his plans, his future, his life. Many worked with him. Not much was said in those meetings of what impressions were being made. The talk centered around Harvard, Watts, clothes, studies, anything, in fact, but who was talking to who. And why, in the first place! It should have seemed natural to believe that sincerity surrounded every meeting, that this sincerity provoke a concern in his wishes. But the Hoodlum would not have sensed this, nor would he have responded. His world was too clouded, too filled with the spectres of his world, *that* world which now included Harvard as well as Watts, which began to space time and memories: so that there were times when he was afraid of going home, afraid of going there and finding that he wanted Cambridge instead. The exact fear he had when first arriving of wanting Watts more than he wanted Cambridge. The Hoodlum *knew* that he was changing, in name and form as well as in belief. The Hoodlum was dying, he was fighting, kicking, yes, but he was also dying. And this is why he was so sad. No one is happy, not very happy, when a part of them dies, when a fragment of the past begins to recede into the mists.

To be sure, he had encountered prejudice. But it was a subtle kind unknown even to its perpetrator. He had gone to the B'Nai B'Rith House at Harvard, for example, for a party given there one evening by the Hillel Foundation. The place was packed. Of the group he was with, there were six altogether, four whites and two Negroes, not much in the way of overt attention was paid. But then, as our Hoodlum stood away from even this group, in a corner, watching the people, hearing the sounds of the party, listening to the wonderment in his own eyes, a small, bespectacled Caucasian fellow strode up to him and, there, from the top of a drink, asked, "Do you feel a little uncomfortable here, if you don't mind my asking?"

"Only if you feel uncomfortable." To know that he did not know that I would not know until the morrow that the B'Nai

B'Rith was a Jewish Foundation. Or that Jews had suffering in common with *us* Negroes, and that they, too, were meeting injustice in the present world.

There were questions that could not be so easily answered, though: What does *your* father do for a living? No, he wasn't a Civil Service employee. Then, he was not unemployed. He could not answer that question. He did not know the answer. My father is a laborer. The hardest kind of worker, because to hustle in the streets, knock someone in the head and take their money, run away, that would be so much easier a way to survive. Always in fear of capture. If it wasn't the police who were after you, it was your wife: Why don't you go out and get a job? Oh, I suppose there ain't any work that's *good enough* for you? Things that prep school kids would not understand, had not been raised to understand, might not ever understand. Why were black men so concerned about being black men? Why did they insist on making things so difficult to explain, making civil rights the perpetual subject of discussion —Watts was forever on the lips of white boys, wanting to know what it was like. Is it really that bad? Have you ever seen anyone shot? Is there really police brutality? Have you every been shot at?

They had never seen the lonely unlit streets of Watts. Had never been afraid at night, typing or reading, of the animal sounds. Look out the window and see the dog packs roaming the streets of the projects, knock over and then forage through garbage cans, no one chasing them away but only watching. Green beast eyes glowing in the night, out of the night, and the moon, the moon's pale light, above your head as you gazed back into those eyes, into their unthinking depths, and heard the low guttural growls of the beast. He feared dogs, a feeling quite unlike even his closest friends on that campus, in that world. Negroes from middle-class backgrounds who had attended prep schools and achieved glowing records. Negroes from South Side Chicago housing projects, who taught him how to light matches against the wind. Harvard Negroes, who believed in themselves and looked on life, all of life, as part of the game. The Education Game: to play it you have to seem it, have to become so much a part of the accepted stereotyped portraiture of the aspiring Negro that you finally become accepted. But acceptance was not really this feeling. It would have been as easy to accept the dog packs. Thoughts of Harvard, of the long-haired, well-groomed dogs that strode, romped through the Freshman Yard— friendly dogs, *cared for* by their owners. Could it be that in the dog packs, in Watts, he saw himself and his friends? So close to fighting over garbage, the garbage that life dumped out to you, in trash cans called haunted schoolyards and wind-swept playgrounds: where the only sound was the continual grating of the rings, the iron rings, suspended by chains, swinging back and forth over the sandpit, the housing projects silhouetted in the gray stormy weather against the horizon—one's face turned toward the projects above the buildings into the grayness of God's Heaven. Where little kids fought over games, spilled blood, and ran in gangs while inside those buildings, locked away from sight of the world, fought the owners of the children: to have the love of a child.

But what did they say whenever faced with this Hoodlum? Of course, thoughts arose concerning his maturity: what is a man that he tells of youth and youth's own fears, of dogs and people and the hardships, the tragedies. Not as if he were singing a song, but because he simply believed that he had lived this way and that in this survival, he had a particular influence which had to be realized sooner or later. There was fear of a growing rift in that Cambridge. Because he feared the eyes of man, the Hoodlum withdrew, regardless of their interest in his story. Tragedy had withdrawn as it only knew how: the universal had been tapped, no matter how slightly or unseemingly, in the lives of all who had grown to know him, and within that human shell another life was being born: I stepped forth, aware that a man can create a ghetto within the confines of his own mind. Stake out the proposed borderlines of blackness and whiteness: move at that instant into the outside world, itself both black and white, a world of externals and appearances: become two people, black and white, not Good and Evil. Learn to immerse oneself into the plights, the stories, of other people because you can tap the extent of sorrow in the lives of all you meet. Tell Negroes to beware of their blackness: it may be but another white man's values. Tell whites of how books, of how *Bleak House*, can become real, the fog a part of your nostrils: your sister pregnant and your mind totally detached from this reality: that you moved intermittently between Harvard and Watts, afraid of committing yourself to one or the other completely. No one could tell me anything. I knew what the answers were. There was only one question that had everyone confused.

It was the middle of the school year. It was the beginning of spring. Christmas was over and so, too, was much of the light-hearted air that had atmospherized Harvard Yard during its opening three months. Now, education had set in and our Hoodlum raised himself from his bed to look out of the window, to take stock of that change in the air, and then, to walk out of the door into the crisp thirty-degree weather before quickly retiring to his room. Damn, it's colder than hell out there! he would mutter—though, of course, the winter had been much colder. He was simply looking for an excuse not to go to class and this coldness was the best excuse he could find. Of course, it would soon be warm, but that did not matter. His bookshelf would always be there, big and with each day's trip to the Harvard Bookstore growing bigger (though we must remember that these book-buying excursions took place in the late afternoon when it had grown commensurately warmer). There was no thought in his mind of attending classes. Was he an ingrate, or a rebel, or a reactionary, some radical, perhaps, if it might not be asking too much, could he well have been simply involved in finding out what life was all about, or is that too simple? If he was a product of the slums, then of what slums, and what sort of product was he?

Did his eyes see Harvard: the Yard and the Yale Game behind, the counseling sessions over with, his position in the movement of things firmly established? No, not really that kind of world. It was too artificial, too involved with the processes of trying to make a better living when all he wanted was to simply let time pass by. He didn't know who Norman Mailer was, though *The Naked and the Dead* was out. Nor had he read James Joyce. *Finnegans Wake*: what was that? Or if one knew who Samuel Beckett and the race-screaming LeRoi Jones (who could sink down into the limpid surfaces of reality and come out with some pretty valid insights into the nature of homosexuality, which scares most college kids) were—then it was just as easy to assume a literary superiority, a greater racial awareness. He was not that involved, in other words, with the world situation at large. You had on your hands a kid who was genuinely wrapped up in trying to make meaning out of a wrecked life instead of scrapping all remembrances of it completely, then having the courage to admit this rejection consciously to himself, and then moving on to restructure a new world. Nothing unusual at all.

To then be aware of what life exacts of you, if one is concerned with this whole business of dying, and it was not the easiest task in the world for the Hoodlum. Many times he found himself using a borrowed joke from a friend to express his morning breakfast greetings in the old freshman dining quarters: "It's your world, squirrel. I'm just trying to get a nut!" And he was, he was in search of an orgasm of physical and spiritual revelation that could not be his consciously during that year because he had not opened himself up to the possibility of there existing other worlds of existence than his own. The typical white rebels were met, these rich kids who had turned away from their parents, and those Cadillacs, black (as opposed to the loud whiteness, the white-on-white-in-white Cadillacs of Watts and any other Negro ghetto in America), which used to turn into the Yard on weekends, parents bringing candy and cookies and other various foodstuffs which sooner or later were eaten by everybody but the parents' kid. Like most poor kids, our man would see these goodies and say nothing. "You'll get tremendous cultural exposure!" one former Jordan teacher had told him before he left for Harvard. He did. In sarcastic, biting ways that might have been seen by others but was felt, registered internally, and then left there to realize itself days, weeks, hours, months, years later: perhaps as a sudden laugh, perhaps as a bitter cursing, perhaps a shame, perhaps, and then in greater proportions, as a concern with the twin shingles of the social measuring-scales upon which poverty and affluence are doled out: some suffer, some die, all of us learn what it is to want more. Another teacher had said, "Do you know what *enough* is?—just a little bit more!"

He was on academic probation—make up your grades or flunk out. Only nine out of that class of twelve hundred flunked out. A lot of others took leaves of absence to study themselves, and there were the perpetual Radcliffe cases: those unnamed medical leaves of absence so that some girl could have her illegitimate baby in peace. A world that was, in retrospect, quite similar to Watts. And yet, because of its tremendous freedom, there were the canoe rides on the Concord River where cold was the name of the air and pretty was the color of the fish, a great deal more warming. Most of the time life back home was cold. Parents here were people you could see and appreciate. Made you wonder why white kids would rebel. If you had the chance, you surely wouldn't walk out on a million-dollar inheritance.

The shocking realization was that this was me, JOHNIE, who had grown up in Watts and had seen policemen literally crack skulls open while women fell to their knees crying like babies at seeing their babies carried off to jail, who had seen his father's house burn to the ground, who had almost become inured to death and blood and tears. Too much of it spoils the novelty. My own morality was not based on a Western system of good and evil, traceable to Plato and Hesiod, Jesus and St. Augustine. Rather, it was a social and cultural orientation to the slums—in which evil was taken for granted and upon it erected a value system of happiness and terror. I knew that I was not alone. My friends, all of us who have been nursed on this world, live according to this system of values. This was something neither Chris Wadsworth, nor Dr. Cotton, nor anyone else in that entire place would have gathered, no farther than seeing a bit of the sun just before it sinks into the sea, and then, until the next day, is lost. They only saw the moon, good people for all that they were, showing human characteristics of love and warmth and sincerity in their work that make definite impressions but which could not at that time be extended into this many-surfaced world.

Some might run the risk of calling it all a dreamworld and they would be wrong, as wrong as those who would call the Hoodlum a racist when all he was, in truth, was a bearer of the imprint from that world. He was beyond even looking back upon his world and calling it sordid, brutal, with a frankness that at times had left him overwhelmed, typical advertising adjectives of revealing books. No, this for him was a dynamism that time and again cost him, cost him friendships and relationships that might have offered a way out of this reality into another: an escape. And he would have been glad for a hand toward escape, though now, when Harvard is superimposed over Watts, though the Hoodlum is placed above my own reflection in the mirror, I suppose there truthfully could have been no escape. Harvard had become a ghost-yard, empty. There were animal sounds in the air. The snow had become brown and slushy. Snow was not pretty, it acted as an obstruction. In his way of travel, in my way, and everyone else's. People were laughing and looking real because they tasted joy denied to me. A man can flunk out of school for many reasons.

A man looking into himself must not look too hard, or the reflection will be encased within Reality's mirror. I saw mine, the entire story called the coming of the Hoodlum. I began to wonder if I might ever escape, so that I would come closer to my own salvation. That is right, for I had become a spiritualist, not a mystic. I had entered Harvard an atheist, who went home Christmas and sat in his mother's church taking notes on the Reverend's sermon and then, at the end of the services, when everyone went up and congratulated the minister on his ministerings, had shown where his dialectics differed considerably from his own exhortations to the good and plenty of the land.

On June 7, 1965, exactly nine months later, I returned to Watts. This time it was for keeps, if anything in life can be applied that label. But the Hoodlum was fired, fire: he believed in God. He had believed in the possibility of all men finally coming together, in truth, he had dedicated himself to some personal ministering of his own to the needs of his friends and companions, with whom he had shared the living experience, Watts. There, within that jet, the mind's eyes traveled both back and forth in time, seeing Harvard before arriving that September 21, 1964, and leaving that June day, seeing Christmas and seeing Jordan High, seeing all that he was. Most of all, understanding that things would have to be different from here on out. Something had happened, he did not know what. But there was one thing that had to be true: he was more than a year older, he had done a lot more than party late at night, or lose his virginity, or take Chinese Philosophy. He had changed. Back home.

The last thing he remembered reading in the Harvard *Crimson* was that applications this year for those 1,200 spots had risen to 6,500. To be sure, there would be more Negroes. It has been getting like that all across the country. But then, that was progress. This, 1965, would be the year, His year: his resolution. And in August of that year, Watts and all of Los Angeles would burn before he began understanding why life was so much dearer than death.

———

Johnie Scott (1948–   ) *was the first young man from Watts, the black community in Los Angeles, to be accepted in an Ivy League college. After the year at Harvard he describes in this essay, he won a scholarship to Stanford University. His essays and poems have appeared in* Harper's, Time, Scholastic, Pageant, *and other magazines. A writer and teacher in the Watts Writers' Workshop since Spring, 1966, he was one of the original "Angry Voices of Watts" on an NBC-TV special. "The Coming of the Hoodlum" was published in* From the Ashes: Voices of Watts *(1967), edited by Budd Schulberg. Mr. Scott, coming from a community largely deprived of the American promise, shares a sense of alienation from college with Henry Adams, wealthy grandson of President John Quincy Adams, whose account of Harvard a century ago follows this essay.*

1. To what degree is Scott's description of his schooling before college an example of what Jules Henry called "learning the nightmare"? What similarities and differences do you see between Scott's and Orwell's schooling and their reactions to it?
2. What is Scott's purpose in giving so many details about life in Watts? What attitudes are expressed and called for by these recurring references to Watts? What kinds of words and sentence structures does Scott tend to use in these descriptive passages? Why?
3. How does Scott demonstrate that "ghettoes are built within the mind"? Why does he flunk out of Harvard?
4. The irony of calling himself "the Hoodlum" becomes particularly clear in the paragraph describing his fear of being killed, which kept him from the easy money to be made by stealing. In what sense, then, is he a "Hoodlum"? What is the tone of

the word as Scott uses it? Why does he so persistently refer to himself in the third person in this intimately personal and reflective essay?

5. *Early in the essay, Scott describes the "cleavage" in himself, "a strange and troubling turmoil born out of the chaos" of Watts. What is this cleavage? How does it relate to the turmoil of Watts, the social and intellectual promise of Harvard? In what way does the cleavage remain at the end of the essay when Scott looks in the mirror and sees "the Hoodlum" as well as "my own reflection in the mirror"?*

Henry Adams

HARVARD COLLEGE

One day in June, 1854, young Adams walked for the last time down the steps of Mr. Dixwell's school in Boylston Place, and felt no sensation but one of unqualified joy that this experience was ended. Never before or afterwards in his life did he close a period so long as four years without some sensation of loss—some sentiment of habit—but school was what in after life he commonly heard his friends denounce as an intolerable bore. He was born too old for it. The same thing could be said of most New England boys. Mentally they never were boys. Their education as men should have begun at ten years old. They were fully five years more mature than the English or European boy for whom schools were made. For the purposes of future advancement, as afterwards appeared, these first six years of a possible education were wasted in doing imperfectly what might have been done perfectly in one, and in any case would have had small value. The next regular step was Harvard College. He was more than glad to go. For generation after generation, Adamses and Brookses and Boylstons and Gorhams had gone to Harvard College, and although none of them, as far as known, had ever done any good there, or thought himself the better for it, custom, social ties, convenience, and, above all, economy, kept each generation in the track. Any other education would have required a serious effort, but no one took Harvard College seriously. All went there because their friends went there, and the College was their ideal of social self-respect.

Harvard College, as far as it educated at all, was a mild and liberal school, which sent young men into the world with all they needed to make respectable citizens, and something of what they wanted to make useful ones. Leaders of men it never tried to make. Its ideals were altogether different. The Unitarian clergy had given to the College a character of moderation, balance, judgment, restraint, what the French called *mesure*; excellent traits, which the College attained with singular success, so that its graduates could commonly be recognized by the stamp, but such a type of character

From *The Education of Henry Adams*. Copyright 1918 by the Massachusetts Historical Society. Selection reprinted by permission of and arrangement with Houghton Mifflin Company, the authorized publishers.

rarely lent itself to autobiography. In effect, the school created a type but not a will. Four years of Harvard College, if successful, resulted in an autobiographical blank, a mind on which only a watermark had been stamped.

The stamp, as such things went, was a good one. The chief wonder of education is that it does not ruin everybody concerned in it, teachers and taught. Sometimes in after life, Adams debated whether in fact it had not ruined him and most of his companions, but, disappointment apart, Harvard College was probably less hurtful than any other university then in existence. It taught little, and that little ill, but it left the mind open, free from bias, ignorant of facts, but docile. The graduate had few strong prejudices. He knew little, but his mind remained supple, ready to receive knowledge.

What caused the boy most disappointment was the little he got from his mates. Speaking exactly, he got less than nothing, a result common enough in education. Yet the College Catalogue for the years 1854 to 1861 shows a list of names rather distinguished in their time. Alexander Agassiz and Phillips Brooks led it; H. H. Richardson and O. W. Holmes helped to close it. As a rule the most promising of all die early, and never get their names into a Dictionary of Contemporaries, which seems to be the only popular standard of success. Many died in the war. Adams knew them all, more or less; he felt as much regard, and quite as much respect for them then, as he did after they won great names and were objects of a vastly wider respect; but, as help towards education, he got nothing whatever from them or they from him until long after they had left college. Possibly the fault was his, but one would like to know how many others shared it. Accident counts for much in companionship as in marriage. Life offers perhaps only a score of possible companions, and it is mere chance whether they meet as early as school or college, but it is more than a chance that boys brought up together under like conditions have nothing to give each other. The Class of 1858, to which Henry Adams belonged, was a typical collection of young New Englanders, quietly penetrating and aggressively commonplace; free from meannesses, jealousies, intrigues, enthusiasms, and passions; not exceptionally quick; not consciously sceptical; singularly indifferent to display, artifice, florid expression, but not hostile to it when it amused them; distrustful of themselves, but little disposed to trust any one else; with not much humor of their own, but full of readiness to enjoy the humor of others; negative to a degree that in the long run became positive and triumphant. Not harsh in manners or judgment, rather liberal and open-minded, they were still as a body the most formidable critics one would care to meet, in a long life exposed to criticism.

They never flattered, seldom praised; free from vanity, they were not intolerant of it; but they were objectiveness itself; their attitude was a law of nature; their judgment beyond appeal, not an act either of intellect or emotion or of will, but a sort of gravitation.

This was Harvard College incarnate, but even for Harvard College, the Class of 1858 was somewhat extreme. Of unity this band of nearly one hundred young men had no keen sense, but they had equally little energy of repulsion. They were pleasant to live with, and above the average of students—German, French, English, or what not—but chiefly because each individual appeared satisfied to stand alone. It seemed a sign of force; yet to stand alone is quite natural when one has no passions; still easier when one has no pains.

Into this unusually dissolvent medium, chance insisted on enlarging Henry Adams's education by tossing a trio of Virginians as little fitted for it as Sioux Indians to a treadmill. By some further affinity, these three outsiders fell into relation with the Bostonians among whom Adams as a schoolboy belonged, and in the end with Adams himself, although they and he knew well how thin an edge of friendship separated them in 1856 from mortal enmity. One of the Virginians was the son of Colonel Robert E. Lee, of the Second United States Cavalry; the two others who seemed instinctively to form a staff for Lee, were town-Virginians from Petersburg. A fourth outsider came from Cincinnati and was half Kentuckian, N. L. Anderson, Longworth on the mother's side. For the first time Adams's education brought him in contact with new types and taught him their values. He saw the New England type measure itself with another, and he was part of the process.

Lee, known through life as "Roony," was a Virginian of the eighteenth century, much as Henry Adams was a Bostonian of the same age. Roony Lee had changed little from the type of his grandfather, Light Horse Harry. Tall, largely built, handsome, genial, with liberal Virginian openness towards all he liked, he had also the Virginian habit of command and took leadership as his natural habit. No one cared to contest it. None of the New Englanders wanted command. For a year, at least, Lee was the most popular and prominent young man in his class, but then seemed slowly to drop into the background. The habit of command was not enough, and the Virginian had little else. He was simple beyond analysis; so simple that even the simple New England student could not realize him. No one knew enough to know how ignorant he was; how childlike; how helpless before the relative complexity of a school. As an animal, the Southerner seemed to have every advantage, but even as an animal he steadily lost ground.

The lesson in education was vital to these young men, who,

within ten years, killed each other by scores in the act of testing their college conclusions. Strictly, the Southerner had no mind; he had temperament. He was not a scholar; he had no intellectual training; he could not analyze an idea, and he could not even conceive of admitting two; but in life one could get along very well without ideas, if one had only the social instinct. Dozens of eminent statesmen were men of Lee's type, and maintained themselves well enough in the legislature, but college was a sharper test. The Virginian was weak in vice itself, though the Bostonian was hardly a master of crime. The habits of neither were good; both were apt to drink hard and to live low lives; but the Bostonian suffered less than the Virginian. Commonly the Bostonian would take some care of himself even in his worst stages, while the Virginian became quarrelsome and dangerous. When a Virginian had brooded a few days over an imaginary grief and substantial whiskey, none of his Northern friends could be sure that he might not be waiting, round the corner, with a knife or pistol, to revenge insult by the dry light of *delirium tremens*; and when things reached this condition, Lee had to exhaust his authority over his own staff. Lee was a gentleman of the old school, and, as everyone knows, gentlemen of the old school drank almost as much as gentlemen of the new school; but this was not his trouble. He was sober even in the excessive violence of political feeling in those years; he kept his temper and his friends under control.

Adams liked the Virginians. No one was more obnoxious to them, by name and prejudice; yet their friendship was unbroken and even warm. At a moment when the immediate future posed no problem in education so vital as the relative energy and endurance of North and South, this momentary contact with Southern character was a sort of education for its own sake; but this was not all. No doubt the self-esteem of the Yankee, which tended naturally to self-distrust, was flattered by gaining the slow conviction that the Southerner, with his slave-owning limitations, was as little fit to succeed in the struggle of modern life as though he were still a maker of stone axes, living in caves, and hunting the *bos primigenius*, and that every quality in which he was strong, made him weaker; but Adams had begun to fear that even in this respect one eighteenth-century type might not differ deeply from another. Roony Lee had changed little from the Virginian of a century before; but Adams was himself a good deal nearer the type of his great-grandfather than to that of a railway superintendent. He was little more fit than the Virginians to deal with a future America which showed no fancy for the past. Already Northern society betrayed a preference for economists over diplomats or soldiers—one might even call it a jealousy—against which two eighteenth-century types had little chance to live, and which they had in common to fear.

Nothing short of this curious sympathy could have brought into close relations two young men so hostile as Roony Lee and Henry Adams, but the chief difference between them as collegians consisted only in their difference of scholarship: Lee was a total failure; Adams a partial one. Both failed, but Lee felt his failure more sensibly, so that he gladly seized the chance of escape by accepting a commission offered him by General Winfield Scott in the force then being organized against the Mormons. He asked Adams to write his letter of acceptance, which flattered Adams's vanity more than any Northern compliment could do, because, in days of violent political bitterness, it showed a certain amount of good temper. The diplomat felt his profession.

If the student got little from his mates, he got little more from his masters. The four years passed at college were, for his purposes, wasted. Harvard College was a good school, but at bottom what the boy disliked most was any school at all. He did not want to be one in a hundred—one per cent of an education. He regarded himself as the only person for whom his education had value, and he wanted the whole of it. He got barely half of an average. Long afterwards, when the devious path of life led him back to teach in his turn what no student naturally cared or needed to know, he diverted some dreary hours of faculty-meetings by looking up his record in the class-lists, and found himself graded precisely in the middle. In the one branch he most needed—mathematics—barring the few first scholars, failure was so nearly universal that no attempt at grading could have had value, and whether he stood fortieth or ninetieth must have been an accident or the personal favor of the professor. Here his education failed lamentably. At best he could never have been a mathematician; at worst he would never have cared to be one; but he needed to read mathematics, like any other universal language, and he never reached the alphabet.

Beyond two or three Greek plays, the student got nothing from the ancient languages. Beyond some incoherent theories of free-trade and protection, he got little from Political Economy. He could not afterwards remember to have heard the name of Karl Marx mentioned, or the title of "Capital." He was equally ignorant of Auguste Comte. These were the two writers of his time who most influenced its thought. The bit of practical teaching he afterwards reviewed with most curiosity was the course in Chemistry, which taught him a number of theories that befogged his mind for a lifetime. The only teaching that appealed to his imagination was a course of lectures by Louis Agassiz on the Glacial Period and Palæontology, which had more influence on his curiosity than the

rest of the college instruction altogether. The entire work of the
four years could have been easily put into the work of any four
months in after life.

Harvard College was a negative force, and negative forces have
value. Slowly it weakened the violent political bias of childhood,
not by putting interests in its place, but by mental habits which
had no bias at all. It would also have weakened the literary bias, if
Adams had been capable of finding other amusement, but the climate kept him steady to desultory and useless reading, till he had
run through libraries of volumes which he forgot even to their
title-pages. Rather by instinct than by guidance, he turned to
writing, and his professors or tutors occasionally gave his English
composition a hesitating approval; but in that branch, as in all the
rest, even when he made a long struggle for recognition, he never
convinced his teachers that his abilities, at their best, warranted
placing him on the rank-list, among the first third of his class. Instructors generally reach a fairly accurate gauge of their scholars'
powers. Henry Adams himself held the opinion that his instructors
were very nearly right, and when he became a professor in his turn,
and made mortifying mistakes in ranking his scholars, he still ob-
stinately insisted that on the whole, he was not far wrong. Student
or professor, he accepted the negative standard because it was the
standard of the school.

He never knew what other students thought of it, or what they
thought they gained from it; nor would their opinion have much
affected his. From the first, he wanted to be done with it, and stood
watching vaguely for a path and a direction. The world outside
seemed large, but the paths that led into it were not many and lay
mostly through Boston, where he did not want to go. As it happened, by pure chance, the first door of escape that seemed to offer
a hope led into Germany, and James Russell Lowell opened it.

Lowell, on succeeding Longfellow as Professor of Belles-Lettres,
had duly gone to Germany, and had brought back whatever he
found to bring. The literary world then agreed that truth survived
in Germany alone, and Carlyle, Matthew Arnold, Renan, Emerson, with scores of popular followers, taught the German faith. The
literary world had revolted against the yoke of coming capitalism—
its money-lenders, its bank directors, and its railway magnates.
Thackeray and Dickens followed Balzac in scratching and biting
the unfortunate middle class with savage ill-temper, much as the
middle class had scratched and bitten the Church and Court for a
hundred years before. The middle class had the power, and held its
coal and iron well in hand, but the satirists and idealists seized the
press, and as they were agreed that the Second Empire was a disgrace to France and a danger to England, they turned to Germany

because at that moment Germany was neither economical nor military, and a hundred years behind western Europe in the simplicity of its standard. German thought, method, honesty, and even taste, became the standards of scholarship. Goethe was raised to the rank of Shakespeare—Kant ranked as a law-giver above Plato. All serious scholars were obliged to become German, for German thought was revolutionizing criticism. Lowell had followed the rest, not very enthusiastically, but with sufficient conviction, and invited his scholars to join him. Adams was glad to accept the invitation, rather for the sake of cultivating Lowell than Germany, but still in perfect good faith. It was the first serious attempt he had made to direct his own education, and he was sure of getting some education out of it; not perhaps anything that he expected, but at least a path.

Singularly circuitous and excessively wasteful of energy the path proved to be, but the student could never see what other was open to him. He could have done no better had he foreseen every stage of his coming life, and he would probably have done worse. The preliminary step was pure gain. James Russell Lowell had brought back from Germany the only new and valuable part of its universities, the habit of allowing students to read with him privately in his study. Adams asked the privilege, and used it to read a little, and to talk a great deal, for the personal contact pleased and flattered him, as that of older men ought to flatter and please the young even when they altogether exaggerate its value. Lowell was a new element in the boy's life. As practical a New Englander as any, he leaned towards the Concord faith rather than towards Boston where he properly belonged; for Concord, in the dark days of 1856, glowed with pure light. Adams approached it in much the same spirit as he would have entered a Gothic Cathedral, for he well knew that the priests regarded him as only a worm. To the Concord Church all Adamses were minds of dust and emptiness, devoid of feeling, poetry or imagination; little higher than the common scourings of State Street; politicians of doubtful honesty; natures of narrow scope; and already, at eighteen years old, Henry had begun to feel uncertainty about so many matters more important than Adamses that his mind rebelled against no discipline merely personal, and he was ready to admit his unworthiness if only he might penetrate the shrine. The influence of Harvard College was beginning to have its effect. He was slipping away from fixed principles; from Mount Vernon Street; from Quincy; from the eighteenth century; and his first steps led toward Concord.

He never reached Concord, and to Concord Church he, like the rest of mankind who accepted a material universe, remained always an insect, or something much lower—a man. It was surely no fault of his that the universe seemed to him real; perhaps—as Mr.

Emerson justly said—it was so; in spite of the long-continued effort of a lifetime, he perpetually fell back into the heresy that if anything universal was unreal, it was himself and not the appearances; it was the poet and not the banker; it was his own thought, not the thing that moved it. He did not lack the wish to be transcendental. Concord seemed to him, at one time, more real than Quincy; yet in truth Russell Lowell was as little transcendental as Beacon Street. From him the boy got no revolutionary thought whatever—objective or subjective as they used to call it—but he got good-humored encouragement to do what amused him, which consisted in passing two years in Europe after finishing the four years of Cambridge.

The result seemed small in proportion to the effort, but it was the only positive result he could ever trace to the influence of Harvard College, and he had grave doubts whether Harvard College influenced even that. Negative results in plenty he could trace, but he tended towards negation on his own account, as one side of the New England mind had always done, and even there he could never feel sure that Harvard College had more than reflected a weakness. In his opinion the education was not serious, but in truth hardly any Boston student took it seriously, and none of them seemed sure that President Walker himself, or President Felton after him, took it more seriously than the students. For them all, the college offered chiefly advantages vulgarly called social, rather than mental.

Unluckily for this particular boy, social advantages were his only capital in life. Of money he had not much, of mind not more, but he could be quite certain that, barring his own faults, his social position would never be questioned. What he needed was a career in which social position had value. Never in his life would he have to explain who he was; never would he have need of acquaintance to strengthen his social standing; but he needed greatly some one to show him how to use the acquaintance he cared to make. He made no acquaintance in college which proved to have the smallest use in after life. All his Boston friends he knew before, or would have known in any case, and contact of Bostonian with Bostonian was the last education these young men needed. Cordial and intimate as their college relations were, they all flew off in different directions the moment they took their degrees. Harvard College remained a tie, indeed, but a tie little stronger than Beacon Street and not so strong as State Street. Strangers might perhaps gain something from the college if they were hard pressed for social connections. A student like H. H. Richardson, who came from far away New Orleans, and had his career before him to chase rather than to guide, might make valuable friendships at college. Certainly Adams made no acquaintance there that he valued in after life so much as Richardson, but still more certainly the college relation had little to do with the later friendship. Life is a narrow valley, and the roads run close together. Adams would have attached himself to Richardson in any case, as he attached himself to John La-Farge or Augustus St. Gaudens or Clarence King or John Hay, none of whom were at Harvard College. The valley of life grew more and more narrow with years, and certain men with common tastes were bound to come together. Adams knew only that he would have felt himself on a more equal footing with them had he been less ignorant, and had he not thrown away ten years of early life in acquiring what he might have acquired in one.

Socially or intellectually, the college was for him negative and in some ways mischievous. The most tolerant man of the world could not see good in the lower habits of the students, but the vices were less harmful than the virtues. The habit of drinking—though the mere recollection of it made him doubt his own veracity, so fantastic it seemed in later life—may have done no great or permanent harm; but the habit of looking at life as a social relation—an affair of society—did no good. It cultivated a weakness which needed no cultivation. If it had helped to make men of the world, or give the manners and instincts of any profession—such as temper, patience, courtesy, or a faculty of profiting by the social defects of opponents—it would have been education better worth having than mathematics or languages; but so far as it helped to make anything, it helped only to make the college standard permanent through life. The Bostonian educated at Harvard College remained a collegian, if he stuck only to what the college gave him. If parents went on generation after generation, sending their children to Harvard College for the sake of its social advantages, they perpetuated an inferior social type, quite as ill-fitted as the Oxford type for success in the next generation.

Luckily the old social standard of the college, as President Walker or James Russell Lowell still showed it, was admirable, and if it had little practical value or personal influence on the mass of students, at least it preserved the tradition for those who liked it. The Harvard graduate was neither American nor European, nor even wholly Yankee; his admirers were few, and his critics many; perhaps his worst weakness was his self-criticism and self-consciousness; but his ambitions, social or intellectual, were not necessarily cheap even though they might be negative. Afraid of serious risks, and still more afraid of personal ridicule, he seldom made a great failure of life, and nearly always led a life more or less worth living. So Henry Adams, well aware that he could not succeed as a scholar, and finding his social position beyond improvement or need of effort, betook himself to the single ambition which otherwise would scarcely have seemed a true outcome of the college, though it was the last remnant of the old Unitarian supremacy. He took to the pen. He wrote.

The College Magazine printed his work, and the College Societies listened to his addresses. Lavish of praise the readers were not; the audiences, too, listened in silence; but this was all the encouragement any Harvard collegian had a reasonable hope to receive; grave silence was a form of patience that meant possible future acceptance; and Henry Adams went on writing. No one cared enough to criticise, except himself who soon began to suffer from reaching his own limits. He found that he could not be this—or that—or the other; always precisely the things he wanted to be. He had not wit or scope or force. Judges always ranked him beneath a rival, if he had any; and he believed the judges were right. His work seemed to him thin, commonplace, feeble. At times he felt his own weakness so fatally that he could not go on; when he had nothing to say, he could not say it, and he found that he had very little to say at best. Much that he then wrote must be still in existence in print or manuscript, though he never cared to see it again, for he felt no doubt that it was in reality just what he thought it. At best it showed only a feeling for form; an instinct of exclusion. Nothing shocked—not even its weakness.

Inevitably an effort leads to an ambition—creates it—and at that time the ambition of the literary student, which almost took place of the regular prizes of scholarship, was that of being chosen as the representative of his class—the Class Orator—at the close of their course. This was political as well as literary success, and precisely the sort of eighteenth-century combination that fascinated an eighteenth-century boy. The idea lurked in his mind, at first as a dream, in no way serious or even possible, for he stood outside the number of what were known as popular men. Year by year, his position seemed to improve, or perhaps his rivals disappeared, until at last, to his own great astonishment, he found himself a candidate. The habits of the college permitted no active candidacy; he and his rivals had not a word to say for or against themselves, and he was never even consulted on the subject; he was not present at any of the proceedings, and how it happened he never could quite divine, but it did happen, that one evening on returning from Boston he received notice of his election, after a very close contest, as Class Orator over the head of the first scholar, who was undoubtedly a better orator and a more popular man. In politics the success of the poorer candidate is common enough, and Henry Adams was a fairly trained politician, but he never understood how he managed to defeat not only a more capable but a more popular rival.

To him the election seemed a miracle. This was no mock-modesty; his head was as clear as ever it was in an indifferent canvass, and he knew his rivals and their following as well as he knew himself. What he did not know, even after four years of education, was Harvard College. What he could never measure was the bewildering impersonality of the men, who, at twenty years old, seemed to set no value either on official or personal standards. Here were nearly a hundred young men who had lived together intimately during four of the most impressionable years of life, and who, not only once but again and again, in different ways, deliberately, seriously, dispassionately, chose as their representatives precisely those of their companions who seemed least to represent them. As far as these Orators and Marshals had any position at all in a collegiate sense, it was that of indifference to the college. Henry Adams never professed the smallest faith in universities of any kind, either as boy or man, nor had he the faintest admiration for the university graduate, either in Europe or in America; as a collegian he was only known apart from his fellows by his habit of standing outside the college; and yet the singular fact remained that this commonplace body of young men chose him repeatedly to express his and their commonplaces. Secretly, of course, the successful candidate flattered himself—and them—with the hope that they might perhaps not be so commonplace as they thought themselves; but this was only another proof that all were identical. They saw in him a representative—the kind of representative they wanted —and he saw in them the most formidable array of judges he could ever meet, like so many mirrors of himself, an infinite reflection of his own shortcomings.

All the same, the choice was flattering; so flattering that it actually shocked his vanity; and would have shocked it more, if possible, had he known that it was to be the only flattery of the sort he was ever to receive. The function of Class Day was, in the eyes of nine-tenths of the students, altogether the most important of the college, and the figure of the Orator was the most conspicuous in the function. Unlike the Orators at regular Commencements, the Class Day Orator stood alone, or had only the Poet for rival. Crowded into the large church, the students, their families, friends, aunts, uncles and chaperones, attended all the girls of sixteen or twenty who wanted to show their summer dresses or fresh complexions, and there, for an hour or two, in a heat that might have melted bronze, they listened to an Orator and a Poet in clergyman's gowns, reciting such platitudes as their own experience and their mild censors permitted them to utter. What Henry Adams said in his Class Oration of 1858 he soon forgot to the last word, nor had it the least value for education; but he naturally remembered what was said of it. He remembered especially one of his eminent uncles or relations remarking that, as the work of so young a man, the oration was singularly wanting in enthusiasm. The young man—always in search of education—asked himself whether, setting rhetoric aside, this absence of enthusiasm was a defect or a merit, since, in either case, it was all that Harvard College taught, and all that the hundred young men, whom he was trying to represent, expressed. Another comment threw more light on the effect of the college education. One of the elderly gentlemen noticed the orator's "perfect self-possession." Self-possession indeed! If Harvard College gave nothing else, it gave calm. For four years each student had been obliged to figure daily before dozens of young men who knew each other to the last fibre. One had done little but read papers to Societies, or act comedy in the Hasty Pudding, not to speak of all sorts of regular exercises, and no audience in future life would ever be so intimately and terribly intelligent as these. Three-fourths of the graduates would rather have addressed the Council of Trent or the British Parliament than have acted Sir Anthony Absolute or Dr. Ollapod before a gala audience of the Hasty Pudding. Self-possession was the strongest part of Harvard College, which certainly taught men to stand alone, so that nothing seemed stranger to its graduates than the paroxysms of terror before the public which often overcame the graduates of European universities. Whether this was, or was not, education, Henry Adams never knew. He was ready to stand up before any audience in America or Europe, with nerves rather steadier for the excitement, but whether he should ever have anything to say, remained to be proved. As yet he knew nothing. Education had not begun.

———

HENRY ADAMS (1838–1918) *had the best instruction and culture that a thriving Boston society could give. Though brought up in the company of the powerful, rich, and famous, sent from the instruction of private tutors to Harvard and the University of Berlin, he felt that rapidly changing times had made his education irrelevant to his needs. His writing includes journalism, fiction (Democracy, 1880; Esther, 1884), biography, essays, history, and his autobiography,* The Education of Henry Adams (1907), *from which this chapter is taken.*

1. *Johnie Scott found Harvard of little use in his attempt "to make meaning out of a wrecked life." Adams found at Harvard, a century before, "an autobiographical blank": "The chief wonder*

of education is that it does not ruin everybody concerned in it, teachers and taught." The message is similar, but the tone is quite different. Examine and describe the similarities and differences in each writer's a) attitude toward himself, b) attitude toward the reader, and c) attitude toward Harvard.

2. Both Adams and Scott refer to themselves in the third person. Why? What is the difference between the ways they refer to themselves, and how does this difference affect tone?

3. "Lee was a gentleman of the old school, and, as every one knows, gentlemen of the old school drank as much as gentlemen of the new school." Who is the "*every one*" Adams assumes as his audience? What is the tone of this passage, and how is it achieved? What is its purpose? Why is there so little humor in Johnie Scott's essay?

4. Adams grudgingly admits that Harvard had some advantages. What were they? Reread the last few pages of Scott's essay to see what he felt he received from his year at Harvard. Compare what each of them gained, and describe the differences and similarities. Did they each, in fact, waste their time at college?

Thomas J. Cottle

THE POLITICS OF RETRIEVAL:
AN OPEN LETTER

[*The letter of solicitation below by R. Dyke Benjamin '59 to his classmates prompted the response of Thomas J. Cottle '59, which follows.*]

Dear Classmate: April 1969
It is with great sadness that I am writing you one of my final letters as your Tenth Reunion Gift Chairman. When I accepted the responsibility of Chairman, it never occurred to me that our Tenth Reunion might be more of a celebration of what Harvard was ten years ago than of what is happening to the College today.

For me, Harvard was an experience which developed my own capacity for intellectual excitement and for contribution to a way of life. Now a segment of the undergraduate body is stressing revolution more than intellectual growth. Rather than striving to develop unique individual approaches to living, this element is striving to impose their group-derived "non-negotiable demands" upon Harvard's leadership.

Since recent events are so foreign to my concept of Harvard, it would be hypocritical for me to solicit another penny from the Class of 1959 IF I did not have hope for the future. However, I am sure that there will continue to be many undergraduates who are anxious to develop their own thoughts and self-expression to the point where they will not have to rely upon group force to initiate change.

Based upon the strong belief that Harvard will continue to be dedicated to the objective of providing each undergraduate with the opportunity to develop his powers of perception and articulation, I ask you to give the College more money—not less. By helping to provide Harvard with

From the *Harvard Alumni Bulletin*, June 9, 1969. Reprinted by permission of the publisher.

adequate resources, we can enable the College to sustain the atmosphere of intellectual vitality which we were privileged to enjoy.

Sincerely yours,
R. DYKE BENJAMIN
New York, 10th Reunion Gift Chairman

Having made it through these last few weeks of witnessing a Harvard struggling to awaken itself from what Kant called the dogmatic slumber, I have been especially troubled and, I might say, a bit angered by your letter. Somehow, I catch in it a plea to return to a time gone by and a logic built upon the pilings of an anachronistic structure. No, I take it all back, I was deeply angered by your letter.

Perhaps the Harvard of ten years ago was, in fact, a delicious place, "developing our capacities for intellectual excitement," but some of us weren't as ready, apparently, as you were. Or, maybe the intellectualism drowned out, or failed to wake up, a whole slew of qualities and activities that I thought went with college, but never quite got. I wasn't ready, that is undeniable, but neither was Harvard in its way, and this is the point I hope somehow to pass on.

Even as I begin to think of the 1950's, I'm not quite able to get a fix on the context into which college experiences should be observed and judged. I know we all prided ourselves in knowing the few Negroes on campus. I know they weren't called blacks in those days. I know, too, that many of the Jewish boys would speak silently together about the one or two of their kind who were diligently trying to get into a club. They spoke of some mystic rotation for some clubs that would determine when a Jew might get in. Certainly the Negroes had no problems. In fact there was no Negro problem in those days. Indeed, the clubs offered no problems either. It all seemed fair enough. After all, the prep school boys came from the families who founded the country, hence they deserved—no, they earned—special rights to be in their clubs, and that's the way it was even if that wasn't quite the way it might ideally be.

So on Mondays we used to walk to class and look at some of our comrades in their army suits, all dressed up like little soldiers and sailors, disappearing to some secret buildings behind the Biological Laboratories that no one ever could locate, or would bother to speak about. They had it good, those guys, it was said. They had their way paid and it didn't really take that much time, and, actually, their summer outfits, in particular, looked rather good on them.

You really wouldn't dare refer to them as "wonks" because they were in the Army and Navy, and they were just as gentle in their khakis or blues as they were Tuesday morning in their dungarees and sport coats. But who, after all, would join if he didn't have to? Who really wanted to march and get all caught up in that authoritarian way of life where they made you get a crew cut, even if the courses were guts? Probably only the poorer kids went out for ROTC, we used to think. And we would reminisce about the anomalous initials. Rotten old tin cans, someone once told me in Chicago.

As incongruous as they seemed, the little soldiers could almost be excused their necessities next to the student-council boys. Now here were the power-hungry guys, so it seemed, anxious to better their extracurricular records for business and law school admissions officers. How often in those shady days of the fifties did we darling products of high-school student governments strut about the Yard snarling over the rather aggressive and abrasive sorts who would run for class marshal or president or representative to some committee? Just whose prestige and well being were they after with their well-groomed Cambridge uniforms and regular two-week-interval haircuts? I ask you that, we'd say. Just who are they trying to kid?

Then there were the days, certainly each of us knew them, when our parents would come to visit. Everyone would welcome parents, to whom they would give that casual and conceited tour through the Yard and the libraries. We would tell them about the greatest collection of books in the world, second only to the Library of Congress and the Bibliotheque. Or was it the third largest in the United States? No, Harvard's scale was the world. It had to be. And we would walk them past the Union and Lamont and point out how no girl could get into Lamont, except of course in the summer because it was one of the few air-conditioned places on campus and, anyway, the summer didn't count because Harvard Summer School would open its door to anyone. I mean, you know, it wasn't really Harvard because all those other kids could come and buy their little Harvard notebooks and green bookbags. It was just so obvious that every boy and girl in America wanted to go to Harvard and probably could have afforded it. And if they couldn't, Harvard would give them a scholarship. Right?

God it was great! I used to show my father the boundaries of Harvard. We would drive down Memorial Drive, the one on the Harvard side of the River, and I used to think how great it was that someday Harvard might own it all. All those little shacks and houses already falling down would all be shoved aside for the monster brain eating its way to Boston and Somerville. If only MIT wouldn't beat us to it. But they couldn't. How could they match our money and power and brains? It would all be ours; and during those drives I would just about believe that it would be mine, too. My father used to ask questions about relocation or dislocation, but those terms, I thought, had to do with the higher economic strategies involved, and no freshman or sophomore could be expected to deal with that. These were issues for my father's friends. It was adult talk.

I think what made school great then was that nothing happened in the world to disturb our Cambridge work and efforts. There were no wars, no problems in cities, no school difficulties. Castro was great. He came to speak once. There was Hungary, but Harvard, we all knew, would open its doors to those sad refugees. And Stevenson, but the country wasn't smart enough to accept him. The country with all those anti-intellectual feelings and envy of Harvard. It was proof of something good and special that he didn't win. It made us all the more special and elite and privileged, but still not like Yale where they had those insidious secret societies or, worse, Princeton where Jews couldn't get in and where colored boys waited on tables in the eating clubs. At least that's what we argued.

School, of course, was often a bit boring, but that's the way school was supposed to be. Relevant materials could be discussed at the dinner table, but the real intellectual stuff came in class. Anyway, it was all preparation for some later events and experiences, and boredom and aloneness were the price you paid for being the best, or, at least, for being in the best place.

Oh Dyke, dear classmate, can't you see how pitifully out of it we were? Can't you truly recall that whispering generation of ours, which actually believed that most anyone had a chance to "make Harvard," or that everyone had parents rich enough to take those immodest tours we doled out. Can't you for a moment taste again that male chauvinism, those feelings we had and the ideologies related to women? And the Jews and the Negroes and the poor? Did we not ignore their worlds or fail to question the condescending, hypocritical, and just generally ghastly way we treated them all? And they, not yet able to scream loud enough to be heard over the melodies of the band or Glee Club or just the sounds our cordovans made on the cobblestones. Do you remember them? Not the ones who came; the other ones. The ones in Roxbury where some of us would go occasionally to tutor a little black-faced boy or girl, and where we would go, too, on Saturday nights, frightened to death, looking for "black meat." Did you know of this? Do you recall the treatment of students from the Midwest and the equally absurd honor paid to sons of great men who lived in great houses? We were so out of it. So pitifully out of it and of everything else that mattered.

Can you for a moment recall what you felt about America then, with all that talk about communism? Did many of us really understand the shudder from the faculty which came from Senator McCarthy and surely was in the winds when we came in that deliciously beautiful September of 1955? Did we know of it, or know the meaning of HUAC and intimidation? Weren't we really spending quite a bit of time collecting lists of famous men of Harvard? Wasn't this really the pastime of many of us? Eliot, Roosevelt, Agee, Bernstein, Emerson. Weren't we hunting for names on the faculty, too, and wasn't there a magical belief that to be with them but for the minutes it takes to walk through the Yard out beyond the Cambridge Common on an icy February morning, would bring us success, accomplishment, dare I say fame? We followed after people then, believing always America to be so fine, not perfect of course, but fine. And we believed, too, that Harvard was just as fine, just as deserving of that casual "I couldn't care less" infatuation we had, and many of us probably still have. We loved it even through the crises when small problems arose that probably were our own faults anyway.

One could go on and on really, describing the utter differences between now and ten years ago, or if they aren't true differences, then the intense variations in historical continuity that make this present generation stand so uniquely apart from one half a generation ago. This probably is one of the most incomprehensible aspects of youth: how can such changes have come about so quickly? On the social level, the changes in fact weren't that sudden, for had we paid the slightest attention to our society, we would have seen it all, and cared for it more than we did. But we were the workers and whisperers, the products of a psychological age, the students who too often let the pleasures and privileges of college spray over us to the exclusion of most everything else. It's nothing short of ironic to look at the two Harvards, ours and theirs, and realize that with all "their" drugs and "turn-ons," our four years were truly what today's students would call an "ego trip." We were so self-satisfied and isolated, protected and removed, as gradually we worked our way to honors and degrees with but the slightest concern for that other world until we got there. How many of us really took that outside more seriously than the inside? It was almost as if the shock and blessed sheen of a Harvard acceptance didn't wear off in time to permit us to enter all the worlds which, in fact, Harvard would have helped us enter.

But no more. The days of self-interest aren't gone, of course, but there are rumblings and explosions now that make it evident that students not only have discovered and rediscovered the structure of society, they want change. They want change even if it means great cost to them. This is the difference. Their notion of care implies sacrifice. They're ambivalent about giving up some things, but they're honestly presenting themselves and their goals and asking us to judge and react. Many no longer play that game of "best behavior" for admissions officers and teachers. They're yanking and pulling the University into the world like never before. If they could, some would mount the whole place on a dolly and wheel it into Roxbury, Watts, Ocean Hill-Brownsville, Washington, and Hanoi.

Their strategies and tactics have been abhorred, vilified, repressed, encouraged, copied, but whatever the results, this is a socially conscious, politicized group of students, who will not abide by an anachronistic Harvard nor tolerate the very sense of privilege so many of us felt and worshipped. If it's a privilege, they say, then let all have a chance, let all have a go at it. Above all, they feel their plans and efforts have worth. I think that their sense of worth is identical to the sense I felt in the 1950's when I thought of my own life style, my own career, my own destiny.

The inevitable dilemma of the alumnus is that his very soul is trapped between two times, two histories. Only naturally does he hope that his donation or his presence at a reunion may either reunite two times, or blot one out so that only his special time remains. To recapture those four extraordinary years, or even just those clear September afternoons before the first registration and first classes, as well as the emerging adolescence that carried the weight of all those hours, would indeed be a lovely and bitter-sweet reward. But it is not to be, for when we turn about, we do not resume, we do not even retrace steps; we merely head our futures on a new course. So, the magic of donation and reunion gain their strength from the engagement they augur for the present, as clumsy and difficult as it seems. We cannot be temporal imperialists, suffocating today's children with the time of our childhoods. We don't really have to forfeit our adolescence and "college days," as smirkingly we used to call them, but we're going to have to let them sit there proudly but still, between high school and young adulthood. And we're going to have to support and teach, argue with, and respond to today's children and, even more, to today. "They" have the advantage, for it's their time and, shockingly, to a great extent, their turf.

I've been harsh, too extreme perhaps, but I speak to myself as much as to you. I, too, want one more peek at a privileged time.

When you come to visit Harvard—and each of us now in many respects is a visitor, our claim having lessened with time—speak with students. Speak with the ones, perhaps, who by their very appearance may trouble you most of all. They are quite something, and if I may don my own alumni vocabulary, you will be quite proud that they now trespass where once you did. How sad it is really that each of us privileged persons has but four swift years to make a kind of mark we cannot make again. Sadder still is the fact that millions of us cannot make any such mark at all.

This is the paradox we overlooked and that our students now have found. The following are excerpts from a letter from a Radcliffe graduating senior. Last year she wrote me she had chosen community work over receiving honors in her Department. She felt the former offered greater worth. This year soon after the strike, she wrote me again: "First, I abhor both sides for using the police as a universal punching bag in what amounts to an intra-class struggle. I did not approve of the tactics of taking the building. But I approved less of calling in the police. Still, the frustration with this society has reached a point of no return for many. (It strikes me at this level: we can find ample justification for spending ten billion dollars a year to murder the Vietnamese but we can't dig up two billion extra dollars to feed our own malnourished people!) This is my inheritance. This is the 'justice,' 'love,' and 'brotherhood' which I can claim a full adult right to. . . .

"How is a twenty-one-year-old woman supposed to be decent, humane, loving, committed, intelligent, while still absorbing the myths of 'justice,' 'love,' and 'brotherhood,' (not to mention 'academic freedom'). . . . Is poetry to be the solace, the escape, or the elitist corruption in my adulthood? Not that I expect you or anyone else to answer these questions. It will be agonizing enough looking for your own answers."

THOMAS J. COTTLE (1937–   ), *a member of Harvard's class of 1959, received the doctorate from the University of Chicago in 1968. He is now Assistant Professor of Social Relations at Harvard. This "open letter" will be included in a book Mr. Cottle is writing, tentatively titled* Hello Moon, Goodbye Childhood.

1. Cottle is "deeply angered" by the tone of Benjamin's letter. What is that tone? What is the comparison Benjamin draws

between the Harvard of 1959 and 1969? Which does he prefer
and why?

2. What is the tone of Cottle's first two paragraphs? The third
paragraph shifts to a different tone to describe his college years;
define this new tone, and show how the third paragraph serves
as a transition. How does Cottle convey the way he feels now
while describing the way it was? What does he mean by "God
it was great!"?

3. Cottle's anger at Benjamin is explicit and obvious. But three
paragraphs from the end, Cottle says, "I speak to myself as
much as to you." Who is the real audience for this open letter?
What attitude toward that audience has Cottle arrived at by the
end of his letter?

4. Compare Cottle's attitude toward Benjamin's letter with the
way he feels about the senior's letter that serves as a conclusion.
Why does he prefer the statement of "agonizing" problems to
what Benjamin offers? What other writers in this section have
rejected solutions in favor of problems?

Jonathan Swift

AN ARGUMENT AGAINST THE ABOLISHING
OF CHRISTIANITY

I am very sensible what a weakness and presumption it is, to reason against the general humor and disposition of the world. I remember it was with great justice, and a due regard to the freedom both of the public and the press, forbidden upon severe penalties to write, or discourse, or lay wagers against the Union, even before it was confirmed by parliament, because that was looked upon as a design, to oppose the current of the people, which, besides the folly of it, is a manifest breach of the fundamental law that makes this majority of opinion the voice of God. In like manner, and for the very same reasons, it may perhaps be neither safe nor prudent to argue against the abolishing of Christianity, at a juncture when all parties appear so unanimously determined upon the point, as we cannot but allow from their actions, their discourses, and their writings. However, I know not how, whether from the affection of singularity, or the perverseness of human nature, but so it unhappily falls out, that I cannot be entirely of this opinion. Nay, although I were sure an order were issued out for my immediate prosecution by the attorney-general, I should still confess that in the present posture of our affairs at home or abroad, I do not yet see the absolute necessity of extirpating the Christian religion from among us.

This perhaps may appear too great a paradox even for our wise and paradoxical age to endure; therefore I shall handle it with all tenderness, and with the utmost deference to that great and profound majority which is of another sentiment.

And yet the curious may please to observe how much the genius of a nation is liable to alter in half an age: I have heard it affirmed for certain by some very old people that the contrary opinion was even in their memories as much in vogue as the other is now; and that a project for the abolishing of Christianity would then have appeared as singular, and been thought as absurd, as it would be at this time to write or discourse in its defense.

From *An Argument to Prove That the Abolishing of Christianity in England May, as Things Now Stand, Be Attended with Some Inconveniences . . .* (1708).

Therefore I freely own that all appearances are against me. The system of the Gospel, after the fate of other systems, is generally antiquated and exploded; and the mass or body of the common people, among whom it seems to have had its latest credit, are now grown as much ashamed of it as their betters; opinions, like fashions, always descending from those of quality to the middle sort, and thence to the vulgar, where at length they are dropped and vanish.

But here I would not be mistaken, and must therefore be so bold as to borrow a distinction from the writers on the other side, when they make a difference between nominal and real Trinitarians. I hope no reader imagines me so weak to stand up in the defense of *real* Christianity, such as used in primitive times (if we may believe the authors of those ages) to have an influence upon men's belief and actions: to offer at the restoring of that would indeed be a wild project; it would be to dig up foundations; to destroy at one blow all the wit, and half the learning of the kingdom; to break the entire frame and constitution of things; to ruin trade, extinguish arts and sciences with the professors of them; in short, to turn our courts, exchanges, and shops into deserts; and would be full as absurd as the proposal of Horace, where he advises the Romans all in a body to leave their city and seek a new seat in some remote part of the world, by way of cure for the corruption of their manners.

Therefore, I think this caution was in itself altogether unnecessary (which I have inserted only to prevent all possibility of caviling), since every candid reader will easily understand my discourse to be intended only in defense of *nominal* Christianity, the other having been for some time wholly laid aside by general consent as utterly inconsistent with our present schemes of wealth and power.

But why we should therefore cast off the name and title of Christians, although the general opinion and resolution be so violent for it, I confess I cannot (with submission) apprehend the consequence necessary. However, since the undertakers propose such wonderful advantages to the nation by this project, and advance many plausible objections against the system of Christianity, I shall briefly consider the strength of both, fairly allow them their greatest weight, and offer such answers as I think most reasonable. After which I will beg leave to show what inconveniences may possibly happen by such an innovation, in the present posture of our affairs.

First, one great advantage proposed by the abolishing of Christianity is, that it would very much enlarge and establish liberty of conscience, that great bulwark of our nation, and of the protestant religion, which is still too much limited by priestcraft, notwithstanding all the good intentions of the legislature, as we have lately found by a severe instance. For it is confidently reported, that two young gentlemen of great hopes, bright wit, and profound judgment, who upon a thorough examination of causes and effects, and by the mere force of natural abilities, without the least tincture of learning, having made a discovery, that there was no God, and generously communicating their thoughts for the good of the public, were some time ago, by an unparalleled severity, and upon I know not what obsolete law, broke only for blasphemy. And as it hath been wisely observed, if persecution once begins, no man alive knows how far it may reach, or where it will end.

In answer to all which, with deference to wiser judgments, I think this rather shows the necessity of a nominal religion among us. Great wits love to be free with the highest objects: and if they cannot be allowed a God to revile or renounce, they will speak evil of dignities, abuse the government, and reflect upon the ministry; which I am sure few will deny to be of much more pernicious consequence, according to the saying of Tiberius, *Deorum offensa diis curae.** As to the particular fact related, I think it is not fair to argue from one instance, perhaps another cannot be produced; yet (to the comfort of all those who may be apprehensive of persecution) blasphemy we know is freely spoken a million of times in every coffee-house and tavern, or wherever else good company meet. It must be allowed indeed, that to break an English freeborn officer only for blasphemy, was, to speak the gentlest of such an action, a very high strain of absolute power. Little can be said in excuse for the general; perhaps he was afraid it might give offense to the allies, among whom, for aught I know, it may be the custom of the country to believe in a God. But if he argued, as some have done, upon a mistaken principle, that an officer who is guilty of speaking blasphemy, may some time or other proceed so far as to raise a mutiny, the consequence is by no means to be admitted; for, surely the commander of an English army is likely to be but ill obeyed, whose soldiers fear and reverence him as little as they do a Deity.

It is further objected against the gospel system, that it obliges men to the belief of things too difficult for free-thinkers, and such who have shaken off the prejudices that usually cling to a confined education. To which I answer, that men should be cautious, how they raise objections which reflect upon the wisdom of the nation. Is not everybody freely allowed to believe whatever he pleases, and to publish his belief to the world whenever he thinks fit, especially if it serves to strengthen the party which is in the right? Would

* An insult to the gods is the concern of the gods.

any indifferent foreigner, who should read the trumpery lately written by Asgil, Tindale, Toland, Coward, and forty more, imagine the Gospel to be our rule of faith, and confirmed by parliaments? Does any man either believe, or say he believes, or desire to have it thought that he says he believes one syllable of the matter? And is any man worse received upon that score, or does he find his want of nominal faith a disadvantage to him in the pursuit of any civil or military employment? What if there be an old dormant statute or two against him? Are they not now obsolete, to a degree that Empson and Dudley themselves if they were now alive, would find it impossible to put them in execution?

It is likewise urged that there are by computation in this kingdom above ten thousand parsons, whose revenues, added to those of my lords the bishops, would suffice to maintain at least two hundred young gentlemen of wit and pleasure, and free-thinking, enemies to priestcraft, narrow principles, pedantry, and prejudices; who might be an ornament to the Court and Town: And then, again, so great a number of able-bodied divines might be a recruit to our fleet and armies. This indeed appears to be a consideration of some weight: but then, on the other side, several things deserve to be considered likewise; as, first, whether it may not be thought necessary that in certain tracts of country, like what we call parishes, there shall be *one* man at least of abilities to read and write. Then it seems a wrong computation, that the revenues of the Church throughout this island would be large enough to maintain two hundred young gentlemen, or even half that number, after the present refined way of living; that is, to allow each of them such a rent, as in the modern form of speech, would make them *easy*. But still there is in this project a greater mischief behind; and we ought to beware of the woman's folly, who killed the hen that every morning laid her a golden egg. For, pray, what would become of the race of men in the next age, if we had nothing to trust to beside the scrofulous, consumptive productions, furnished by our men of wit and pleasure, when, having squandered away their vigor, health, and estate, they are forced by some disagreeable marriage to piece up their broken fortunes, and entail rottenness and politeness on their posterity? Now, here are ten thousand persons reduced by the wise regulations of Henry the Eighth, to the necessity of a low diet and moderate exercise, who are the only great restorers of our breed, without which the nation would in an age or two become one great hospital.

Another advantage proposed by the abolishing of Christianity is the clear gain of one day in seven, which is now entirely lost, and consequently the kingdom one seventh less considerable in trade, business, and pleasure; beside the loss to the public of so many stately structures now in the hands of the clergy, which might be converted into theatres, exchanges, market-houses, common dormitories, and other public edifices.

I hope I shall be forgiven a hard word, if I call this a perfect cavil. I readily own there hath been an old custom, time out of mind, for people to assemble in the churches every Sunday, and that shops are still frequently shut, in order, as it is conceived, to preserve the memory of that ancient practice; but how this can prove a hindrance to business or pleasure, is hard to imagine. What if the men of pleasure are forced, one day in the week, to game at home instead of the chocolate-house? Are not the taverns and coffee-houses open? Can there be a more convenient season for taking a dose of physick? Are fewer claps got upon Sundays than other days? Is not that the chief day for traders to sum up the accounts of the week, and for lawyers to prepare their briefs? But I would fain know how it can be pretended that the churches are misapplied. Where are more appointments and rendezvous of gallantry? Where more care to appear in the foremost box with greater advantage of dress? Where more meetings for business? Where more bargains driven of all sorts? And where so many conveniences or incitements to sleep?

There is one advantage greater than any of the foregoing, proposed by the abolishing of Christianity: that it will utterly extinguish parties among us, by removing those factious distinctions of High and Low Church, of Whig and Tory, Presbyterian and Church of England, which are now so many grievous clogs upon public proceedings, and are apt to prefer the gratifying themselves, or depressing their adversaries, before the most important interest of the state.

I confess, if it were certain that so great an advantage would redound to the nation by this expedient, I would submit and be silent: but will any man say, that if the words *whoring, drinking, cheating, lying, stealing,* were by act of parliament ejected out of the English tongue and dictionaries, we should all awake next morning chaste and temperate, honest and just, and lovers of truth? Is this a fair consequence? Or, if the physicians would forbid us to pronounce the words *pox, gout, rheumatism* and *stone,* would that expedient serve like so many talismans to destroy the diseases themselves? Are party and faction rooted in men's hearts no deeper than phrases borrowed from religion, or founded upon no firmer principles? And is our language so poor that we cannot find other terms to express them? Are *envy, pride, avarice,* and *ambition* such ill nomenclators, that they cannot furnish appellations for their owners? Will not *heydukes* and *mamalukes, mandarins* and *patshaws,* or any other words formed at pleasure, serve to distinguish those who are in the ministry from others who would be in it if they could? What, for instance, is easier than to vary the form of speech, and instead of the word *church*, make it a question in politics, whether the Monument be in danger? Because religion was nearest at hand to furnish a few convenient phrases, is our invention so barren we can find no others? Suppose, for argument sake, that the Tories favored Margarita, the Whigs Mrs. Tofts, and the Trimmers Valentini, would not *Margaritians*, *Toftians* and *Valentinians* be very tolerable marks of distinction? The *Prasini* and *Veneti*, two most virulent factions in Italy, began (if I remember right) by a distinction of colors in ribbons, which we might do with as good a grace about the dignity of the blue and the green, and would serve as properly to divide the Court, the Parliament, and the Kingdom between them, as any terms of art whatsoever borrowed from religion. And therefore I think there is little force in this objection against Christianity, or prospect of so great an advantage as is proposed in the abolishing of it.

It is again objected, as a very absurd ridiculous custom, that a set of men should be suffered, much less employed and hired, to bawl one day in seven against the lawfulness of those methods most in use toward the pursuit of greatness, riches and pleasure, which are the constant practice of all men alive on the other six. But this objection is, I think, a little unworthy so refined an age as ours. Let us argue this matter calmly. I appeal to the breast of any polite freethinker, whether in the pursuit of gratifying a predominant passion, he hath not always felt a wonderful incitement, by reflecting it was a thing forbidden: and therefore we see, in order to cultivate this taste, the wisdom of the nation hath taken special care that the ladies should be furnished with prohibited silks, and the men with prohibited wine. And indeed, it were to be wished that some other prohibitions were promoted, in order to improve the pleasures of the town; which, for want of such expedients, begin already, as I am told, to flag and grow languid, giving way daily to cruel inroads from the spleen.

It is likewise proposed as a great advantage to the public, that if we once discard the system of the Gospel, all religion will of course be banished for ever; and consequently, along with it, those grievous prejudices of education, which under the names of *virtue, conscience, honor, justice,* and the like, are so apt to disturb the peace of human minds, and the notions whereof are so hard to be eradicated by right reason or freethinking, sometimes during the whole course of our lives. Here first I observe how difficult it is to get rid of a phrase which the world is once grown fond of, although the occasion that first produced it be entirely taken away. For several years past, if a man had but an ill-favored nose, the deep-thinkers of the age would some way or other contrive to impute the cause to the prejudice of his education. From this fountain were said to be derived all our foolish notions of justice, piety, love of our country, all our opinions of God, or a future state, Heaven, Hell, and the like; and there might formerly perhaps have been some pretense for this charge. But so effectual care hath been since taken to remove those prejudices, by an entire change in the methods of education, that (with honor I mention it to our polite innovators) the young gentlemen who are now on the scene, seem to have not the least tincture left of those infusions, or string of those weeds; and, by consequence, the reason for abolishing nominal Christianity upon that pretext, is wholly ceased.

For the rest, it may perhaps admit a controversy, whether the banishing of all notions of religion whatsoever, would be convenient for the vulgar. Not that I am in the least of opinion with those who hold religion to have been the invention of politicians, to keep the lower part of the world in awe by the fear of invisible powers; unless mankind were then very different from what it is now: For I look upon the mass or body of our people here in England to be as freethinkers, that is to say, as staunch unbelievers, as any of the highest rank. But I conceive some scattered notions about a superior power to be of singular use for the common people, as furnishing excellent materials to keep children quiet when they grow peevish, and providing topics of amusement in a tedious winter night.

Lastly, it is proposed as a singular advantage, that the abolishing of Christianity will very much contribute to the uniting of Protestants, by enlarging the terms of communion so as to take in all sorts of dissenters, who are now shut out of the pale upon account of a few ceremonies which all sides confess to be things indifferent: that this alone will effectually answer the great ends of a scheme for comprehension, by opening a large noble gate, at which all bodies may enter; whereas the chaffering with dissenters, and dodging about this or the other ceremony, is but like opening a few wickets, and leaving them at jar, by which no more than one can get in at a time, and that, not without stooping, and sideling, and squeezing his body.

To all this I answer that there is one darling inclination of mankind, which usually affects to be a retainer to religion, although she be neither its parent, its godmother, or its friend; I mean the spirit of opposition, that lived long before Christianity, and can easily subsist without it. Let us, for instance, examine wherein the opposition of sectaries among us consists; we shall find Christianity to have no share in it at all. Does the Gospel anywhere prescribe a starched, squeezed countenance, a stiff, formal gait, a singularity of manners and habit, or any affected modes of speech different

from the reasonable part of mankind? Yet, if Christianity did lend
its name to stand in the gap, and to employ or divert these humors,
they must of necessity be spent in contraventions to the laws of the
land, and disturbance of the public peace. There is a portion of enthusiasm assigned to every nation, which, if it hath not proper objects to work on, will burst out, and set all into a flame. If the quiet
of a state can be bought by only flinging men a few ceremonies to
devour, it is a purchase no wise man would refuse. Let the mastiffs
amuse themselves about a sheep-skin stuffed with hay, provided it
will keep them from worrying the flock. The institution of convents
abroad seems in one point a strain of great wisdom, there being few
irregularities in human passions, which may not have recourse
to vent themselves in some of those orders, which are so many re-
treats for the speculative, the melancholy, the proud, the silent, the
politic and the morose, to spend themselves, and evaporate the
noxious particles; for each of whom we in this island are forced to
provide a several sect of religion, to keep them quiet: and whenever Christianity shall be abolished, the legislature must find some
other expedient to employ and entertain them. For what imports it
how large a gate you open, if there will be always left a number who
place a pride and a merit in refusing to enter?

Having thus considered the most important objections against
Christianity and the chief advantages proposed by the abolishing
thereof, I shall now with equal deference and submission to wiser
judgments as before, proceed to mention a few inconveniences that
may happen, if the Gospel should be repealed; which perhaps the
projectors may not have sufficiently considered.

And first, I am very sensible how much the gentlemen of wit
and pleasure are apt to murmur, and be choked at the sight of so
many draggled-tail parsons, that happen to fall in their way, and
offend their eyes; but at the same time, these wise reformers do not
consider what an advantage and felicity it is, for great wits to be always provided with objects of scorn and contempt, in order to exercise and improve their talents, and divert their spleen from falling
on each other or on themselves; especially when all this may be done
without the least imaginable danger to their persons.

And to urge another argument of a parallel nature: if Christianity were once abolished, how could the freethinkers, the strong
reasoners, and the men of profound learning, be able to find another subject so calculated in all points whereon to display their
abilities? What wonderful productions of wit should we be deprived of, from those whose genius by continual practice hath been
wholly turned upon raillery and invectives against religion, and
would therefore never be able to shine or distinguish themselves
upon any other subject! We are daily complaining of the great de-

cline of wit among us, and would we take away the greatest, perhaps the only, topic we have left? Who would ever have suspected Asgill for a wit, or Toland for a philosopher, if the inexhaustible stock of Christianity had not been at hand to provide them with materials? What other subject, through all art or nature, could have produced Tindal for a profound author, or furnished him with readers? It is the wise choice of the subject that alone adorns and distinguishes the writer. For, had a hundred such pens as these been employed on the side of religion, they would have immediately sunk into silence and oblivion.

Nor do I think it wholly groundless, or my fears altogether imaginary, that the abolishing of Christianity may perhaps bring the Church into danger, or at least put the senate to the trouble of another securing vote. I desire I may not be mistaken: I am far from presuming to affirm or think that the Church is in danger at present, or as things now stand; but we know not how soon it may be so when the Christian religion is repealed. As plausible as this project seems, there may a dangerous design lurk under it: Nothing can be more notorious, than that the Atheists, Deists, Socinians, Antitrinitarians, and other subdivisions of freethinkers, are persons of little zeal for the present ecclesiastical establishment: Their declared opinion is for repealing the Sacramental Test: they are very indifferent with regard to ceremonies; nor do they hold the *jus divinum* of Episcopacy. Therefore this may be intended as one politic step toward altering the constitution of the Church Established, and setting up Presbytery in the stead, which I leave to be further considered by those at the helm.

In the last place, I think nothing can be more plain, than that by this expedient, we shall run into the evil we chiefly pretend to avoid; and that the abolishment of the Christian religion will be the readiest course we can take to introduce popery. And I am the more inclined to this opinion, because we know it has been the constant practice of the Jesuits to send over emissaries with instructions to personate themselves members of the several prevailing sects among us. So it is recorded, that they have at sundry times appeared in the guise of Presbyterians, Anabaptists, Independents and Quakers, according as any of these were most in credit; so, since the fashion hath been taken up of exploding religion, the popish missionaries have not been wanting to mix with the freethinkers; among whom, Toland the great oracle of the Antichristians is an Irish priest, the son of an Irish priest; and the most learned and ingenious author of a book called "The *Rights* of the Christian Church," was in a proper juncture reconciled to the Romish faith, whose true son, as appears by a hundred passages in his treatise, he still continues. Perhaps I could add some others to the number;

but the fact is beyond dispute, and the reasoning they proceed by is right: for, supposing Christianity to be extinguished, the people will never be at ease till they find out some other method of worship; which will as infallibly produce superstition, as this will end in popery.

And therefore, if notwithstanding all I have said, it shall still be thought necessary to have a bill brought in for repealing Christianity, I would humbly offer an amendment; that instead of the word, Christianity, may be put religion in general; which I conceive will much better answer all the good ends proposed by the projectors of it. For, as long as we leave in being a God and his providence, with all the necessary consequences which curious and inquisitive men will be apt to draw from such premises, we do not strike at the root of the evil, although we should ever so effectually annihilate the present scheme of the Gospel: for of what use is freedom of thought, if it will not produce freedom of action, which is the sole end, how remote soever in appearance, of all objections against Christianity? And, therefore, the freethinkers consider it as a sort of edifice, wherein all the parts have such a mutual dependence on each other, that if you happen to pull out one single nail, the whole fabric must fall to the ground. This was happily expressed by him who had heard of a text brought for proof of the Trinity, which in an ancient manuscript was differently read; he thereupon immediately took the hint, and by a sudden deduction of a long *sorites*, most logically concluded, "Why, if it be as you say, I may safely whore and drink on, and defy the parson." From which, and many the like instances easy to be produced, I think nothing can be more manifest than that the quarrel is not against any particular points of hard digestion in the Christian system, but against religion in general; which, by laying restraints on human nature, is supposed the great enemy to the freedom of thought and action.

Upon the whole, if it shall still be thought for the benefit of Church and State, that Christianity be abolished, I conceive, however, it may be more convenient to defer the execution to a time of peace, and not venture in this conjuncture to disoblige our allies, who, as it falls out, are all Christians, and many of them, by the prejudices of their education, so bigoted, as to place a sort of pride in the appellation. If upon being rejected by them, we are to trust an alliance with the Turk, we shall find ourselves much deceived: for, as he is too remote, and generally engaged in war with the Persian emperor, so his people would be more scandalized at our infidelity, than our Christian neighbors. Because, the Turks are not only strict observers of religious worship, but what is worse, believe a God; which is more than is required of us even while we preserve the name of Christians.

To conclude: Whatever some may think of the great advantages to trade by this favorite scheme, I do very much apprehend, that in six months time after the act is passed for the extirpation of the Gospel, the Bank, and East-India Stock, may fall at least one *per cent*. And since that is fifty times more than ever the wisdom of our age thought fit to venture for the preservation of Christianity, there is no reason we should be at so great a loss, merely for the sake of destroying it.

———

JONATHAN SWIFT (1667–1745) *is best known as author of the bitterly comic satire* Gulliver's Travels (1726). *As dean of the cathedral of St. Patrick in Dublin, he felt keenly the miserable condition of the Irish poor and the hyprocrisy of the establishment in England that permitted and encouraged such misery. Although he wrote much poetry, and non-satirical prose, his fierce command over prose satire was the principal weapon he used to fight the institutional hypocrisy he hated. "I have ever hated all nations, professions, and communities, and all my love is toward individuals," he wrote Alexander Pope. "I hate and detest that animal called man, although I heartily love John, Peter, Thomas, and so forth." Frequently, as in "An Argument Against Abolishing Christianity" (1708), Swift chose a persona, a supposed author, whose invented personality expresses reasonable ideas which we are asked to reject; Swift manipulates our attitudes towards the persona and his arguments with great care so that we can perceive the real argument being made by the real author.*

1. *Swift is pretending that an act of Parliament to abolish Christianity is about to be passed, to great public acclaim. He then invents a speaker, who presents the argument against the act. Put aside, for the moment, the real argument Swift is making, and describe this speaker. What kind of language does he use? What kinds of arguments does he present, and on what premises are they based? What is important to him? Why has Swift chosen such a voice to present his ideas?*
2. *How do you discover that Swift is making a wholly different argument than his speaker? Analyze several sentences to show how Swift's voice and ideas become clear, even though the speaker is portrayed as someone wholly indifferent to Swift's*

concept of Christianity and sense of values.

3. *The speaker lists objections to Christianity. How valid are these objections? "The gospel system . . . obliges men to the belief of things too difficult for free thinkers," says the speaker. In the second century* A.D., *Tertullian's answer to this problem was, "I believe because it is absurd." What is the speaker's response in Swift's essay? What is the real object of Swift's satire here?*

4. *Describe the two sets of values that come into conflict in this satire. What are the advantages for a writer in using satire and irony, instead of straightforward analysis? What are the problems?*

N. O. Brown

APOCALYPSE: THE PLACE OF MYSTERY IN
THE LIFE OF THE MIND

        I didn't know whether I should appear be-
fore you—there is a time to show and a time to hide; there is a time
to speak, and also a time to be silent. What time is it? It is fifteen
years since H. G. Wells said Mind was at the End of its Tether—
with a frightful queerness come into life: there is no way out or
around or through, he said; it is the end. It is because I think mind
is at the end of its tether that I would be silent. It is because I
think there is a way out—a way down and out—the title of Mr.
John Senior's new book on the occult tradition in literature—that
I will speak.

Mind at the end of its tether: I can guess what some of you are
thinking—*his* mind is at the end of its tether—and this could be;
it scares me but it deters me not. The alternative to mind is certainly madness. Our greatest blessings, says Socrates in the *Phae-
drus*, come to us by way of madness—provided, he adds, that the
madness comes from the god. Our real choice is between holy and
unholy madness: open your eyes and look around you—madness is
in the saddle anyhow. Freud is the measure of our unholy madness,
as Nietzsche is the prophet of the holy madness, of Dionysus, the
mad truth. Dionysus has returned to his native Thebes; mind—at
the end of its tether—is another Pentheus, up a tree. Resisting
madness can be the maddest way of being mad.

And there is a way out—the blessed madness of the maenad and
the bacchant: "Blessed is he who has the good fortune to know the
mysteries of the gods, who sanctifies his life and initiates his soul,
a bacchant on the mountains, in holy purifications." It is possible to
be mad and to be unblest; but it is not possible to get the blessing
without the madness; it is not possible to get the illuminations
without the derangement. Derangement is disorder: the Dionysian
faith is that order as we have known it is crippling, and for cripples;
that what is past is prologue; that we can throw away our crutches

Reprinted from the May, 1961 issue of *Harper's Magazine* by permission of the
author. Copyright © 1961, by Harper's Magazine, Inc.

and discover the supernatural power of walking; that human history goes from man to superman.

No superman I; I come to you not as one who has supernatural powers, but as one who seeks for them, and who has some notions which way to go to find them.

Sometimes—most times—I think that the way down and out leads out of the university, out of the academy. But perhaps it is rather that we should recover the academy of earlier days—the Academy of Plato in Athens, the Academy of Ficino in Florence, Ficino who says, "The spirit of the god Dionysus was believed by the ancient theologians and Platonists to be the ecstasy and abandon of disencumbered minds, when partly by innate love, partly at the instigation of the god, they transgress the natural limits of intelligence and are miraculously transformed into the beloved god himself: where, inebriated by a certain new draft of nectar and by an immeasurable joy, they rage, as it were, in a bacchic frenzy. In the drunkenness of this Dionysian wine, our Dionysius (the Areopagite) expresses his exultation. He pours forth enigmas, he sings in dithyrambs. To penetrate the profundity of his meanings, to imitate his quasi-Orphic manner of speech, we too require the divine fury."

At any rate the point is first of all to find again the mysteries. By which I do not mean simply the sense of wonder—that sense of wonder which is indeed the source of all true philosophy—by mystery I mean secret and occult; therefore unpublishable; therefore outside the university as we know it; but not outside Plato's Academy, or Ficino's.

Why are mysteries unpublishable? First because they cannot be put into words, at least not the kind of words which earned you your Phi Beta Kappa keys. Mysteries display themselves in words only if they can remain concealed; this is poetry, isn't it? We must return to the old doctrine of the Platonists and Neo-Platonists, that poetry is veiled truth; as Dionysus is the god who is both manifest and hidden; and as John Donne declared, with the Pillar of Fire goes the Pillar of Cloud. This is also the new doctrine of Ezra Pound, who says: "Prose is not education but the outer courts of the same. Beyond its doors are the mysteries. Eleusis. Things not to be spoken of save in secret. The mysteries self-defended, the mysteries that cannot be revealed. Fools can only profane them. The dull can neither penetrate the secretum nor divulge it to others." The mystic academies, whether Plato's or Ficino's, knew the limitations of words and drove us on beyond them, to go over, to go under, to the learned ignorance, in which God is better honored and loved by silence than by words, and better seen by closing the eyes to images than by opening them.

And second, mysteries are unpublishable because only some can see them, not all. Mysteries are intrinsically esoteric, and as such an offense to democracy: is not publicity a democratic principle? Publication makes it republican—a thing of the people. The pristine academies were esoteric and aristocratic, self-consciously separate from the profane vulgar. Democratic resentment denies that there can be anything that can't be seen by everybody; in the democratic academy truth is subject to public verification; truth is what any fool can see. This is what is meant by the so-called scientific method: so-called science is the attempt to democratize knowledge —the attempt to substitute method for insight, mediocrity for genius, by getting a standard operating procedure. The great equalizers dispensed by the scientific method are the tools, those analytical tools. The miracle of genius is replaced by the standardized mechanism. But fools with tools are still fools, and don't let your Phi Beta Kappa key fool you. Tibetan prayer wheels are another way of arriving at the same result: the degeneration of mysticism into mechanism—so that any fool can do it. Perhaps the advantage is with Tibet: for there the mechanism is external while the mind is left vacant; and vacancy is not the worst condition of the mind. And the resultant prayers make no futile claim to originality or immortality; being nonexistent, they do not have to be catalogued or stored.

The sociologist Simmel sees showing and hiding, secrecy and publicity, as two poles, like Yin and Yang, between which societies oscillate in their historical development. I sometimes think I see that civilizations originate in the disclosure of some mystery, some secret; and expand with the progressive publication of their secret; and end in exhaustion when there is no longer any secret, when the mystery has been divulged, that is to say profaned. The whole story is illustrated in the difference between ideogram and alphabet. The alphabet is indeed a democratic triumph; and the enigmatic ideogram, as Ezra Pound has taught us, is a piece of mystery, a piece of poetry, not yet profaned. And so there comes a time—I believe we are in such a time—when civilization has to be renewed by the discovery of new mysteries, by the undemocratic but sovereign power of the imagination, by the undemocratic power which makes poets the unacknowledged legislators of mankind, the power which makes all things new.

The power which makes all things new is magic. What our time needs is mystery: what our time needs is magic. Who would not say that only a miracle can save us? In Tibet the degree-granting institution is, or used to be, the College of Magic Ritual. It offers courses in such fields as clairvoyance and telepathy; also (attention physics majors) internal heat: internal heat is a yoga bestowing supernatural control over body temperature. Let me succumb for a moment to the fascination of the mysterious East and tell you of the examination procedure for the course in internal heat. Candidates assemble naked, in midwinter, at night, on a frozen Himalayan lake. Beside each one is placed a pile of wet frozen undershirts; the assignment is to wear, until they are dry, as many as possible of these undershirts before dawn. Where the power is real, the test is real, and the grading system dumfoundingly objective. I say no more. I say no more; Eastern Yoga does indeed demonstrate the existence of supernatural powers, but it does not have the particular power our Western society needs; or rather I think that each society has access only to its own proper powers; or rather each society will only get the kind of power it knows how to ask for.

The Western consciousness has always asked for freedom: the human mind was born free, or at any rate born to be free, but everywhere it is in chains; and now at the end of its tether. It will take a miracle to free the human mind: because the chains are magical in the first place. We are in bondage to authority outside ourselves: most obviously—here in a great university it must be said—in bondage to the authority of books. There is a Transcendentalist anticipation of what I want to say in Emerson's Phi Beta Kappa address on the American Scholar:

"The books of an older period will not fit this. Yet hence arises a grave mischief. The sacredness which attaches to the act of creation, the act of thought, is transferred to the record. Instantly the book becomes noxious: the guide is a tyrant. The sluggish and perverted mind of the multitude having once received this book, stands upon it, and makes an outcry if it is destroyed. Colleges are built on it. Meek young men grow up in libraries. Hence, instead of Man Thinking, we have the bookworm. I had better never see a book than to be warped by its attraction clean out of my own orbit, and make a satellite instead of a system. The one thing in the world, of value, is the active soul."

How far this university is from that ideal is the measure of the defeat of our American dream.

This bondage to books compels us not to see with our own eyes; compels us to see with the eyes of the dead, with dead eyes. Whitman, likewise in a Transcendentalist sermon, says, "You shall no longer take things at second or third hand, nor look through the eyes of the dead, nor feed on the specters in books." There is a hex on us, the specters in books, the authority of the past; and to exorcise these ghosts is the great work of magical self-liberation. Then the eyes of the spirit would become one with the eyes of the body, and god would be in us, not outside. God in us: *entheos*: enthusiasm; this is the essence of the holy madness. In the fire of the holy madness even books lose their gravity, and let themselves go up into the flame: "Properly," says Ezra Pound, "we should read for power. Man reading should be man intensely alive. The book should be a ball of light in one's hand."

I began with the name of Dionysus; let me be permitted to end with the name of Christ: for the power I seek is also Christian. Nietzsche indeed said the whole question was Dionysus versus Christ; but only the fool will take these as mutually exclusive opposites. There is a Dionysian Christianity, an apocalyptic Christianity, a Christianity of miracles and revelations. And there always have been some Christians for whom the age of miracle and revelation is not over; Christians who claim the spirit; enthusiasts. The power I look for is the power of enthusiasm; as condemned by John Locke; as possessed by George Fox, the Quaker; through whom the houses were shaken; who saw the channel of blood running down the streets of the city of Litchfield; to whom, as a matter of fact, was even given the magic internal heat—"The fire of the Lord was so in my feet, and all around me, that I did not matter to put on my shoes any more."

Read again the controversies of the seventeenth century and discover our choice: we are either in an age of miracles, says Hobbes, miracles which authenticate fresh revelations; or else we are in an age of reasoning from already received Scripture. Either miracle or Scripture. George Fox, who came up in spirit through the flaming sword into the paradise of God, so that all things were new, he being renewed to the state of Adam which he was in before he fell, sees that none can read Moses aright without Moses' spirit; none can read John's words aright, and with a true understanding of them, but in and with the same divine spirit by which John spake them, and by his burning shining light which is sent from God. Thus the authority of the past is swallowed up in new creation; the word is made flesh. We see with our own eyes and to see with our own eyes is second sight. To see with our own eyes is second sight.

> Twofold Always. May God us keep
> From single vision and Newton's sleep.

NORMAN O. BROWN (1913–   ) *is best known as the author of* Life Against Death *(1959) and* Love's Body *(1966). He has taught at Nebraska Wesleyan, Wesleyan University, the University of Rochester, and, now, the University of California, Santa Cruz.*

Since 1950, he has devoted himself to the psychoanalytical study of history, and he has become a profound critic of what he calls "the Western traditions of morality and rationality." In a prefatory note to Love's Body, Brown says "Apocalypse: The Place of Mystery in the Life of the Mind" records "a shaking of the foundations; and faintly foreshadows, like false dawn, the end."

1. This address was delivered before the Phi Beta Kappa chapter of Columbia University in 1960. How would you describe Brown's attitude toward his audience of elite faculty and honor students? For example, discuss the apparently humble first sentence, with its Biblical echoes followed by "What time is it?"; the attack on the scientific method and "fools with tools are still fools, and don't let your Phi Beta Kappa key fool you." Why does Brown choose to establish such a relationship with his audience? What role has he chosen for himself?

2. After defining the necessary mysteries as unpublishable, and condemning "bondage to books," Brown opens his last paragraph with an imperative: "Read again the controversies of the seventeenth century and discover our choice." Is Brown inconsistent, or is there a connection between these attitudes toward the printed word? How does his attitude toward books relate to his attitude toward the audience?

3. What is the relation between this mystical analysis of the university and Jules Henry's sociological analysis of the schools? Is there a similarity between what they find to be missing?

4. Here, Brown speaks of the university in the language of a religious prophet. In the previous essay, Swift spoke of religion in the language of a blunt man of business. How does this kind of tonal decision help a writer bring outside values to bear upon an institution? Is there a connection between religious and educational institutions; between the attacks of Brown and Swift on these institutions?

Part Three CONTROLLING

MEANING: LARGE SMALL EXPERIENCES

We sometimes feel that only wonderful and unusual experiences can be of interest to others; in truth, however, our lives are interesting or humdrum not because of the extraordinary things that do or do not happen, but because of the way we see and respond to the ordinary things that happen all of the time.

But to discover and convey the meaning in small events requires writing skill that does not come easily. An ordinary incident must be conveyed without exaggeration, and the fullness of its meaning must be made clear without forcing or absurdity. For this to happen, the relationship to the reader—the tone of the writing—needs to be defined and controlled with care, so the reader responds to event and analysis without finding the event trivial and the analysis irresponsible. The reader is always, legitimately, asking why he should spend his time reading an essay; when the essay is about an admittedly ordinary personal experience, this question becomes the most important one the writer must handle. To write about an undeserved spanking, as Mary McCarthy does; or a spanking deserved but not received, as Edmund Gosse does; or a minor incident in Burma; or a baseball game; or a closed carnival, is to face directly the challenge of tone: how can the writer so relate to the reader that he will follow clearly, be interested in, and respect what the writer has to say?

To be aware of this problem is itself a kind of solution to it. No single answer can apply to all subjects, as the selections in this section make amply clear. But to ask why a reader should want to read about a small event is to ask the central question about the essay or any essay: a writer must have something to say to someone before an essay can exist at all. Thus Edmund Gosse has something to say about the way a child discovers his own identity, Mary

McCarthy *urges us to think about tyranny and the psychology of concentration camps, John Updike asks us to understand our attitudes toward heroes, and so on.*

Writing about apparently ordinary events asks the writer and reader to work together to see the meaning beneath the surface of the usual, and it asks the writer to attend specifically to the problem of ordering and controlling meaning in his prose. With a subject matter not in itself of obvious importance you are forced to attend carefully to the demands of relevance and coherence. A writer alert to the need of his reader to follow an argument or an idea will not wander off to irrelevant topics, or fail to connect his ideas clearly.

One way to notice the different ways the writers of the selections here control their meaning is to contrast their tones. Notice the extraordinary difference between the ways Edmund Gosse and Mary McCarthy see their childhood:

> *But of all the thoughts which rushed upon my savage and undeveloped little brain at this crisis, the most curious was that I had found a companion and a confidant in myself.*
> —GOSSE

> *If we had been clever, we would have refused this bait and paraded our misery, but we were too simple to do anything but seize the moment and play out a whole year's playtime in this gala hour and a half. Such techniques, of course, are common in concentration camps and penal institutions, where the same sound calculation of human nature is made.*
> —MCCARTHY

When Gosse looks back at himself, he almost seems embarrassed, apologetic. Writing before Freud taught us to take childhood seriously, he sees himself as barely human ("my savage and undeveloped little brain"), and hardly worth the attention of a serious adult. Nonetheless, somehow this savage child was in the process of becoming a proper and educated citizen, and doing so by making discoveries about himself and his parents. Thus, Gosse is caught in an unresolvable dilemma: while unable to use grown-up language to describe his young life, he is fascinated by, and asks the reader to be interested in, a growth process he instinctively feels to be of real importance: "We attribute, I believe, too many moral ideas to little children. It is obvious that in this tremendous juncture, I ought to have been urged forward by good instincts, or held back by naughty ones." The overstatement of "tremendous," the patronization of "naughty," the resistance to investigate too deeply the obviously hostile motivation of the boy's destructiveness, all show Gosse blocked by his Victorian attitudes from seeing too clearly his own childhood. And yet the events he describes show the child's instinctive life with a force that commands our attention. In rebellion against his father and a repressive society, demonstrated in part by Gosse's own language, the boy in fact does become human.

Mary McCarthy has no trouble at all taking her childhood seriously. The childhood simplicity she describes is neither that of a savage nor of an undeveloped human; she was, if anything, too fully human, not sufficiently "clever" to scheme in ways that came naturally to her Uncle Myers. She asks us to feel sympathy for the children, playing in a frenzy to compensate for their deprivation, and to see their condition with a sadness close to that we bring to sufferers in concentration camps. The children, far from savage, fully express "human nature," and what they suffer helps us understand the psychology of tyranny, the consent of the tyrannized, as a human phenomenon. Just as Edmund Gosse expresses in his choice of words a society unable to relate to children effectively, Mary McCarthy's language embodies a world helpless before outrage. In both cases we are asked to see how the human spirit can survive and perhaps even profit from severely restrictive conditions; the essays are important because the survival of an individual represents the endurance of values we are asked to treasure and honor. And in both cases we can observe how writers sensitive to tone gain a kind of control over their past by writing about this past in such a way as to inquire what it meant to them and what it can mean to a reader.

Edmund Gosse

FATHER AND SON

In the course of this, my sixth year, there happened a series of minute and soundless incidents which, elementary as they may seem when told, were second in real importance to none in my mental history. The recollection of them confirms me in the opinion that certain leading features in each human soul are inherent to it, and cannot be accounted for by suggestion or training. In my own case, I was most carefully withdrawn, like Princess Blanchefleur in her marble fortress, from every outside influence whatever, yet to me the instinctive life came as unexpectedly as her lover came to her in the basket of roses. What came to me was the consciousness of self, as a force and as a companion, and it came as the result of one or two shocks, which I will relate.

In consequence of hearing so much about an Omniscient God, a being of supernatural wisdom and penetration who was always with us, who made, in fact, a fourth in our company, I had come to think of Him, not without awe, but with absolute confidence. My Father and Mother, in their serene discipline of me, never argued with one another, never even differed; their wills seemed absolutely one. My Mother always deferred to my Father, and in his absence spoke of him to me, as if he were all-wise. I confused him in some sense with God; at all events I believed that my Father knew everything and saw everything. One morning in my sixth year, my Mother and I were alone in the morning-room, when my Father came in and announced some fact to us. I was standing on the rug, gazing at him, and when he made this statement, I remember turning quickly, in embarrassment, and looking into the fire. The shock to me was as that of a thunderbolt, for what my Father had said "was not true." My Mother and I, who had been present at the trifling incident, were aware that it had not happened exactly as it had been reported to him. My Mother gently told him so, and he accepted the correction. Nothing could possibly have been more trifling to my parents, but to me it meant an epoch. Here was the appalling discovery, never suspected before, that my Father was not as God, and did not know everything. The shock was not caused by any suspicion that he was not telling the truth, as it appeared to him, but by the awful proof that he was not, as I had supposed, omniscient.

This experience was followed by another, which confirmed the first, but carried me a great deal further. In our little back-garden, my Father had built up a rockery for ferns and mosses, and from the water-supply of the house he had drawn a leaden pipe so that it pierced upwards through the rockery and produced, when a tap was turned, a pretty silvery parasol of water. The pipe was exposed somewhere near the foot of the rockery. One day, two workmen, who were doing some repairs, left their tools during the dinner-hour in the back-garden, and as I was marching about I suddenly thought that to see whether one of these tools could make a hole in the pipe would be attractive. It did make such a hole, quite easily, and then the matter escaped my mind. But a day or two afterwards, when my Father came in to dinner, he was very angry. He had turned the tap, and instead of the fountain arching at the summit, there had been a rush of water through a hole at the foot. The rockery was absolutely ruined.

Of course I realised in a moment what I had done, and I sat frozen with alarm, waiting to be denounced. But my Mother remarked on the visit of the plumbers two or three days before, and my Father instantly took up the suggestion. No doubt that was it; the mischievous fellows had thought it amusing to stab the pipe and spoil the fountain. No suspicion fell on me; no question was asked of me. I sat there, turned to stone within, but outwardly sympathetic and with unchecked appetite.

We attribute, I believe, too many moral ideas to little children. It is obvious that in this tremendous juncture, I ought to have been urged forward by good instincts, or held back by naughty ones. But I am sure that the fear which I experienced for a short time, and which so unexpectedly melted away, was a purely physical one. It had nothing to do with the motions of a contrite heart. As to the destruction of the fountain, I was sorry about that, for my own sake, since I admired the skipping water extremely, and had had no idea that I was spoiling its display. But the emotions which now thronged within me, and which led me, with an almost unwise alacrity, to seek solitude in the back-garden, were not moral at all, they were intellectual. I was not ashamed of having successfully—and so surprisingly—deceived my parents by my crafty silence; I looked upon that as a providential escape, and dismissed all further thought of it. I had other things to think of.

In the first place, the theory that my Father was omniscient or infallible was now dead and buried. He probably knew very little; in this case he had not known a fact of such importance that if you did not know that, it could hardly matter what you knew. My Father, as a deity, as a natural force of immense prestige, fell in my eyes to a human level. In future, his statements about things in general need not be accepted implicitly. But of all the thoughts which rushed upon my savage and undeveloped little brain at this crisis, the most curious was that I had found a companion and a confidant in myself. There was a secret in this world and it belonged to me and to a somebody who lived in the same body with me. There were two of us, and we could talk with one another. It is difficult to define impressions so rudimentary, but it is certain that it was in this dual form that the sense of my individuality now suddenly descended upon me, and it is equally certain that it was a great solace to me to find a sympathiser in my own breast.

My public baptism was the central event of my whole childhood. Everything, since the earliest dawn of consciousness, seemed to have been leading up to it. Everything, afterwards, seemed to be leading down and away from it. The practice of immersing communicants on the sea-beach at Oddicombe had now been completely abandoned, but we possessed as yet no tank for a baptismal purpose in our own Room. The Room in the adjoining town, however, was really quite a large chapel, and it was amply provided with the needful conveniences. It was our practice, therefore, at this time, to claim the hospitality of our neighbours. Baptisms were made an occasion for friendly relations between the two congregations, and led to pleasant social intercourse. I believe that the ministers and elders of the two meetings arranged to combine their forces at these times, and to baptize communicants from both congregations.

The minister of the town meeting was Mr. S., a very handsome old gentleman, of venerable and powerful appearance. He had snowy hair and a long white beard, but from under shaggy eyebrows there blazed out great black eyes which warned the beholder that the snow was an ornament and not a sign of decrepitude. The eve of my baptism at length drew near; it was fixed for October 12, almost exactly three weeks after my tenth birthday. I was dressed in old clothes, and a suit of smarter things was packed up in a carpet-bag. After night-fall, this carpet-bag, accompanied by my Father, myself, Miss Marks and Mary Grace, was put in a four-wheeled cab, and driven, a long way in the dark, to the chapel of our friends. There we were received, in a blaze of lights, with a pressure of hands, with a murmur of voices, with ejaculations and even with tears, and were conducted, amid unspeakable emotion, to places of honour in the front row of the congregation.

The scene was one which would have been impressive, not merely to such hermits as we were, but even to worldly persons accustomed to life and to its curious and variegated experiences. To me it was dazzling beyond words, inexpressibly exciting, an initiation to every kind of publicity and glory. There were many candidates, but the rest of them,—mere grown-up men and women,— gave thanks aloud that it was their privilege to follow where I led. I was the acknowledged hero of the hour. Those were days when newspaper enterprise was scarcely in its infancy, and the event owed nothing to journalistic effort. In spite of that, the news of this remarkable ceremony, the immersion of a little boy of ten years old "as an adult," had spread far and wide through the county in the course of three weeks. The chapel of our hosts was, as I have said, very large; it was commonly too large for their needs, but on this night it was crowded to the ceiling, and the crowd had come— as every soft murmurer assured me—to see *me*.

There were people there who had travelled from Exeter, from Dartmouth, from Totnes, to witness so extraordinary a ceremony. There was one old woman of eighty-five who had come, my neighbours whispered to me, all the way from Moreton-Hampstead, on purpose to see me baptized. I looked at her crumpled countenance with amazement, for there was no curiosity, no interest visible in it. She sat there perfectly listless, looking at nothing, but chewing between her toothless gums what appeared to be a jujube.

In the centre of the chapel-floor a number of planks had been taken up, and revealed a pool which might have been supposed to be a small swimming-bath. We gazed down into this dark square of mysterious waters, from the tepid surface of which faint swirls of vapour rose. The whole congregation was arranged, tier above tier, about the four straight sides of this pool; every person was able to see what happened in it without any unseemly struggling or standing on forms. Mr. S. now rose, an impressive hieratic figure, commanding attention and imploring perfect silence. He held a small book in his hand, and he was preparing to give out the number of a hymn, when an astounding incident took place.

There was a great splash, and a tall young woman was perceived to be in the baptismal pool, her arms waving above her head, and her figure held upright in the water by the inflation of the air underneath her crinoline, which was blown out like a bladder, as in some extravagant old fashion-plate. Whether her feet touched the bottom of the font I cannot say, but I suppose they did so. An indescribable turmoil of shrieks and cries followed on this extraordinary apparition. A great many people excitedly called upon other people to be calm, and an instance was given of the remark of James Smith that

> He who, in quest of quiet, "Silence!" hoots
> Is apt to make the hubbub he imputes.

The young woman, in a more or less fainting condition, was presently removed from the water, and taken into the sort of tent which was prepared for candidates. It was found that she herself had wished to be a candidate and had earnestly desired to be baptized, but that this had been forbidden by her parents. On the supposition that she fell in by accident, a pious coincidence was detected in this affair; the Lord had pre-ordained that she should be baptized in spite of all opposition. But my Father, in his shrewd way, doubted. He pointed out to us, next morning, that, in the first place, she had not, in any sense, been baptized, as her head had not been immersed; and that, in the second place, she must have deliberately jumped in, since, had she stumbled and fallen forward, her hands and face would have struck the water, whereas they remained quite dry. She belonged, however, to the neighbour congregation, and we had no responsibility to pursue the inquiry any further.

Decorum being again secured, Mr. S., with unimpaired dignity, proposed to the congregation a hymn, which was long enough to occupy them during the preparations for the actual baptism. He then retired to the vestry, and I (for I was to be the first to testify) was led by Miss Marks and Mary Grace into the species of tent of which I have just spoken. Its pale sides seemed to shake with the jubilant singing of the saints outside, while part of my clothing was removed and I was prepared for immersion. A sudden cessation of the hymn warned us that the Minister was now ready, and we emerged into the glare of lights and faces to find Mr. S. already standing in the water up to his knees. Feeling as small as one of our microscopical specimens, almost infinitesimally tiny as I descended into his Titanic arms, I was handed down the steps to him. He was dressed in a kind of long surplice, underneath which—as I could not, even in that moment, help observing—the air gathered in long bubbles which he strove to flatten out. The end of his noble beard he had tucked away; his shirt-sleeves were turned up at the wrist.

The entire congregation was now silent, so silent that the uncertain splashing of my feet as I descended seemed to deafen me. Mr. S., a little embarrassed by my short stature, succeeded at length in securing me with one palm on my chest and the other between my shoulders. He said, slowly, in a loud, sonorous voice that seemed to enter my brain and empty it, "I baptize thee, my Brother, in the name of the Father and of the Son and of the Holy Ghost!" Having intoned this formula, he then gently flung me backwards until I was wholly under the water, and then—as he brought me up again, and tenderly steadied my feet on the steps of the font, and delivered me, dripping and spluttering, into the anxious hands of the women, who hurried me to the tent—the whole assembly broke forth in a thunder of song, a pæan of praise to God for this manifestation of his marvellous goodness and mercy. So great was the enthusiasm, that it could hardly be restrained so as to allow the other candidates, the humdrum adults who followed in my wet and glorious footsteps, to undergo a ritual about which, in their case, no one in the congregation pretended to be able to take even the most languid interest.

My Father's happiness during the next few weeks it is now pathetic to me to look back upon. His sterness melted into a universal complaisance. He laughed and smiled, he paid to my opinions the tribute of the gravest consideration, he indulged—utterly unlike his wont—in shy and furtive caresses. I could express no wish that he did not attempt to fulfil, and the only warning which he cared to give me was one, very gently expressed, against spiritual pride.

This was certainly required, for I was puffed out with a sense of my own holiness. I was religiously confidential with my Father, condescending with Miss Marks (who I think had given up trying to make it all out), haughty with the servants, and insufferably patronising with those young companions of my own age with whom I was now beginning to associate.

I would fain close this remarkable episode on a key of solemnity, but alas! if I am to be loyal to the truth, I must record that some of the other little boys presently complained to Mary Grace that I put out my tongue at them in mockery, during the service in the Room, to remind them that I now broke bread as one of the Saints and that they did not.

———

EDMUND GOSSE (1849–1928) *called* Father and Son (1907) *"the record of a struggle between two temperaments, two consciences and almost two epochs." Born to middle-aged, almost fanatically devout parents, he was cut off from friends his own age, surrounded by taboos, and restricted in his reading to pious materials. His mother, who died when he was seven, imagined him as a future missionary, and, if lucky, a martyr; his father, who brought him up, mixed a warm affection with severe religious plans: "I had rather see him a warm devoted man of God than the brightest scholar," he wrote to his son's schoolmaster.*

Young Gosse, to his father's dismay, began early to make a worldly career as essayist and scholar. Their relationship mellowed in later years. In 1887, when Gosse was on his way to distinction as a writer, he wrote to a friend that his father "is wonderfully sweet and gentle, wonderfully mellowed at last by the softening hand of age; and I have felt an affection for him and a pleasure in his company, this visit, that I am afraid I never really felt before. And so, in the evening there is light."

Gosse's books include many literary studies, a dozen biographies, and two romances. This selection is from Father and Son, his best-known work.

1. In the first paragraph of this selection, Gosse deals with a problem of tone that is always present for an autobiographer. What is the problem, and how well does Gosse solve it?

2. The preface to this section discusses Gosse's attitude toward himself as he describes the fountain incident when he was six. Discuss the baptism scene; how seriously does Gosse consider himself as a ten-year-old? Why is he telling us about the baptism?

3. What does the baptism mean to the adults; to the boy; to the writer looking back? What is the writer's relation to his readers, and what attitude does he ask his readers to take toward the baptism?

4. Discuss the tone of some of Gosse's descriptive terms at the start of the baptism scene: "inexpressibly exciting," "mysterious waters," "astounding incident," "indescribable turmoil," etc. Why does he use this kind of language here, and elsewhere? What is the relationship of such language to that describing the old lady chewing the jujube, or the boy sticking out his tongue? What kind of meaning emerges out of the last two paragraphs, showing the boy "puffed out with a sense of my own holiness"? Does this meaning emerge out of the scene, or the choice of words for the scene, or are they, in effect, the same?

Mary McCarthy

A TIN BUTTERFLY

We both had enviable possessions and did not have them. In the closet in my bedroom, high on the top shelf, beyond my reach even standing on a chair, was a stack of cardboard doll boxes, containing wonderful French dolls, dressed by my Seattle grandmother in silks, laces, and satins, with crepe-de-Chine underwear and shoes with high heels. These and other things were sent us every year at Christmastime, but my aunt had decreed that they were all too good for us, so they remained in their boxes and wrappings, *verboten*, except on the rare afternoon, perhaps once in a twelvemonth or so, when a relation or a friend of the family would come through from the West, and then down would come the dolls, out would come the baseball gloves and catchers' masks and the watches and the shiny cars and the doll houses, and we would be set to playing with these things on the floor of the living room while the visitor tenderly looked on. As soon as the visitor left, bearing a good report of our household, the dolls and watches and cars would be whisked away, to come out again for the next emergency. If we had been clever, we would have refused this bait and paraded our misery, but we were too simple to do anything but seize the moment and play out a whole year's playtime in this gala hour and a half. Such techniques, of course, are common in concentration camps and penal institutions, where the same sound calculation of human nature is made. The prisoners snatch at their holiday; they trust their guards and the motto *"Carpe diem"* more than they do the strangers who have come to make the inspection. Like all people who have been mistreated, we were wary of being taken in; we felt uneasy about these visitors—Protestants from Seattle—who might be much worse than our uncle and aunt. The latter's faults, at any rate, we knew. Moreover, we had been subjected to propaganda: we had been threatened with the Seattle faction, time and again, by our uncle, who used to jeer and say to us, *"They'*d make you toe the chalk line."

The basis, I think, of my aunt's program for us was in truth

From *Memories of a Catholic Girlhood* by Mary McCarthy. First published in *The New Yorker*. Copyright 1951, © 1957 by Mary McCarthy. Reprinted by permission of Harcourt, Brace & World, Inc.

totalitarian: she was idealistically bent on destroying our privacy. She imagined herself as enlightened in comparison with our parents, and a super-ideal of health, cleanliness, and discipline softened in her own eyes the measures she applied to attain it. A nature not unkindly was warped by bureaucratic zeal and by her subservience to her husband, whose masterful autocratic hand cut through our nonsense like a cleaver. The fact that our way of life resembled that of an orphan asylum was not a mere coincidence; Aunt Margaret strove purposefully toward a corporate goal. Like most heads of institutions, she longed for the eyes of Argus. To the best of her ability, she saw to it that nothing was hidden from her. Even her health measures had this purpose. The aperients we were continually dosed with guaranteed that our daily processes were open to her inspection, and the monthly medical checkup assured her, by means of stethoscope and searchlight and tongue depressor, that nothing was happening inside us to which she was not privy. Our letters to Seattle were written under her eye, and she scrutinized our homework sharply, though her arithmetic, spelling, and grammar were all very imperfect. We prayed, under supervision, for a prescribed list of people. And if we were forbidden companions, candy, most toys, pocket money, sports, reading, entertainment, the aim was not to make us suffer but to achieve efficiency. It was simpler to interdict other children than to inspect all the children with whom we might want to play. From the standpoint of efficiency, our lives, in order to be open, had to be empty; the books we might perhaps read, the toys we might play with figured in my aunt's mind, no doubt, as what the housewife calls "dust catchers" —around these distractions, dirt might accumulate. The inmost folds of consciousness, like the belly button, were regarded by her as unsanitary. Thus, in her spiritual outlook, my aunt was an early functionalist.

Like all systems, my aunt's was, of course, imperfect. Forbidden to read, we told stories, and if we were kept apart, we told them to ourselves in bed. We made romances out of our schoolbooks, even out of the dictionary, and read digests of novels in the *Book of Knowledge* at school. My uncle's partiality for my youngest brother was a weakness in him, as was my aunt Mary's partiality for me. She was supposed to keep me in her room, sewing on squares of cheap cotton, making handkerchiefs with big, crude, ugly hems, and ripping them out and making them over again, but though she had no feeling for art or visual beauty (she would not even teach me to darn, which is an art, or to do embroidery, as the nuns did later on, in the convent), she liked to talk of the old days in Chicago and to read sensational religious fiction in a magazine called the *Extension*, which sometimes she let me take to my room, with a caution against being caught. And on the Sunday walks that my uncle headed, at the end of an interminable streetcar ride, during which my bigger brothers had to scrunch down to pass for under six, there were occasions on which he took us (in military order) along a wooded path, high above the Mississippi River, and we saw late-spring harebells and, once, a coral-pink snake. In Minnehaha Park, a favorite resort, we were allowed to play on the swings and to examine the other children riding on the ponies or on a little scenic railway. Uncle Myers always bought himself a box of Cracker Jack, which we watched him eat and delve into, to find the little favor at the bottom—a ritual we deeply envied, for, though we sometimes had popcorn at home (Myers enjoyed popping it) and even, once or twice, homemade popcorn balls with molasses, we had never had more than a taste of this commercial Cracker Jack, with peanuts in it, which seemed to us the more valuable because *he* valued it and would often come home eating a box he had bought at a ball game. But one Sunday, Uncle Myers, in full, midsummer mood, wearing his new pedometer, bought my brother Sheridan a whole box for himself.

Naturally, we envied Sheridan—the only blond among us, with fair red-gold curls, while the rest of us were all pronounced brunets, with thick black brows and lashes—as we watched him, the lucky one, munch the sticky stuff and fish out a painted tin butterfly with a little pin on it at the bottom. My brothers clamored around him, but I was too proud to show my feelings. Sheridan was then about six years old, and this butterfly immediately became his most cherished possession—indeed, one of the few he had. He carried it about the house with him all the next week, clutched in his hand or pinned to his shirt, and my two other brothers followed him, begging him to be allowed to play with it, which slightly disgusted me, at the age of ten, for I knew that I was too sophisticated to care for tin butterflies and I felt in this whole affair the instigation of my uncle. He was relishing my brothers' performance and saw to it, strictly, that Sheridan clung to his rights in the butterfly and did not permit anybody to touch it. The point about this painted tin butterfly was not its intrinsic value; it was the fact that it was virtually the only toy in the house that had not been, so to speak, socialized, but belonged privately to one individual. Our other playthings—a broken-down wooden swing, an old wagon, a dirty sandbox, and perhaps a fire engine or so and some defaced blocks and twisted second-hand train tracks in the attic—were held by us all in common, the velocipedes we had brought with us from Seattle having long ago foundered, and the skipping rope, the jacks, the few marbles, and the pair of rusty roller skates that were given us being decreed to be the property of all. Hence, for a full week this

butterfly excited passionate emotions, from which I held myself stubbornly apart, refusing even to notice it, until one afternoon, at about
four o'clock, while I was doing my weekly chore of dusting the
woodwork, my white-haired aunt Mary hurried softly into my room
and, closing the door behind her, asked whether I had seen Sheridan's butterfly.

The topic wearied me so much that I scarely lifted my head,
answering no, shortly, and going on with my dusting. But Aunt
Mary was gently persistent: Did I know that he had lost it? Would
I help her look for it? This project did not appeal to me but in
response to some faint agitation in her manner, something almost
pleading, I put down my dustcloth and helped her. We went all
over the house, raising carpets, looking behind curtains, in the
kitchen cupboards, in the Victrola, everywhere but in the den,
which was closed, and in my aunt's and uncle's bedroom. Somehow
—I do not know why—I did not expect to find the butterfly, partly,
I imagine, because I was indifferent to it and partly out of the fatal-
ism that all children have toward lost objects, regarding them as
irretrievable, vanished into the flux of things. At any rate I was
right: we did not find it and I went back to my dusting, vindicated.
Why should I have to look for Sheridan's stupid butterfly, which he
ought to have taken better care of? "Myers is upset," said Aunt
Mary, still hovering, uneasy and diffident, in the doorway. I made a
slight face, and she went out, plaintive, remonstrant, and sighing,
in her pale, high necked, tight-buttoned dress.

It did not occur to me that I was suspected of stealing this toy,
even when Aunt Margaret, five minutes later, burst into my room
and ordered me to come and look for Sheridan's butterfly. I protested that I had already done so, but she paid my objections no
heed and seized me roughly by the arm. "Then do it again, Miss,
and mind that you find it." Her voice was rather hoarse and her
whole furrowed iron-gray aspect somewhat tense and disarrayed, yet
I had the impression that she was not angry with me but with something in outer reality—what one would now call fate or contin-
gency. When I had searched again, lackadaisically, and again found
nothing, she joined in with vigor, turning everything upside down.
We even went into the den, where Myers was sitting, and searched
all around him, while he watched us with an ironical expression, fill-
ing his pipe from a Bull Durham sack. We found nothing, and Aunt
Margaret led me upstairs to my room, which I ransacked while she
stood and watched me. All at once, when we had finished with my
bureau drawers and my closet, she appeared to give up. She sighed
and bit her lips. The door cautiously opened and Aunt Mary came
in. The two sisters looked at each other and at me. Margaret
shrugged her shoulders. "She hasn't got it, I do believe," she said.

She regarded me then with a certain relaxing of her thick wrinkles, and her heavy-skinned hand, with its wedding ring, came down on my shoulder. "Uncle Myers thinks you took it," she said in a rusty whisper, like a spy or a scout. The consciousness of my own innocence, combined with a sense of being let into the confederacy of the two sisters, filled me with excitement and self-importance. "But I didn't, Aunt Margaret," I began proclaiming, making the most of my moment. "What would I want with his silly old butterfly?" The two sisters exchanged a look. "That's what I said, Margaret!" exclaimed old Aunt Mary sententiously. Aunt Margaret frowned; she adjusted a bone hairpin in the coiled rings of her unbecoming coiffure. "Mary Therese," she said to me, solemnly, "if you know anything about the butterfly, if one of your brothers took it, tell me now. If we don't find it, I'm afraid Uncle Myers will have to punish you." "He *can't* punish me, Aunt Margaret," I insisted, full of righteousness. "Not if I didn't do it and *you* don't think I did it." I looked up at her, stagily trustful, resting gingerly on this solidarity that had suddenly appeared between us. Aunt Mary's pale old eyes watered. "You mustn't let Myers punish her, Margaret, if you don't think she's done wrong." They both glanced up at the Murillo Madonna that was hanging on my stained wall. Intelligence passed between them and I was sure that, thanks to our Holy Mother, Aunt Margaret would save me. "Go along, Mary Therese," she said hoarsely. "Get yourself ready for dinner. And don't you say a word of this to your uncle when you come downstairs."

When I went down to dinner, I was exultant, but I tried to hide it. Throughout the meal, everyone was restrained; Herdie was in the dumps about his butterfly, and Preston and Kevin were silent, casting covert looks at me. My brothers, apparently, were wondering how I had avoided punishment, as the eldest, if for no other reason. Aunt Margaret was rather flushed, which improved her appearance slightly. Uncle Myers had a cunning look, as though events would prove him right. He patted Sheridan's golden head from time to time and urged him to eat. After dinner, the boys filed into the den behind Uncle Myers, and I helped Aunt Margaret clear the table. We did not have to do the dishes, for at this time there was a "girl" in the kitchen. As we were lifting the white tablecloth and the silence pad, we found the butterfly—pinned to the silence pad, right by my place.

My hash was settled then, though I did not know it. I did not catch the significance of its being found at *my* place. To Margaret, however, this was grimly conclusive. She had been too "easy," said her expression; once again Myers had been right. Myers went through the formality of interrogating each of the boys in turn

("No, sir," "No, sir," "No, sir") and even, at my insistence, of calling in the Swedish girl from the kitchen. Nobody knew how the butterfly had got there. It had not been there before dinner, when the girl set the table. My judges therefore concluded that I had had it hidden on my person and had slipped it under the tablecloth at dinner, when nobody was looking. This unanimous verdict maddened me, at first simply as an indication of stupidity—how could they be so dense as to imagine that I would hide it by my own place, where it was sure to be discovered? I did not really believe that I was going to be punished on such ridiculous evidence, yet even I could form no theory of how the butterfly had come there. My first base impulse to accuse the maid was scoffed out of my head by reason. What would a grownup want with a silly six-year-old's toy? And the very unfairness of the condemnation that rested on me made me reluctant to transfer it to one of my brothers. I kept supposing that the truth somehow would out, but the interrogation suddenly ended and every eye avoided mine.

Aunt Mary's dragging step went up the stairs, the boys were ordered to bed, and then, in the lavatory, the whipping began. Myers beat me with the strop, until his lazy arm tired; whipping is hard work for a fat man, out of condition, with a screaming, kicking, wriggling ten-year-old in his grasp. He went out and heaved himself, panting, into his favorite chair and I presumed that the whipping was over. But Aunt Margaret took his place, striking harder than he, with a hairbrush, in a businesslike, joyless way, repeating, "Say you did it, Mary Therese, say you did it." As the blows fell and I did not give in, this formula took on an intercessory note, like a prayer. It was clear to me that she was begging me to surrender and give Myers his satisfaction, for my own sake, so that the whipping could stop. When I finally cried out "All right!" she dropped the hairbrush with a sigh of relief; a new doubt of my guilt must have been visiting her, and my confession set everything square. She led me in to my uncle, and we both stood facing him, as Aunt Margaret, with a firm but not ungentle hand on my shoulder, whispered, "Just tell him, 'Uncle Myers, I did it,' and you can go to bed." But the sight of him, sprawling in his leather chair, complacently waiting for this, was too much for me. The words froze on my tongue. I could not utter them to *him*. Aunt Margaret urged me on, reproachfully, as though I were breaking our compact, but as I looked straight at him and assessed his ugly nature, I burst into yells. "I didn't! I didn't!" I gasped, between screams. Uncle Myers shot a vindictive look at his wife, as though he well understood that there had been collusion between us. He ordered me back to the dark lavatory and symbolically rolled up his sleeve. He laid on the strop decisively, but this time I was beside myself, and when Aunt

Margaret hurried in and tried to reason with me, I could only answer with wild cries as Uncle Myers, gasping also, put the strop back on its hook. "You take her," he articulated, but Aunt Margaret's hairbrush this time was perfunctory, after the first few angry blows that punished me for having disobeyed her. Myers did not take up the strop again; the whipping ended, whether from fear of the neighbors or of Aunt Mary's frail presence upstairs or sudden guilty terror, I do not know; perhaps simply because it was past my bedtime.

I finally limped up to bed, with a crazy sense of inner victory, like a saint's, for I had not recanted, despite all they had done or could do to me. It did not occur to me that I had been unchristian in refusing to answer a plea from Aunt Margaret's heart and conscience. Indeed, I rejoiced in the knowledge that I had *made* her continue to beat me long after she must have known that I was innocent; this was her punishment for her condonation of Myers. The next morning, when I opened my eyes on the Murillo Madonna and the Baby Stuart, my feeling of triumph abated; I was afraid of what I had done. But throughout that day and the next, they did not touch me. I walked on air, incredulously and, no doubt, somewhat pompously, seeing myself as a figure from legend: my strength was *as* the strength of ten because my *heart* was pure! Afterward, I was beaten, in the normal routine way, but the question of the butterfly was closed forever in that house.

In my mind, there was, and still is, a connection between the butterfly and our rescue, by our Protestant grandfather, which took place the following year, in the fall or early winter. Already defeated, in their own view, or having ceased to care what became of us, our guardians, for the first time, permitted two of us, my brother Kevin and me, to be alone with this strict, kindly lawyer, as we walked the two blocks between our house and our grandfather McCarthy's. In the course of our walk, between the walls of an early snow, we told Grandpa Preston everything, overcoming our fears and fixing our minds on the dolls, the baseball gloves, and the watches. Yet, as it happened, curiously enough, albeit with a certain aptness, it was not the tale of the butterfly or the other atrocities that chiefly impressed him as he followed our narration with precise legal eyes but the fact that I was not wearing my glasses. I was being punished for breaking them in a fall on the school playground by having to go without; and I could not see why my account of this should make him flush up with anger—to me it was a great relief to be free of those disfiguring things. But he shifted his long, lantern jaw and, settling our hands in his, went straight as a writ up my grandfather McCarthy's front walk. Hence it was on a question

of health that this good American's alarms finally alighted; the
rest of what we poured out to him he either did not believe or
feared to think of, lest he had to deal with the problem of evil.

On health grounds, then, we were separated from Uncle Myers,
who disappeared back into Elkhart with his wife and Aunt Mary.
My brothers were sent off to the sisters in a Catholic boarding
school, with the exception of Sheridan, whom Myers was permitted
to bear away with him, like a golden trophy. Sheridan's stay, however, was of short duration. Very soon, Aunt Mary died, followed
by Aunt Margaret, followed by Uncle Myers; within five years, still
in the prime of life, they were all gone, one, two, three, like nine-
pins. For me, a new life began, under a happier star. Within a few
weeks after my Protestant grandfather's visit, I was sitting in a com-
partment with him on the train, watching the Missouri River go
westward to its source, wearing my white-gold wrist watch and a
garish new red hat, a highly nervous child, fanatical against Protestants, who, I explained to Grandpa Preston, all deserved to be
burned at the stake. In the dining car, I ordered greedily, lamb
chops, pancakes, sausages, and then sat, unable to eat them. "Her
eyes," observed the waiter, "are bigger than her stomach."

Six or seven years later, on one of my trips east to college, I
stopped in Minneapolis to see my brothers, who were all together
now, under the roof of a new and more indulgent guardian, my
uncle Louis, the handsomest and youngest of the McCarthy uncles.
All the old people were dead; my grandmother McCarthy, but
recently passed away, had left a fund to erect a chapel in her name
in Texas, a state with which she had no known connection. Sitting
in the twilight of my uncle Louis' screened porch, we sought a common ground for our reunion and found it in Uncle Myers. It was
then that my brother Preston told me that on the famous night of
the butterfly, he had seen Uncle Myers steal into the dining room
from the den and lift the tablecloth, with the tin butterfly in his
hand.

———

Mary McCarthy (1912–   ) *describes her early life fully in*
Memories of a Catholic Girlhood (1957), *from which this essay is
taken. Her parents died when she was six, and she was raised by
grandparents, uncles, and aunts. After leaving Vassar College, she
began writing articles and reviews, then became an editor for the*
Partisan Review 1937–1948. *Her novels include* The Company She
Keeps (1942), The Groves of Academe (1952), *and* The Group

(1963). During recent years, she has been living mainly in Paris, and writing for The New York Review of Books.

1. The essay begins with a paragraph filled with concrete descriptions of the forbidden toys. But words such as "decreed," "verboten," "emergency," "concentration camps and penal institutions," "propaganda" all suggest that something of large significance is at issue. What is the tone of these words and phrases, and what attitude do they ask the reader to take towards the scene described in such detail? What makes the tone of this passage different from Edmund Gosse's tone in the preceding essay?

2. Aunt Margaret is described in the second paragraph as "idealistically bent on destroying our privacy." What is the "idea" behind this special use of "idealistically," and what attitude are we expected to have toward this idea? What is shown to be in conflict with "system" and "efficiency," most obviously in the third paragraph?

3. Notice the severe control over self-pity in this essay. "Myers beat me with the strop, until his lazy arm tired; whipping is hard work for a fat man, out of condition, with a screaming, kicking, wriggling ten-year-old in his grasp." Why does Miss McCarthy ask us to focus upon the sufferings of the tyrant, instead of her own agony as a child? What is her attitude toward herself as a child?

4. We are only given hints about Uncle Myers' reasons for hiding the tin butterfly at the child's place. Why did he do it? Why does the author not want our attention to linger on this issue?

5. Grandfather McCarthy does not want to think of the situation at Uncle Myers' "lest he have to deal with the problem of evil." The author seems here to suggest that the incident reveals something disturbing about the nature and source of evil. To what degree does the essay structure such an idea?

George Orwell

SHOOTING AN ELEPHANT

In Moulmein, in Lower Burma, I was hated by large numbers of people—the only time in my life that I have been important enough for this to happen to me. I was sub-divisional police officer of the town, and in an aimless, petty kind of way anti-European feeling was very bitter. No one had the guts to raise a riot, but if a European woman went through the bazaars alone somebody would probably spit betel juice over her dress. As a police officer I was an obvious target and was baited whenever it seemed safe to do so. When a nimble Burman tripped me up on the football field and the referee (another Burman) looked the other way, the crowd yelled with hideous laughter. This happened more than once. In the end the sneering yellow faces of young men that met me everywhere, the insults hooted after me when I was at a safe distance, got badly on my nerves. The young Buddhist priests were the worst of all. There were several thousands of them in the town and none of them seemed to have anything to do except stand on street corners and jeer at Europeans.

All this was perplexing and upsetting. For at that time I had already made up my mind that imperialism was an evil thing and the sooner I chucked up my job and got out of it the better. Theoretically—and secretly, of course—I was all for the Burmese and all against their oppressors, the British. As for the job I was doing, I hated it more bitterly than I can perhaps make clear. In a job like that you see the dirty work of Empire at close quarters. The wretched prisoners huddling in the stinking cages of the lock-ups, the grey, cowed faces of the long-term convicts, the scarred buttocks of the men who had been flogged with bamboos—all these oppressed me with an intolerable sense of guilt. But I could get nothing into perspective. I was young and ill-educated and I had had to think out my problems in the utter silence that is imposed on every Englishman in the East. I did not even know that the British Empire is dying, still less did I know that it is a great deal better than the younger empires that are going to supplant it. All I knew was that I was stuck between my hatred of the empire I served and my rage against the evil-spirited little beasts who tried to make my job impossible. With one part of my mind I thought of the British Raj as an unbreakable tyranny, as something clamped down, *in saecula saeculorum,* upon the will of prostrate peoples; with another part I thought that the greatest joy in the world would be to drive a bayonet into a Buddhist priest's guts. Feelings like these are the normal by-products of imperialism; ask any Anglo-Indian official, if you can catch him off duty.

One day something happened which in a roundabout way was enlightening. It was a tiny incident in itself, but it gave me a better glimpse than I had had before of the real nature of imperialism— the real motives for which despotic governments act. Early one morning the sub-inspector at a police station the other end of the town rang me up on the phone and said that an elephant was ravaging the bazaar. Would I please come and do something about it? I did not know what I could do, but I wanted to see what was happening and I got on to a pony and started out. I took my rifle, an old .44 Winchester and much too small to kill an elephant, but I thought the noise might be useful *in terrorem.* Various Burmans stopped me on the way and told me about the elephant's doings. It was not, of course, a wild elephant, but a tame one which had gone "must." It had been chained up, as tame elephants always are when their attack of "must" is due, but on the previous night it had broken its chain and escaped. Its mahout, the only person who could manage it when it was in that state, had set out in pursuit, but he had taken the wrong direction and was now twelve hours' journey away, and in the morning the elephant had suddenly reappeared in the town. The Burmese population had no weapons and were quite helpless against it. It had already destroyed somebody's bamboo hut, killed a cow and raided some fruit-stalls and devoured the stock; also it had met the municipal rubbish van, and, when the driver jumped out and took to his heels, had turned the van over and inflicted violence upon it.

The Burmese sub-inspector and some Indian constables were waiting for me in the quarter where the elephant had been seen. It was a very poor quarter, a labyrinth of squalid bamboo huts, thatched with palm-leaf, winding all over a steep hillside. I remember that it was a cloudy, stuffy morning at the beginning of the rains. We began questioning the people as to where the elephant had gone, and, as usual, failed to get any definite information. That is invariably the case in the East; a story always sounds clear enough at a distance, but the nearer you get to the scene of events the vaguer it becomes. Some of the people said that the elephant had gone in one direction, some said that he had gone in another, some professed not even to have heard of any elephant. I had almost made up my mind that the whole story was a pack of lies, when we heard yells a little distance away. There was a loud, scandalized cry of "Go away, child! Go away this instant!" and an old woman with a switch in her hand came round the corner of a hut, violently shooing away a crowd of naked children. Some more women followed, clicking their tongues and exclaiming; evidently there was something there that the children ought not to have seen. I rounded the hut and saw a man's dead body sprawling in the mud. He was an Indian, a black Dravidian coolie, almost naked, and he could not have been dead many minutes. The people said that the elephant had come suddenly upon him round the corner of the hut, caught him with its trunk, put its foot on his back and ground him into the earth. This was the rainy season and the ground was soft, and his face had scored a trench a foot deep and a couple of yards long. He was lying on his belly with arms crucified and head sharply twisted to one side. His face was coated with mud, the eyes wide open, the teeth bared and grinning with an expression of unendurable agony. (Never tell me, by the way, that the dead look peaceful. Most of the corpses I have seen looked devilish.) The friction of the great beast's foot had stripped the skin from his back as neatly as one skins a rabbit. As soon as I saw the dead man I sent an orderly to a friend's house nearby to borrow an elephant rifle. I had already sent back the pony, not wanting it to go mad with fright and throw me if it smelled the elephant.

The orderly came back in a few minutes with a rifle and five cartridges, and meanwhile some Burmans had arrived and told us that the elephant was in the paddy fields below, only a few hundred yards away. As I started forward practically the whole population of the quarter flocked out of the houses and followed me. They had seen the rifle and were all shouting excitedly that I was going to shoot the elephant. They had not shown much interest in the elephant when he was merely ravaging their homes, but it was different now that he was going to be shot. It was a bit of fun to them, as it would be to an English crowd; besides they wanted the meat. It made me vaguely uneasy. I had no intention of shooting the elephant—I had merely sent for the rifle to defend myself if necessary—and it is always unnerving to have a crowd following you. I marched down the hill, looking and feeling a fool, with the rifle over my shoulder and an ever-growing army of people jostling at my heels. At the bottom, when you got away from the huts, there was a metalled road and beyond that a miry waste of paddy fields a thousand yards across, not yet ploughed but soggy from the first rains and dotted with coarse grass. The elephant was standing eighty yards from the road, his left side towards us. He took not the slight-est notice of the crowd's approach. He was tearing up bunches of grass, beating them against his knees to clean them and stuffing them into his mouth.

I had halted on the road. As soon as I saw the elephant I knew with perfect certainty that I ought not to shoot him. It is a serious matter to shoot a working elephant—it is comparable to destroying a huge and costly piece of machinery—and obviously one ought not to do it if it can possibly be avoided. And at that distance, peace-fully eating, the elephant looked no more dangerous than a cow. I thought then and I think now that his attack of "must" was already passing off; in which case he would merely wander harmlessly about until the mahout came back and caught him. Moreover, I did not in the least want to shoot him. I decided that I would watch him for a little while to make sure that he did not turn savage again, and then go home.

But at that moment I glanced round at the crowd that had fol-lowed me. It was an immense crowd, two thousand at the least and growing every minute. It blocked the road for a long distance on either side. I looked at the sea of yellow faces above the garish clothes—faces all happy and excited over this bit of fun, all certain that the elephant was going to be shot. They were watching me as they would watch a conjurer about to perform a trick. They did not like me, but with the magical rifle in my hands I was momentarily worth watching. And suddenly I realized that I should have to shoot the elephant after all. The people expected it of me and I had got to do it; I could feel their two thousand wills pressing me forward, irresistibly. And it was at this moment, as I stood there with the rifle in my hands, that I first grasped the hollowness, the futility of the white man's dominion in the East. Here was I, the white man with his gun, standing in front of the unarmed native crowd—seemingly the leading actor of the piece; but in reality I was only an absurd puppet pushed to and fro by the will of those yellow faces behind. I perceived in this moment that when the white man turns tyrant it is his own freedom that he destroys. He becomes a sort of hollow, posing dummy, the conventionalized figure of a sahib. For it is the condition of his rule that he shall spend his life in trying to impress the "natives," and so in every crisis he has got to do what the "natives" expect of him. He wears a mask, and his face grows to fit it. I had got to shoot the elephant. I had committed myself to doing it when I sent for the rifle. A sahib has got to act like a sahib; he has got to appear resolute, to know his own mind and do definite things. To come all that way, rifle in hand, with two thou-sand people marching at my heels, and then to trail feebly away, having done nothing—no, that was impossible. The crowd would laugh at me. And my whole life, every white man's life in the East, was one long struggle not to be laughed at.

But I did not want to shoot the elephant. I watched him beating his bunch of grass against his knees, with that preoccupied grandmotherly air that elephants have. It seemed to me that it would be murder to shoot him. At that age I was not squeamish about killing animals, but I had never shot an elephant and never wanted to. (Somehow it always seems worse to kill a *large* animal.) Besides, there was the beast's owner to be considered. Alive, the elephant was worth at least a hundred pounds; dead, he would only be worth the value of his tusks, five pounds, possibly. But I had got to act quickly. I turned to some experienced-looking Burmans who had been there when we arrived, and asked them how the elephant had been behaving. They all said the same thing: he took no notice of you if you left him alone, but he might charge if you went too close to him.

It was perfectly clear to me what I ought to do. I ought to walk up to within, say, twenty-five yards of the elephant and test his behavior. If he charged, I could shoot; if he took no notice of me, it would be safe to leave him until the mahout came back. But also I knew that I was going to do no such thing. I was a poor shot with a rifle and the ground was soft mud into which one would sink at every step. If the elephant charged and I missed him, I should have about as much chance as a toad under a steam-roller. But even then I was not thinking particularly of my own skin, only the watchful yellow faces behind. For at that moment, with the crowd watching me, I was not afraid in the ordinary sense, as I would have been if I had been alone. A white man mustn't be frightened in front of "natives"; and so, in general, he isn't frightened. The sole thought in my mind was that if anything went wrong those two thousand Burmans would see me pursued, caught, trampled on and reduced to a grinning corpse like that Indian up the hill. And if that happened it was quite probable that some of them would laugh. That would never do. There was only one alternative. I shoved the cartridges into the magazine and lay down on the road to get a better aim.

The crowd grew very still, and a deep, low, happy sigh, as of people who see the theatre curtain go up at last, breathed from innumerable throats. They were going to have their bit of fun after all. The rifle was a beautiful German thing with cross-hair sights. I did not then know that in shooting an elephant one should shoot to cut an imaginary bar running from ear-hole to ear-hole. I ought therefore, as the elephant was sideways on, to have aimed straight at his ear-hole; actually I aimed several inches in front of this, thinking the brain would be further forward.

When I pulled the trigger I did not hear the bang or feel the kick—one never does when a shot goes home—but I heard the devilish roar of glee that went up from the crowd. In that instant, in too short a time, one would have thought, even for the bullet to get there, a mysterious, terrible change had come over the elephant. He neither stirred nor fell, but every line of his body had altered. He looked suddenly stricken, shrunken, immensely old, as though the frightful impact of the bullet had paralysed him without knocking him down. At last, after what seemed a long time—it might have been five seconds, I dare say—he sagged flabbily to his knees. His mouth slobbered. An enormous senility seemed to have settled upon him. One could have imagined him thousands of years old. I fired again into the same spot. At the second shot he did not collapse but climbed with desperate slowness to his feet and stood weakly upright, with legs sagging and head drooping. I fired a third time. That was the shot that did for him. You could see the agony of it jolt his whole body and knock the last remnant of strength from his legs. But in falling he seemed for a moment to rise, for as his hind legs collapsed beneath him he seemed to tower upwards like a huge rock toppling, his trunk reaching skywards like a tree. He trumpeted, for the first and only time. And then down he came, his belly towards me, with a crash that seemed to shake the ground even where I lay.

I got up. The Burmans were already racing past me across the mud. It was obvious that the elephant would never rise again, but he was not dead. He was breathing very rhythmically with long rattling gasps, his great mound of a side painfully rising and falling. His mouth was wide open—I could see far down into caverns of pale pink throat. I waited a long time for him to die, but his breathing did not weaken. Finally I fired my two remaining shots into the spot where I thought his heart must be. The thick blood welled out of him like red velvet, but still he did not die. His body did not even jerk when the shots hit him, the tortured breathing continued without a pause. He was dying, very slowly and in great agony, but in some world remote from me where not even a bullet could damage him further. I felt that I had got to put an end to that dreadful noise. It seemed dreadful to see the great beast lying there, powerless to move and yet powerless to die, and not even to be able to finish him. I sent back for my small rifle and poured shot after shot into his heart and down his throat. They seemed to make no impression. The tortured gasps continued as steadily as the ticking of a clock.

In the end I could not stand it any longer and went away. I heard later that it took him half an hour to die. Burmans were arriving with dahs and baskets even before I left, and I was told they had stripped his body almost to the bones by the afternoon.

Afterwards, of course, there were endless discussions about the shooting of the elephant. The owner was furious, but he was only an Indian and could do nothing. Besides, legally I had done the right thing, for a mad elephant has to be killed, like a mad dog, if its owner fails to control it. Among the Europeans opinion was divided. The older men said I was right, the younger men said it was a damn shame to shoot an elephant for killing a coolie, because an elephant was worth more than any damn Coringhee coolie. And afterwards I was very glad that the coolie had been killed; it put me legally in the right and it gave me a sufficient pretext for shooting the elephant. I often wondered whether any of the others grasped that I had done it solely to avoid looking a fool.

———

GEORGE ORWELL *uses many of his experiences as a colonial official from 1922 to 1927 in* Burmese Days *(1934). A major character in the novel at one point talks about "the murder of an elephant which he had perpetrated some years earlier." The tone of that reference seems sharper than that of this essay, written about the same time; certainly the essay allowed Orwell to focus some of his complex feelings about imperialism and his own role in it, and thus make the incident itself a way of talking about a major issue of political morality.*

1. *What is the attitude toward the Burmese expressed in the first paragraph? Does it contrast in any way with the relationship set up between writer and reader? Do these attitudes shift by the end of the essay?*
2. *What are some of the conflicts that lead to the sense of guilt and confusion of the second paragraph?*
3. *The last sentence of the third paragraph speaks in one tone ("[the elephant] had turned the van over and inflicted violence upon it") but the end of the next paragraph changes tone: "I had already sent back the pony, not wanting it to go mad with fright and throw me if it smelled the elephant." Describe each tone; what has caused the change?*
4. *What metaphors become prominent as Orwell describes his*

motives for killing the elephant? How do they affect our attitudes toward his act? Why does he kill the elephant?

5. The last paragraph gives a series of opinions about the meaning
of his act; including two of his own. Which is most corrupt?
Are any of them right?

John Updike

HUB FANS BID KID ADIEU

Fenway Park, in Boston, is a lyric little band-box of a ballpark. Everything is painted green and seems in curiously sharp focus, like the inside of an old-fashioned peeping-type Easter egg. It was built in 1912 and rebuilt in 1934, and offers, as do most Boston artifacts, a compromise between Man's Euclidean determinations and Nature's beguiling irregularities. Its right field is one of the deepest in the American League, while its left field is the shortest; the high left-field wall, three hundred and fifteen feet from home plate along the foul line, virtually thrusts its surface at right-handed hitters. On the afternoon of Wednesday, September 28th, as I took a seat behind third base, a uniformed groundkeeper was treading the top of this wall, picking batting-practice home runs out of the screen, like a mushroom gatherer seen in Wordsworthian perspective on the verge of a cliff. The day was overcast, chill, and uninspirational. The Boston team was the worst in twenty-seven seasons. A jangling medley of incompetent youth and aging competence, the Red Sox were finishing in seventh place only because the Kansas City Athletics had locked them out of the cellar. They were scheduled to play the Baltimore Orioles, a much nimbler blend of May and December, who had been dumped from pennant contention a week before by the insatiable Yankees. I, and 10,453 others, had shown up primarily because this was the Red Sox's last home game of the season, and therefore the last time in all eternity that their regular left fielder, known to the headlines as TED, KID, SPLINTER, THUMPER, TW, and, most cloyingly, MISTER WONDERFUL, would play in Boston. "WHAT WILL WE DO WITHOUT TED?" HUB FANS ASK ran the headline on a newspaper being read by a bulb-nosed cigar smoker a few rows away. Williams' retirement had been announced, doubted (he had been threatening retirement for years), confirmed by Tom Yawkey, the Red Sox owner, and at last widely accepted as the sad but probable truth. He was forty-two and had redeemed his abysmal season of 1959 with a—considering his advanced age—fine one. He had been giving away his gloves and bats and had grudgingly consented to a sentimental ceremony today. This was not necessarily his last game; the Red Sox were scheduled to travel to New York and wind up the season with three games there.

I arrived early. The Orioles were hitting fungos on the field. The day before, they had spitefully smothered the Red Sox, 17-4, and neither their faces nor their drab gray visiting-team uniforms seemed very gracious. I wondered who had invited them to the party. Between our heads and the lowering clouds a frenzied organ was thundering through, with an appositeness perhaps accidental, "You *maaaade* me love you, I didn't wanna do it, I didn't wanna do it . . ."

The affair between Boston and Ted Williams has been no mere summer romance; it has been a marriage, composed of spats, mutual disappointments, and, toward the end, a mellowing hoard of shared memories. It falls into three stages, which may be termed Youth, Maturity, and Age; or Thesis, Antithesis, and Synthesis; or Jason, Achilles, and Nestor.

First, there was the by now legendary epoch when the young bridegroom came out of the West, announced "All I want out of life is that when I walk down the street folks will say 'There goes the greatest hitter who ever lived.'" The dowagers of local journalism attempted to give elementary deportment lessons to this child who spake as a god, and to their horror were themselves rebuked. Thus began the long exchange of backbiting, bat-flipping, booing, and spitting that has distinguished Williams' public relations. The spitting incidents of 1957 and 1958 and the similar dockside courtesies that Williams has now and then extended to the grandstand should be judged against this background: the left-field stands at Fenway for twenty years have held a large number of customers who have bought their way in primarily for the privilege of showering abuse on Williams. Greatness necessarily attracks debunkers, but in Williams' case the hostility has been systematic and unappeasable. His basic offense against the fans has been to wish that they weren't there. Seeking a perfectionist's vacuum, he has quixotically desired to sever the game from the ground of paid spectatorship and publicity that supports it. Hence his refusal to tip his cap to the crowd or turn the other cheek to newsmen. It has been a costly theory—it has probably cost him, among other evidences of good will, two Most Valuable Player awards, which are voted by reporters—but he has held to it from his rookie year on. While his critics, oral and literary, remained beyond the reach of his discipline, the opposing pitchers were accessible, and he spanked them to the tune of .406 in 1941. He slumped to .356 in 1942 and went off to war.

In 1946, Williams returned from three years as a Marine pilot to the second of his baseball avatars, that of Achilles, the hero of incomparable prowess and beauty who nevertheless was to be found sulking in his tent while the Trojans (mostly Yankees) fought through to the ships. Yawkey, a timber and mining maharajah, had surrounded his central jewel with many gems of slightly lesser water, such as Bobby Doerr, Dom DiMaggio, Rudy York, Birdie Tebbetts, and Johnny Pesky. Throughout the late forties, the Red Sox were the best paper team in baseball, yet they had little three-dimensional to show for it, and if this was a tragedy, Williams was Hamlet. A succinct review of the indictment—and a fair sample of appreciative sports-page prose—appeared the very day of Williams' valedictory, in a column by Huck Finnegan in the Boston *American* (no sentimentalist, Huck):

> Williams' career, in contrast [to Babe Ruth's], has been a series of failures except for his averages. He flopped in the only World Series he ever played in (1946) when he batted only .200. He flopped in the playoff game with Cleveland in 1948. He flopped in the final game of the 1949 season with the pennant hinging on the outcome (Yanks 5, Sox 3). He flopped in 1950 when he returned to the lineup after a two-month absence and ruined the morale of a club that seemed pennant-bound under Steve O'Neil. It has always been Williams' records first, the team second, and the Sox non-winning record is proof enough of that.

There are answers to all this, of course. The fatal weakness of the great Sox slugging teams was not-quite-good-enough pitching rather than Williams' failure to hit a home run every time he came to bat. Again, Williams' depressing effect on his teammates has never been proved. Despite ample coaching to the contrary, most insisted that they *liked* him. He has been generous with advice to any player who asked for it. In an increasingly combative baseball atmosphere, he continued to duck beanballs docilely. With umpires he was gracious to a fault. This courtesy itself annoyed his critics, whom there was no pleasing. And against the ten crucial games (the seven World Series games with the St. Louis Cardinals, the 1948 playoff with the Cleveland Indians, and the two-game series with the Yankees at the end of the 1949 season, winning either one of which would have given the Red Sox the pennant) that make up the Achilles' heel of Williams' record, a mass of statistics can be set showing that day in and day out he was no slouch in the clutch. The correspondence columns of the Boston papers now and then suffer a sharp flurry of arithmetic on this score; indeed, for Williams to have distributed all his hits so they did nobody else any good would constitute a feat of placement unparalleled in the annals of selfishness.

Whatever residue of truth remains of the Finnegan charge those of us who love Williams must transmute as best we can, in our own personal crucibles. My personal memories of Williams begin when I was a boy in Pennsylvania, with two last-place teams in Philadelphia to keep me company. For me, "W'ms, lf" was a figment of the box scores who always seemed to be going 3-for-5. He radiated, from afar, the hard blue glow of high purpose. I remember listening over the radio to the All-Star Game of 1946, in which Williams hit two singles and two home runs, the second one off a Rip Sewell "blooper" pitch; it was like hitting a balloon out of the park. I remember watching one of his home runs from the bleachers of Shibe Park; it went over the first baseman's head and rose meticulously along a straight line and was still rising when it cleared the fence. The trajectory seemed qualitatively different from anything anyone else might hit. For me, Williams is the classic ballplayer of the game on a hot August weekday, before a small crowd, when the only thing at stake is the tissue-thin difference between a thing done well and a thing done ill. Baseball is a game of the long season, of relentless and gradual averaging-out. Irrelevance—since the reference point of most individual games is remote and statistical—always threatens its interest, which can be maintained not by the occasional heroics that sportswriters feed upon but by players who always *care*; who care, that is to say, about themselves and their art. Insofar as the clutch hitter is not a sportswriter's myth, he is a vulgarity, like a writer who writes only for money. It may be that, compared to managers' dreams such as Joe DiMaggio and the always helpful Stan Musial, Williams is an icy star. But of all team sports, baseball, with its graceful intermittences of action, its immense and tranquil field sparsely settled with poised men in white, its dispassionate mathematics, seems to me best suited to accommodate, and be ornamented by, a loner. It is an essentially lonely game. No other player visible to my generation has concentrated within himself so much of the sport's poignance, has so assiduously refined his natural skills, has so constantly brought to the plate that intensity of competence that crowds the throat with joy.

By the time I went to college, near Boston, the lesser stars Yawkey had assembled around Williams had faded, and his craftsmanship, his rigorous pride, had become itself a kind of heroism. This brittle and temperamental player developed an unexpected quality of persistence. He was always coming back—back from Korea, back from a broken collarbone, a shattered elbow, a bruised heel, back from drastic bouts of flu and ptomaine poisoning. Hardly a season went by without some enfeebling mishap, yet he always came back, and always looked like himself. The delicate mechanism of timing and power seemed locked, shockproof, in some case outside his body. In addition to injuries, there were a heavily publicized divorce, and the usual storms with the press, and the Williams Shift—the maneuver, custom-built by Lou Boudreau, of the Cleveland Indians, whereby three infielders were concentrated on the right side of the infield, where a left-handed pull hitter like Williams generally hits the ball. Williams could easily have learned to punch singles through the vacancy on his left and fattened his average hugely. This was what Ty Cobb, the Einstein of average, told him to do. But the game had changed since Cobb; Williams believed that his value to the club and to the game was as a slugger, so he went on pulling the ball, trying to blast it through three men, and paid the price of perhaps fifteen points of lifetime average. Like Ruth before him, he bought the occasional home run at the cost of many directed singles—a calculated sacrifice certainly not, in the case of a hitter as average-minded as Williams, entirely selfish.

After a prime so harassed and hobbled, Williams was granted by the relenting fates a golden twilight. He became at the end of his career perhaps the best *old* hitter of the century. The dividing line came between the 1956 and the 1957 seasons. In September of the first year, he and Mickey Mantle were contending for the batting championship. Both were hitting around .350, and there was no one else near them. The season ended with a three-game series between the Yankees and the Sox, and, living in New York then, I went up to the Stadium. Williams was slightly shy of the four hundred at-bats needed to qualify; the fear was expressed that the Yankee pitchers would walk him to protect Mantle. Instead, they pitched to him—a wise decision. He looked terrible at the plate, tired and discouraged and unconvincing. He never looked very good to me in the Stadium. (Last week, in *Life*, Williams, a sportswriter himself now, wrote gloomily of the Stadium, "There's the bigness of it. There are those high stands and all those people smoking—and, of course, the shadows. . . . It takes at least one series to get accustomed to the Stadium and even then you're not sure.") The final outcome in 1956 was Mantle .353, Williams .345.

The next year, I moved from New York to New England, and it made all the difference. For in September of 1957, in the same situation, the story was reversed. Mantle finally hit .365; it was the best season of his career. But Williams, though sick and old, had run away from him. A bout of flu had laid him low in September. He emerged from his cave in the Hotel Somerset haggard but irresistible; he hit four successive pinch-hit home runs. "I feel terrible," he confessed, "but every time I take a swing at the ball it goes out of the park." He ended the season with thirty-eight home runs and an average of .388, the highest in either league since his own .406, and, coming from a decrepit man of thirty-nine, an even more supernal figure. With eight or so of the "leg hits" that a younger man would have beaten out, it would have been .400. And the next year, Williams, who in 1949 and 1953 had lost batting championships by decimal whiskers to George Kell and Mickey Vernon, sneaked in behind his teammate Pete Runnels and filched his sixth title, a bargain at .328.

In 1959, it seemed all over. The dinosaur thrashed around in the .200 swamp for the first half of the season, and was even benched ("rested," Manager Mike Higgins tactfully said). Old foes like the late Bill Cunningham began to offer batting tips. Cunningham thought Williams was jiggling his elbows; in truth, Williams' neck was so stiff he could hardly turn his head to look at the pitcher. When he swung, it looked like a Calder mobile with one thread cut; it reminded you that since 1953 Williams' shoulders had been wired together. A solicitous pall settled over the sports pages. In the two decades since Williams had come to Boston, his status had imperceptibly shifted from that of a naughty prodigy to that of a municipal monument. As his shadow in the record books lengthened, the Red Sox teams around him declined, and the entire American League seemed to be losing life and color to the National. The inconsistency of the new super-stars—Mantle, Colavito, and Kaline—served to make Williams appear all the more singular. And off the field, his private philanthropy—in particular, his zealous chairmanship of the Jimmy Fund, a charity for children with cancer—gave him a civic presence somewhat like that of Richard Cardinal Cushing. In religion, Williams appears to be a humanist, and a selective one at that, but he and the Cardinal, when their good works intersect and they appear in the public eye together, make a handsome and heartening pair.

Humiliated by his '59 season, Williams determined, once more, to come back. I, as a specimen Williams partisan, was both glad and fearful. All baseball fans believe in miracles; the question is, how *many* do you believe in? He looked like a ghost in spring training. Manager Jurges warned us ahead of time that if Williams didn't come through he would be benched, just like anybody else. As it turned out, it was Jurges who was benched. Williams entered the 1960 season needing eight home runs to have a lifetime total of 500; after one time at bat in Washington, he needed seven. For a stretch, he was hitting a home run every second game that he played. He passed Lou Gehrig's lifetime total, then the number 500, then Mel Ott's total, and finished with 521, thirteen behind Jimmy Foxx, who alone stands between Williams and Babe Ruth's unapproachable 714. The summer was a statistician's picnic. His two-thousandth walk came and went, his eighteen-hundredth run

batted in, his sixteenth All-Star Game. At one point, he hit a home
run off a pitcher, Don Lee, off whose father, Thornton Lee, he had
hit a home run a generation before. The only comparable season for
a forty-two-year-old man was Ty Cobb's in 1928. Cobb batted .323
and hit one homer. Williams batted .316 but hit twenty-nine
homers.

In sum, though generally conceded to be the greatest hitter of
his era, he did not establish himself as "the greatest hitter who
ever lived." Cobb, for average, and Ruth, for power, remain su-
preme. Cobb, Rogers Hornsby, Joe Jackson, and Lefty O'Doul,
among players since 1900, have higher lifetime averages than Williams' .344. Unlike Foxx, Gehrig, Hack Wilson, Hank Greenberg,
and Ralph Kiner, Williams never came close to matching Babe
Ruth's season home-run total of sixty. In the list of major-league
batting records, not one is held by Williams. He is second in walks
drawn, third in home runs, fifth in lifetime averages, sixth in runs
batted in, eighth in runs scored and in total bases, fourteenth in
doubles, and thirtieth in hits. But if we allow him merely average
seasons for the four-plus seasons he lost to two wars, and add another season for the months he lost to injuries, we get a man who
in all the power totals would be second, and not a very distant
second, to Ruth. And if we further allow that these years would
have been not merely average but prime years, if we allow for all
the months when Williams was playing in sub-par condition, if
we permit his early and later years in baseball to be some sort of
index of what the middle years could have been, if we give him a
right-field fence that is not, like Fenway's, one of the most distant
in the league, and if—the least excusable "if"—we imagine him
condescending to outsmart the Williams Shift, we can defensibly
assemble, like a colossus induced from the sizable fragments that
do remain, a statistical figure not incommensurate with his grandiose
ambition. From the statistics that are on the books, a good case
can be made that in the *combination* of power and average Williams is first; nobody else ranks so high in both categories. Finally,
there is the witness of the eyes; men whose memories go back to
Shoeless Joe Jackson—another unlucky natural—rank him and Williams together as the best-looking hitters they have seen. It was
for our last look that ten thousand of us had come.

Two girls, one of them with pert buckteeth and eyes as black
as vest buttons, the other with white skin and flesh-colored hair,
like an underdeveloped photograph of a redhead, came and sat on
my right. On my other side was one of those frowning, chestless
young-old men who can frequently be seen, often wearing sailor
hats, attending ball games alone. He did not once open his program
but instead tapped it, rolled up, on his knee as he gave the game

his disconsolate attention. A young lady, with freckles and a depressed, dainty nose that by an optical illusion seemed to thrust her lips forward for a kiss, sauntered down into the box seats and with striking aplomb took a seat right behind the roof of the Oriole dugout. She wore a blue coat with a Northeastern University emblem sewed to it. The girls beside me took it into their heads that this was Williams' daughter. She looked too old to me, and why would she be sitting behind the visitors' dugout? On the other hand, from the way she sat there, staring at the sky and French-inhaling, she clearly was *some*-body. Other fans came and eclipsed her from view. The crowd looked less like a weekday ballpark crowd than like the folks you might find in Yellowstone National Park, or emerging from automobiles at the top of scenic Mount Mansfield. There were a lot of competitively well-dressed couples of tourist age, and not a few babes in arms. A row of five seats in front of me was abruptly filled with a woman and four children, the youngest of them two years old, if that. Someday, presumably, he could tell his grandchildren that he saw Williams play. Along with these tots and second-honeymooners, there were Harvard freshmen, giving off that peculiar nervous glow created when a quantity of insouciance is saturated with insecurity; thick-necked Army officers with brass on their shoulders and lead in their voices; pepperings of priests; perfumed bouquets of Roxbury Fabian fans; shiny salesmen from Albany and Fall River; and those gray, hoarse men—taxi-drivers, slaughterers, and bartenders—who will continue to click through the turnstiles long after everyone else has deserted to television and tramporamas. Behind me, two young male voices blossomed, cracking a joke about God's five proofs that Thomas Aquinas exists—typical Boston College levity;

The batting cage was trundled away. The Orioles fluttered to the sidelines. Diagonally across the field, by the Red Sox dugout, a cluster of men in overcoats were festering like maggots. I could see a splinter of white uniform, and Williams' head, held at a self-deprecating and evasive tilt. Williams' conversational stance is that of a six-foot-three-inch man under a six-foot ceiling. He moved away to the patter of flash bulbs, and began playing catch with a young Negro outfielder named Willie Tasby. His arm, never very powerful, had grown lax with the years, and his throwing motion was a kind of muscular drawl. To catch the ball, he flicked his glove hand onto his left shoulder (he batted left but threw right, as every schoolboy ought to know) and let the ball plop into it comically. This catch session with Tasby was the only time all afternoon I saw him grin.

A tight little flock of human sparrows who, from the lambent and pampered pink of their faces could only have been Boston politicians moved toward the plate. The loudspeakers mammothly coughed as someone huffed on the microphone. The ceremonies began. Curt Gowdy, the Red Sox radio and television announcer, who sounds like everybody's brother-in-law, delivered a brief sermon, taking the two words "pride" and "champion" as his text. It began, "Twenty-one years ago, a skinny kid from San Diego, California . . ." and ended, "I don't think we'll ever see another like him." Robert Tibolt, chairman of the board of the Greater Boston Chamber of Commerce, presented Williams with a big Paul Revere silver bowl. Harry Carlson, a member of the sports committee of the Boston Chamber, gave him a plaque, whose inscription he did not read in its entirety, out of deference to Williams' distaste for this sort of fuss. Mayor Collins presented the Jimmy Fund with a thousand-dollar check.

Then the occasion himself stooped to the microphone, and his voice sounded, after the others, very Californian; it seemed to be coming, excellently amplified, from a great distance, adolescently young and as smooth as a butternut. His thanks for the gifts had not died from our ears before he glided, as if helplessly, into "In spite of all the terrible things that have been said about me by the maestros of the keyboard up there . . ." He glanced up at the press rows suspended above home plate. (All the Boston reporters, incidentally, reported the phrase as "knights of the keyboard," but I heard it as "maestros" and prefer it that way.) The crowd tittered, appalled. A frightful vision flashed upon me, of the press gallery pelting Williams with erasers, of Williams clambering up the foul screen to slug journalists, of a riot, of Mayor Collins being crushed. ". . . And they *were* terrible things," Williams insisted, with level melancholy, into the mike. "I'd like to forget them, but I can't." He paused, swallowed his memories, and went on, "I want to say that my years in Boston have been the greatest thing in my life." The crowd, like an immense sail going limp in a change of wind, sighed with relief. Taking all the parts himself, Williams then acted out a vivacious little morality drama in which an imaginary tempter came to him at the beginning of his career and said, "Ted, you can play anywhere you like." Leaping nimbly into the role of his younger self (who in biographical actuality had yearned to be a Yankee), Williams gallantly chose Boston over all the other cities, and told us that Tom Yawkey was the greatest owner in baseball and we were the greatest fans. We applauded ourselves heartily. The umpire came out and dusted the plate. The voice of doom announced over the loudspeakers that after Williams' retirement his uniform number, 9, would be permanently retired—the first time the Red Sox had so honored a player. We cheered. The national anthem was played. We cheered. The game began.

Williams was third in the batting order, so he came up in the bottom of the first inning, and Steve Barber, a young pitcher who was not yet born when Williams began playing for the Red Sox, offered him four pitches, at all of which he disdained to swing, since none of them were within the strike zone. This demonstrated simultaneously that Williams' eyes were razor-sharp and that Barber's control wasn't. Shortly, the bases were full, with Williams on second. "Oh, I hope he gets held up at third! That would be wonderful," the girl beside me moaned, and, sure enough, the man at bat walked and Williams was delivered into our foreground. He struck the pose of Donatello's David, the third-base bag being Goliath's head. Fiddling with his cap, swapping small talk with the Oriole third baseman (who seemed delighted to have him drop in), swinging his arms with a sort of prancing nervousness, he looked fine—flexible, hard, and not unbecomingly substantial through the middle. The long neck, the small head, the knickers whose cuffs were worn down near his ankles—all these points, often observed by caricaturists, were visible in the flesh.

One of the collegiate voices behind me said, "He looks old, doesn't he, old; big deep wrinkles in his face . . ."

"Yeah," the other voice said, "but he looks like an old hawk, doesn't he?"

With each pitch, Williams danced down the baseline, waving his arms and stirring dust, ponderous but menacing, like an attacking goose. It occurred to about a dozen humorists at once to shout "Steal home! Go, go!" Williams' speed afoot was never legendary. Lou Clinton, a young Sox outfielder, hit a fairly deep fly to center field. Williams tagged up and ran home. As he slid across the plate, the ball, thrown with unusual heft by Jackie Brandt, the Oriole center fielder, hit him on the back.

"Boy, he was really loafing, wasn't he?" one of the boys behind me said.

"It's cold," the other explained. "He doesn't play well when it's cold. He likes heat. He's a hedonist."

The run that Williams scored was the second and last of the inning. Gus Triandos, of the Orioles, quickly evened the score by plunking a home run over the handy left-field wall. Williams, who had had this wall at his back for twenty years, played the ball flawlessly. He didn't budge. He just stood there, in the center of the little patch of grass that his patient footsteps had worn brown, and, limp with lack of interest, watched the ball pass overhead. It was not a very interesting game. Mike Higgins, the Red Sox manager, with nothing to lose, had restricted his major-league players to the left-field line—along with Williams, Frank Malzone, a firstrate third baseman, played the game—and had peopled the rest of the terrain with unpredictable youngsters fresh, or not so fresh, off the farms. Other than Williams' recurrent appearances at the plate, the *maladresse* of the Sox infield was the sole focus of suspense; the second baseman turned every grounder into a juggling act, while the shortstop did a breathtaking impersonation of an open window. With this sort of assistance, the Orioles wheedled their way into a 4-2 lead. They had early replaced Barber with another young pitcher, Jack Fisher. Fortunately (as it turned out), Fisher is no cutie; he is willing to burn the ball through the strike zone, and inning after inning this tactic punctured Higgins' string of test balloons.

Whenever Williams appeared at the plate—pounding the dirt from his cleats, gouging a pit in the batter's box with his left foot, wringing resin out of the bat handle with his vehement grip, switching the stick at the pitcher with an electric ferocity—it was like having a familiar Leonardo appear in a shuffle of *Saturday Evening Post* covers. This man, you realized—and here, perhaps, was the difference, greater than the difference in gifts—really intended to hit the ball. In the third inning, he hoisted a high fly to deep center. In the fifth, we thought he had it; he smacked the ball hard and high into the heart of his power zone, but the deep right field in Fenway and the heavy air and a casual east wind defeated him. The ball died. Al Pilarcik leaned his back against the big "380" painted on the right-field wall and caught it. On another day, in another park, it would have been gone. (After the game, Williams said, "I didn't think I could hit one any harder than that. The conditions weren't good.")

The afternoon grew so glowering that in the sixth inning the arc lights were turned on—always a wan sight in the daytime, like the burning headlights of a funeral procession. Aided by the gloom, Fisher was slicing through the Sox rookies, and Williams did not come to bat in the seventh. He was second up in the eighth. This was almost certainly his last time to come to the plate in Fenway Park, and instead of merely cheering, as we had at his three previous appearances, we stood, all of us—stood and applauded. Have you ever heard applause in a ballpark? Just applause —no calling, no whistling, just an ocean of handclaps, minute after minute, burst after burst, crowding and running together in continuous succession like the pushes of surf at the edge of the sand. It was a sombre and considered tumult. There was not a boo in it. It seemed to renew itself out of a shifting set of memories as the kid, the Marine, the veteran of feuds and failures and injuries, the friend of children, and the enduring old pro evolved down the bright tunnel of twenty-one summers toward this moment. At last, the umpire signalled for Fisher to pitch; with the other players, he had been frozen in position. Only Williams had moved during the ovation, switching his bat impatiently, ignoring everything except his cherished task. Fisher wound up, and the applause sank into a hush.

Understand that we were a crowd of rational people. We knew that a home run cannot be produced at will; the right pitch must be perfectly met and luck must ride with the ball. Three innings before, we had seen a brave effort fail. The air was soggy; the season was exhausted. Nevertheless, there will always lurk, around a corner in a pocket of our knowledge of the odds, an indefensible hope, and this was one of the times, which you now and then find in sports, when a density of expectation hangs in the air and plucks an event out of the future.

Fisher, after his unsettling wait, was wide with the first pitch. He put the second one over, and Williams swung mightily and missed. The crowd grunted, seeing that classic swing, so long and smooth and quick, exposed, naked in its failure. Fisher threw the third time, Williams swung again, and there it was. The ball climbed on a diagonal line into the vast volume of air over center field. From my angle, behind third base, the ball seemed less an object in flight than the tip of a towering, motionless construct, like the Eiffel Tower or the Tappan Zee Bridge. It was in the books while it was still in the sky. Brandt ran back to the deepest corner of the outfield grass; the ball descended behind his reach and struck in the crotch where the bullpen met the wall, bounced chunkily, and, as far as I could see, vanished.

Like a feather caught in a vortex, Williams ran around the square of bases at the center of our beseeching screaming. He ran as he always ran out home runs—hurriedly, unsmiling, head down, as if our praise were a storm of rain to get out of. He didn't tip his cap. Though we thumped, wept, and chanted "We want Ted" for minutes after he hid in the dugout, he did not come back. Our noise for some seconds passed beyond excitement into a kind of immense open anguish, a wailing, a cry to be saved. But immortality is nontransferable. The papers said that the other players, and even the umpires on the field, begged him to come out and acknowledge us in some way, but he never had and did not now. Gods do not answer letters.

Every true story has an anticlimax. The men on the field refused to disappear, as would have seemed decent, in the smoke of Williams' miracle. Fisher continued to pitch, and escaped further harm. At the end of the inning, Higgins sent Williams out to his left-field position, then instantly replaced him with Carrol Hardy, so we had a long last look at Williams as he ran out there and then back, his uniform jogging, his eyes steadfast on the ground. It was nice, and we were grateful, but it left a funny taste.

One of the scholasticists behind me said, "Let's go. We've seen everything. I don't want to spoil it." This seemed a sound aesthetic decision. Williams' last word had been so exquisitely chosen, such a perfect fusion of expectation, intention, and execution, that already it felt a little unreal in my head, and I wanted to get out before the castle collapsed. But the game, though played by clumsy midgets under the feeble glow of the arc lights, began to tug at my attention, and I loitered in the runway until it was over. Williams' homer had, quite incidentally, made the score 4-3. In the bottom of the ninth inning, with one out, Marlin Coughtry, the second-base juggler, singled. Vic Wertz, pinch-hitting, doubled off the left-field wall, Coughtry advancing to third. Pumpsie Green walked, to load the bases. Willie Tasby hit a double-play ball to the third baseman, but in making the pivot throw Billy Klaus, an ex-Red Sox infielder, reverted to form and threw the ball past the first baseman and into the Red Sox dugout. The Sox won, 5-4. On the car radio as I drove home I heard that Williams had decided not to accompany the team to New York. So he knew how to do even that, the hardest thing. Quit.

———

JOHN UPDIKE (1932–   ) *became a staff writer for* The New Yorker *after leaving Harvard, and continues to contribute articles and stories to what he calls "the best of possible magazines." His best-known novels are* Rabbit, Run *(1960),* The Centaur *(1963), and* Couples *(1968), but he prefers his short stories to them; "if I had to give anybody one book of [mine] it would be the Vintage* Olinger Stories *[1964]," he told the* Paris Review *in 1968.*

This essay was printed originally in The New Yorker, *October 22, 1960, less than a month after Ted Williams' last game with the Red Sox.*

1. What is the tone of the title? What is Updike's attitude toward journalists in this essay? What kinds of words describe them? How does the journalistic prose quoted in paragraph 5 differ from Updike's? How does this essay differ from a usual newspaper account of a game?

2. One way to consider the writer's problem in this essay is to ask how he gets from the "Kid" of the title to the sentence, "Gods do not answer letters." One fairly obvious device he uses

is to bring in allusions outside baseball, such as the mythological names in paragraph three. Find several other ways in which the author "earns" the kind of meaning he attaches to Williams.

3. What is the function of the details and descriptions (the statistics, the other fans, Williams' stance as a runner, the sound system, for example)? In what sense do these details work for or against the various means of establishing "greatness" you noticed in question 2?

4. What is the tone of the references to the other ballplayers? The other fans? The politicians at the ceremony at home plate? What is the attitude the writer takes to himself (". . . we were the greatest fans. We applauded ourselves heartily.")? What is the value for ordinary people of contemplation of the kind of hero Updike creates in Williams?

James Joyce

ARABY

North Richmond Street, being blind, was a quiet street except at the hour when the Christian Brothers' School set the boys free. An uninhabited house of two storeys stood at the blind end, detached from its neighbours in a square ground. The other houses of the street, conscious of decent lives within them, gazed at one another with brown imperturbable faces.

The former tenant of our house, a priest, had died in the back drawing-room. Air, musty from having been long enclosed, hung in all the rooms, and the waste room behind the kitchen was littered with old useless papers. Among these I found a few paper-covered books, the pages of which were curled and damp: *The Abbot,* by Walter Scott, *The Devout Communicant* and *The Memoirs of Vidocq.* I liked the last best because its leaves were yellow. The wild garden behind the house contained a central apple-tree and a few straggling bushes under one of which I found the late tenant's rusty bicycle-pump. He had been a very charitable priest; in his will he had left all his money to institutions and the furniture of his house to his sister.

When the short days of winter came dusk fell before we had well eaten our dinners. When we met in the street the houses had grown sombre. The space of sky above us was the colour of ever-changing violet and towards it the lamps of the street lifted their feeble lanterns. The cold air stung us and we played till our bodies glowed. Our shouts echoed in the silent street. The career of our play brought us through the dark muddy lanes behind the houses where we ran the gantlet of the rough tribes from the cottages, to the back doors of the dark dripping gardens where odours arose from the ashpits, to the dark odorous stables where a coachman smoothed and combed the horse or shook music from the buckled harness. When we returned to the street light from the kitchen windows had filled the areas. If my uncle was seen turning the corner we hid in the shadow until we had seen him safely housed. Or if Mangan's sister came out on the doorstep to call her brother in to his tea we watched her from our shadow peer up and down the street. We waited to see whether she would remain or go in and, if she remained, we left our shadow and walked up to Mangan's steps resignedly. She was waiting for us, her figure defined by the light from the half-opened door. Her brother always teased her before he obeyed and I stood by the railings looking at her. Her dress swung as she moved her body and the soft rope of her hair tossed from side to side.

Every morning I lay on the floor in the front parlour watching her door. The blind was pulled down to within an inch of the sash so that I could not be seen. When she came out on the doorstep my heart leaped. I ran to the hall, seized my books and followed her. I kept her brown figure always in my eye and, when we came near the point at which our ways diverged, I quickened my pace and passed her. This happened morning after morning. I had never spoken to her, except for a few casual words, and yet her name was like a summons to all my foolish blood.

Her image accompanied me even in places the most hostile to romance. On Saturday evenings when my aunt went marketing I had to go to carry some of the parcels. We walked through the flaring streets, jostled by drunken men and bargaining women, amid the curses of labourers, the shrill litanies of shop-boys who stood on guard by the barrels of pigs' cheeks, the nasal chanting of street-singers, who sang a *come-all-you* about O'Donovan Rossa, or a ballad about the troubles in our native land. These noises converged in a single sensation of life for me: I imagined that I bore my chalice safely through a throng of foes. Her name sprang to my lips at moments in strange prayers and praises which I myself did not understand. My eyes were often full of tears (I could not tell why) and at times a flood from my heart seemed to pour itself out into my bosom. I thought little of the future. I did not know whether I would ever speak to her or not or, if I spoke to her, how I could tell her of my confused adoration. But my body was like a harp and her words and gestures were like fingers running upon the wires.

One evening I went into the back drawing-room in which the priest had died. It was a dark rainy evening and there was no sound in the house. Through one of the broken panes I heard the rain impinge upon the earth, the fine incessant needles of water playing in the sodden beds. Some distant lamp or lighted window gleamed below me. I was thankful that I could see so little. All my senses seemed to desire to veil themselves and, feeling that I was about to slip from them, I pressed the palms of my hands together until they trembled, murmuring: *O love! O love!* many times.

At last she spoke to me. When she addressed the first words to

me I was so confused that I did not know what to answer. She asked
me was I going to *Araby*. I forget whether I answered yes or no. It
would be a splendid bazaar, she said; she would love to go.

—And why can't you? I asked.

While she spoke she turned a silver bracelet round and round
her wrist. She could not go, she said, because there would be a re-
treat that week in her convent. Her brother and two other boys
were fighting for their caps and I was alone at the railings. She held
one of the spikes, bowing her head towards me. The light from the
lamp opposite our door caught the white curve of her neck, lit up
her hair that rested there and, falling, lit up the hand upon the
railing. It fell over one side of her dress and caught the white
border of a petticoat, just visible as she stood at ease.

—It's well for you, she said.

—If I go, I said, I will bring you something.

What innumerable follies laid waste my waking and sleeping
thoughts after that evening! I wished to annihilate the tedious
intervening days. I chafed against the work of school. At night in
my bedroom and by day in the classroom her image came between
me and the page I strove to read. The syllables of the word *Araby*
were called to me through the silence in which my soul luxuriated
and cast an Eastern enchantment over me. I asked for leave to go
to the bazaar on Saturday night. My aunt was surprised and hoped
it was not some Freemason affair. I answered few questions in class.
I watched my master's face pass from amiability to sternness; he
hoped I was not beginning to idle. I could not call my wandering
thoughts together. I had hardly any patience with the serious work
of life which, now that it stood between me and my desire, seemed
to me child's play, ugly monotonous child's play.

On Saturday morning I reminded my uncle that I wished to go
to the bazaar in the evening. He was fussing at the hallstand, looking for the hat-brush, and answered me curtly:

—Yes, boy, I know.

As he was in the hall I could not go into the front parlour and
lie at the window. I left the house in bad humour and walked
slowly towards the school. The air was pitilessly raw and already
my heart misgave me.

When I came home to dinner my uncle had not yet been home.
Still it was early. I sat staring at the clock for some time and, when
its ticking began to irritate me, I left the room. I mounted the
staircase and gained the upper part of the house. The high cold
empty gloomy rooms liberated me and I went from room to room
singing. From the front window I saw my companions playing below
in the street. Their cries reached me weakened and indistinct and,
leaning my forehead against the cool glass, I looked over at the

dark house where she lived. I may have stood there for an hour, seeing nothing but the brown-clad figure cast by my imagination, touched discreetly by the lamplight at the curved neck, at the hand upon the railings and at the border below the dress.

When I came downstairs again I found Mrs. Mercer sitting at the fire. She was an old garrulous woman, a pawnbroker's widow, who collected used stamps for some pious purpose. I had to endure the gossip of the tea-table. The meal was prolonged beyond an hour and still my uncle did not come. Mrs. Mercer stood up to go: she was sorry she couldn't wait any longer, but it was after eight o'clock and she did not like to be out late, as the night air was bad for her. When she had gone I began to walk up and down the room, clenching my fists. My aunt said:

—I'm afraid you may put off your bazaar for this night of Our Lord.

At nine o'clock I heard my uncle's latchkey in the halldoor. I heard him talking to himself and heard the hallstand rocking when it had received the weight of his overcoat. I could interpret these signs. When he was midway through his dinner I asked him to give me the money to go to the bazaar. He had forgotten.

—The people are in bed and after their first sleep now, he said.

I did not smile. My aunt said to him energetically:

—Can't you give him the money and let him go? You've kept him late enough as it is.

My uncle said he was very sorry he had forgotten. He said he believed in the old saying: *All work and no play makes Jack a dull boy.* He asked me where I was going and, when I had told him a second time he asked me did I know *The Arab's Farewell to his Steed*. When I left the kitchen he was about to recite the opening lines of the piece to my aunt.

I held a florin tightly in my hand as I strode down Buckingham Street towards the station. The sight of the streets thronged with buyers and glaring with gas recalled to me the purpose of my journey. I took my seat in a third-class carriage of a deserted train. After an intolerable delay the train moved out of the station slowly. It crept onward among ruinous houses and over the twinkling river. At Westland Row Station a crowd of people pressed to the carriage doors; but the porters moved them back, saying that it was a special train for the bazaar. I remained alone in the bare carriage. In a few minutes the train drew up beside an improvised wooden platform. I passed out on to the road and saw by the lighted dial of a clock that it was ten minutes to ten. In front of me was a large building which displayed the magical name.

I could not find any sixpenny entrance and, fearing that the bazaar would be closed, I passed in quickly through a turnstile, handing a shilling to a weary-looking man. I found myself in a big hall girdled at half its height by a gallery. Nearly all the stalls were closed and the greater part of the hall was in darkness. I recognised a silence like that which pervades a church after a service. I walked into the centre of the bazaar timidly. A few people were gathered about the stalls which were still open. Before a curtain, over which the words *Café Chantant* were written in coloured lamps, two men were counting money on a salver. I listened to the fall of the coins.

Remembering with difficulty why I had come I went over to one of the stalls and examined porcelain vases and flowered tea-sets. At the door of the stall a young lady was talking and laughing with two young gentlemen. I remarked their English accents and listened vaguely to their conversation.

—O, I never said such a thing!

—O, but you did!

—O, but I didn't!

—Didn't she say that?

—Yes. I heard her.

—O, there's a . . . fib!

Observing me the young lady came over and asked me did I wish to buy anything. The tone of her voice was not encouraging; she seemed to have spoken to me out of a sense of duty. I looked humbly at the great jars that stood like eastern guards at either side of the dark entrance to the stall and murmured:

—No, thank you.

The young lady changed the position of one of the vases and went back to the two young men. They began to talk of the same subject. Once or twice the young lady glanced at me over her shoulder.

I lingered before her stall, though I knew my stay was useless, to make my interest in her wares seem the more real. Then I turned away slowly and walked down the middle of the bazaar. I allowed the two pennies to fall against the sixpence in my pocket. I heard a voice call from one end of the gallery that the light was out. The upper part of the hall was now completely dark.

Gazing up into the darkness I saw myself as a creature driven and derided by vanity; and my eyes burned with anguish and anger.

———

JAMES JOYCE (1882–1941) *attended the Christian Brothers' School on North Richmond Street in Dublin. When Joyce was twelve, from May 14–17, 1894, a bazaar called "Araby" came to Dublin; this "Grand Oriental Fête" cost one shilling for supposedly Eastern entertainment and shops. The childhood experience gave Joyce the frame of this story from the collection* Dubliners *(1914); the disillusionment he associates with the experience recurs in various ways in his three major novels,* A Portrait of the Artist as a Young Man *(1914–15),* Ulysses *(1922), and* Finnegans Wake *(1939).*

1. *In the Introduction to this book we are told that "James Joyce asks us to value a child's tears over a closed carnival because those tears help us see the meaning of growing up in an environment hostile to the imagination." How does Joyce convey this hostile environment to the reader?*

2. *What does the carnival Araby mean to the boy, to the aunt and uncle, to the reader? What connection is there for the boy between the appeal of Araby and that of Mangan's sister?*

3. *The boy says ". . . her name was like a summons to all my foolish blood." "Her name sprang to my lips at moments in strange prayers and praises which I did not understand." Why are we never told what Mangan's sister's name really is? What does the boy mean by "foolish blood" and "strange prayers and praises which I did not understand?"*

4. *Joyce uses church imagery to describe the boy's feelings about Mangan's sister. What does this imagery tell the reader about the boy's feelings about the church? Does Joyce, the adult writer, have an attitude toward the church that he is trying to convey to the reader in this story?*

5. *Joyce makes frequent references to darkness and light, vision and blindness. Why do the children prefer the shadows? Why is the boy "thankful that I could see so little"? Why is Mangan's sister "defined by the light from the half-opened door"? Why does Joyce also show Araby half dark?*

6. *Reread the closing paragraph. What is there about growing up in this world that causes anger? Anguish? How has the boy been driven by vanity? Derided by vanity?*

7. *To what degree has the story given the incident of the closed carnival enough meaning to carry the emotional weight of the last paragraph? Just before the last paragraph is the following sentence: "I heard a voice call from one end of the gallery that the light was out." What, if anything, does the last paragraph add to this already strong ending?*

Appendix REWRITING FOR

CONTROL OF TONE

A professional writer knows that only a small part of his job is done when his first draft is finished; ten or fifteen revisions are not unusual, and to salvage large parts of a first draft is a kind of triumph. Certainly no writer is likely to do very successful writing unless he adopts some of the habits of the professional and learns to rewrite thoroughly and carefully.

No one can give a ready or easy formula for rewriting. The process of creation from conception through outlining through early drafts to a final outline and final draft is very complicated. Each writer must finally choose the procedures which best allow him to understand and demonstrate his best thoughts on his topic.

After all, revision is most valuable if it serves the writer as well as the reader. To replace a vague word or an incoherent paragraph with the precise word or a developed idea is not merely a matter of pleasing a more or less interested reader; it is thinking itself. Rewriting is usually a matter of finding out what you really want to say by a search for the right words and the most effective organization.

The concept of tone, which this text has been examining from many points of view, does offer a valuable way to conceive of rewriting. Whatever method you use to revise your work, you need to be sure that your relationship to your reader is in fact the one you want, that your attitude toward your subject is clear and appropriate, that you have something to say worth hearing about your topic. Unless these three problems are solved, no amount of rewriting will turn a poor paper into a good one.

The student paper printed here dramatically demonstrates the kind of change that can take place when questions of tone are considered part of the revision process. The major change from first to second draft occurs in the writer's attitude toward the other boys *in the scout troop. The almost ritualistic condemnation of them, sometimes inappropriately bitter, changes to one of sympathetic understanding as a result of more careful and original thought. As the writer examines his attitude toward the boys, he also realizes the nicely ambiguous value of the "space exploration" of his topic: adolescent boys are necessarily involved in exploring their own worlds, even when they are supposedly finding out about planetary space. Perhaps the scout leader knew what he was doing after all.*

As his attitude towards the subject becomes more understanding and less bitter, the writer's relationship to the reader changes also. The humorless spoil-sport of the first draft, who seems rather a stuffy and unpleasant prig, changes to a relaxed and intelligent fellow who knows what is really happening: "This is hardly the sort of meeting that would be expected of this type of group" becomes "He understood that in the strange, exciting world of the sixteen year old, self-exploration is much more intriguing than a journey into the world of science." And finally the rather pointless condemnation of the scout troop becomes an interesting and clever account of human vitality conquering scientific fact.

Robert Farr

EXPLORER POST 14: NOT INTELLECTUALLY PREPARED (first draft)

I was a member of Explorer Post 14 for two years. We were a rather unorthodox Explorer post in that we wore no uniforms, had a constitution, elected officers, and had a nuclear physicist for a scout master. Also, we did not go on camping trips, hikes and other things of this type that one would normally associate with Scouting. On the contrary, we studied, heard lectures and saw films on math and science and worked on science projects, or at least that's what we were supposed to do.

We actually did hear lectures and see films, but having a serious discussion about any subject or working on a project, that was out of the question. I believe that this will become clear as I describe one of our typical meetings.

We would meet at Aerospace about 7:30 P.M. every other Wednesday night. Before the meeting began there was always a period of utter havoc. Loud talk and laughter, writing on the blackboard, making paper airplanes and other juvenile actions were common until the scoutmaster arrived. We then began the meeting with the flag salute which was led by the president of the Post. We quickly passed over the subjects of new and old business, project discussions, future plans and other things of relative unimportance. We would then have a film or a lecture followed by a short, abortive discussion. This was not always the case. At times we did have lengthy intelligent discussions, but these were rare. Then we would adjourn the meeting and all go home. This is hardly the sort of meeting that would be expected of this type of group.

Another good example is projects. Each member of the group was expected to work on a project, individually or with another member. The only thing was, nobody ever worked on projects. With a group of this type, one would expect the members to be eager to work on projects and present them to other members for discussion, but this was just too much work.

I don't believe that the failure of our group to function as it was

Reprinted by permission of the author.

originally planned can be blamed on our scoutmaster as might at first be believed. On the contrary, I believe it was a direct result of the attitudes of the majority of the members toward doing anything that appeared to be work. Part of the members were the playboy type. They received good grades in school but preferred to chase around and go on dates three or four times a week rather than spend a little extra time working on a project or preparing a topic for a general discussion. Others were just plain lazy. All of the members had above average intelligence and the ability to think and reason, but thinking was just too much like work. Thus, it appears to me that the members of this group were not intellectually prepared for an Explorer program of this type as it was originally designed.

Robert Farr

EXPLORER POST 14: THE NEW WORLD

(second draft)

Explorer Post 14 customarily met in a room at Aerospace usually used by scientists to discuss such vital subjects as defense projects and space exploration. The walls of the spacious, well-lighted room were blank, except for the west wall which was decorated by a map of the world showing all of the routes taken by the early explorers to the New World. But this map was covered by a large motion picture screen whose pale blankness gave the room an air of sterility.

The twelve sixteen-year old boys supposedly gathered together for the purpose of exploring the world of math and science. But actually this was just a guise for their real purpose—the exploration of the novel, quick-paced world of the teenager.

The meeting began, supposedly, with the flag salute. Actually the meeting began fifteen minutes earlier as the group gathered in the room that was to be their uncharted world for the next hour and a half. In these first fifteen minutes, the initial exploration began with the boys testing each other with silly comments about the day's activities at school and home. W. T. Smith III, the leader of the particular expedition, pulled the blackboard out to the middle of the room and began to map out their course. As it turned out, the map resembled the figure of Bridget Bardot and therefore was appropriately named The French Curve. About this time, Dr. Nordin, the nuclear physicist-scout master, entered the room, and the expedition reached a temporary impasse.

After the flag salute, the lights went out and the motion picture screen flashed with brilliant colors and the blank walls reverberated with the sounds of a film entitled "The Exploration of the Moon and Beyond." It was the story of the men and the spacecraft that would someday soon venture into the black reaches of space to explore the moon and the Earth's nearest neighbors, Mars and Venus. As the film ended, the bright lights again flicked on, and Dr. Nordin engaged the boys in a discussion of space exploration that lasted about twenty minutes.

But then the inevitable happened. The screen came down revealing the world map. The temporary impasse overcome, the boys returned to their exploration with more vigor than before. Their path led them to cars, the date W. T. had the night before and girls in general. But soon they were forced to end their journey for the meeting was at an end.

During the last part of the meeting, Dr. Nordin had just sat with the boys, laughing with them and only occasionally entering a comment of his own. Why had he done this? Why didn't he try to make the boys continue their discussion along more intellectually oriented lines? The reason is simple. He understood that in the strange, exciting world of the sixteen year old, self exploration is much more intriguing than a journey into the world of science. For it is at this age when a person must find himself so that someday he will be a mature individual both mentally and physically. So each week Dr. Nordin took up the role of a silent guide so that a group of sixteen year old boys could engage in the exploration of life.

Robert Farr *wrote and rewrote this paper as a college freshman in 1967. He graduated as a major in mathematics from the California State College, San Bernardino, in 1970.*

1. *The object here is to discover the process by which the writer moved from first to second draft. Notice first of all some of the terms or phrases which establish his relationship to the troop in the first draft: "that's what we were supposed to do" (par. 1), "that was out of the question" (par. 2). Find at least one such indication of attitude in each of the other paragraphs. Define the writer's relationship to the troop.*

2. *Look closely at the passive verbs in the first draft: "we were supposed to do" (par. 1), "that would be expected of this type group" (par. 2), "as it was originally planned" (par. 4), "as it was originally designed" (par. 4). Who are those doing the supposing, expecting, planning, designing? Try turning these verbs from passive to active; what happens?*

3. *Notice the word "intelligent" in paragraph 2 of the first draft, and the phrase "intellectually prepared" in the title and the last sentence. What does the writer mean and what attitudes does he imply? How do you feel about someone who uses such terms with such meanings for a group of sixteen-year-olds? Notice the*

different tone of "intellectually-oriented" in the last paragraph
of the second draft.

4. The fourth paragraph of the first draft begins "Another good
example is projects." Good example of what? Say the sentence
out loud, and aim for the right tone of voice. Does it tend toward a whine, as if there were a list of grievances? To what
degree does this sentence help define the author-reader relationship throughout the first draft?

5. The author certainly has something to say in the first draft.
What is it? His attitudes toward topic and reader are also
clearly defined. What are they? What does a close consideration of tone suggest about possible ways of reconsidering the
meaning of the topic?

6. How has the relationship of the author to the troop changed in
the second draft? Find specific words and phrases that indicate
this different relationship. How does this relationship affect
your feelings about the writer and your respect for what he has
to say?

7. What does the writer in the second draft now feel is worth
demonstrating about the troop meetings? Is it more interesting
than what he said in the first draft? How has the changed tone
led to a changed concept of topic?

8. Notice the kinds of verbs in the second draft, most obviously in
paragraphs 4 and 5. What do verbs such as "flashed," "reverberated," "venture," "explore" do to the tone? How do these
reflect the changed tone and the new concept of topic?

9. Both drafts are organized more or less chronologically, that is,
they follow the schedule of a troop meeting from start to finish.
But the structure seems more purposeful in the second draft, as
a comparison of the fourth paragraphs shows. Describe how the
difference in tones leads to a difference in structure (refer to
question 4).

10. The first paragraph of the second draft was the last part of this
paper to be written. (Many writers routinely write their open-
ings last. Why?) What does this first paragraph accomplish besides setting the location of the meeting? Is there a connection
between the map covered by a blank screen and the topic of
the paper? How does the opening establish the tone?